World University Library

The World University Library is an international series of books, each of which has been specially commissioned. The authors are leading scientists and scholars from all over the world who, in an age of increasing specialisation, see the need for a broad, up-to-date presentation of their subject. The aim is to provide authoritative introductory books for university students which will be of interest also to the general reader. The series is published in Britain, France, Germany, Holland, Italy, Spain, Sweden and the United States.

Frontispiece. Village children in Dahomey gather for the distribution of food.

J. L. Sampedro

Decisive Forces in World Economics

translated from the Spanish
by S. E. Nodder

World University Library

McGraw-Hill Book Company
New York Toronto

Library of Congress Catalog Card Number: 67-14683
Phototypeset by BAS Printers Limited, Wallop, Hampshire, England
Printed by Officine Grafiche Arnoldo Mondadori, Verona, Italy

Contents

1 Introduction: an unsettled world

Every morning, millions of us take a look at life in our newspapers. We need to keep abreast of events since we live in an age in which, as Ortega y Gasset said,

> we do not know what is happening to us, and this is just what is happening to us; modern man is beginning to lose his bearings; he is beyond his country, *dépaysé*, cast into a new environment that resembles an unknown land. Such an existential emotion always takes hold of men in momentous periods of history.

We open our papers anticipating disaster – monetary devaluation perhaps, or political revolution, or nuclear war, or proof of flying saucers. The man in the street may well read his paper simply to find out whether the princess got married or what is showing at the movies. But he is very well aware (or at least a dark and apprehensive little corner of his consciousness is aware) that whatever he may be looking for, his peace of mind can be shattered by a great black headline. He knows that he is living in a period of crisis; he is aware that he is crossing a precarious bridge between bygone stability and a new, indeterminate phase.

It is true that the same thing has happened before. But there have also been times of greater calm. Many people remember that their parents led reasonably tranquil lives, without the constant torture of anxiety. They had their tribulations and their griefs, of course, but they were comforted in setback and hardship not only by religion but by the assurance of the unchanging structure of a stable world.

Today this stability is changing only too rapidly and we find we have to move in an environment totally different from the one we were taught to recognise in childhood. The cadet who trained for cavalry charges has become a general commanding airborne divisions. The scientist has graduated from electricity to nuclear physics, the doctor from the pulse to the electrocardiogram, the scholar from his book-lined study to the microfilm library, the housewife from the sink and scrubbing brush to detergents and the washing-machine – or even to the office or factory.

The same trend is to be found everywhere. As Valéry wrote, we find ourselves taking part in a never-ending card-game in which, throughout our lives, the hands change, the rules of the game alter and even the players are replaced by others. What was once proven fact no longer offers us security. Science itself, which to the ancients gave promise of happiness and knowledge, disturbs us with each new discovery. Five hundred years ago we were living securely at the centre of the universe. Suddenly we began to rotate round the sun, but our alarm was quietened by the thought that at least we were living a logical clockwork existence, perfectly explained by savants like Newton and Laplace. Today the sun and its satellites are a mere handful of dust in a galaxy whose diameter is a hundred thousand light years; and this is just one of something like a hundred thousand million galaxies, the nearest of which is Andromeda, 2·2 million light years away. And in this age of the quasar (newly discovered worlds, too big to be stars and too dense to be galaxies) the scientists are offering our scepticism no fewer than three contradictory theories regarding the universe: Hoyle's representation of a continuous galactic creation commensurate with the disappearance of existing galaxies, Lemaître's indefinite expansion theory and Robertson and Tolman's hypothesis of a universe in a state of rhythmical expansion and contraction.

Where, in all this mysterious infinity, can a secure anchorage be found? Emphatically not in economics. Even in this sphere, the theme of the present book, the pillars of the temples have come crashing down more than once in a short space of time. Some years ago, the French newspapers carried the story of a harmless madman who escaped from the sanatorium where he had been maintained by his family since 1914. After walking up and down the streets for a time, bewildered by the awful traffic, he entered a restaurant. He had no money, of course, but on his watch-chain he wore a gold napoleon as a charm and remembered that he had often enjoyed a real feast for something less than twenty francs. His trepidation was indescribable when he was presented with a bill for 2,200 francs. Without daring to protest, he detached the coin from his chain and very humbly handed it to the waiter, who began a whispered colloquy with the manager. And just when the wretched diner was expecting the storm to break, it turned out that they were accepting his payment with the utmost civility and were giving him back into the bargain almost 2,000 francs. Two thousand francs and a meal for a coin worth only twenty! The madman left his change on the table and fled back to his place of detention, where at least he was safe from the madmen outside. How can the economy fail to have suffered vicissitudes, if there have been such alterations in the value of money, the very foundation of security? Every reader has heard of the shattering inflation which befell the German mark after the First World War and of the great world slump of the 'thirties, with all its economic and social consequences. I make no attempt here to list all the re-alignments of the political, ideological and social boundaries which have taken place in the last fifty years, because the most important of them will be analysed in this book. At this juncture I wish only to impress on the reader the acuteness of the transformation undergone by the economic fabric of life.

As we shall see, that liberal economy which had been recognised as a signal victory for social organisation, has lagged behind and in its place has come state control of the economy accompanied, in some countries, by the public ownership of capital and the control of all producer industries as a function of the state. Astounding technical progress has been achieved. But we feel that we are the prisoners of its results. We find innumerable flaws in the very organisation which is the source of so many advances; and the people of the most affluent nations appear to us to be lacking above all in that one commodity so priceless for the enjoyment of life: time. They earn their living at a far higher material level than ever before but they have no time in which to live. They have progressively reduced the length of the working day but they end up slaves to overtime and organised leisure. They take sleeping-pills to counter excitement or tension, which they then have to offset with stimulants to enable them to face their daily tasks. Viewed as a whole the economy of the advanced countries seems to function

Stamps on a letter sent within Berlin in September, 1923, amounting to 30,000 M. In face value they range from 50 M (the highest in a series issued in December 1922) to 20,000 M (from a series surcharged from 5,000 to 2,000,000). Eventually it was impossible to keep pace, and stamps were printed without values, inserting them at a second printing up to 50,000,000,000 M. New stamps in gold currency were issued from 1 December.

like a bicycle whose rider is compelled to keep on pedalling merely to stay on his machine. New expedients have to be created for stimulating demand in order to consume an output whose growth, of necessity, increases annually.

I am no pessimist, as will be clearly realised later on, and I hasten to insist that mankind is making progress and that the economy is the product of organisation and not mere chaos. But though the world is no doubt advancing, it is suffering the tremendous contradictions inherent in every period of crisis. This was underlined by the UN when it officially labelled the 1960s 'The

Berlin shop window, 1923. By now there was an acute shortage of money. Banks were unable to give credit, and many firms went bankrupt. The painted sign 'We need money' echoed the cry of the whole country.

United Nations Development Decade', in a document beginning with these words:

It is an extraordinary fact that at a time when affluence is beginning to be the condition, or at least the potential condition, of whole countries and regions rather than of a few favoured individuals, and when scientific feats are becoming possible which beggar mankind's wildest dreams of the past, more people in the world are suffering from hunger and want than ever before. Such a situation is so intolerable and so contrary to the best interests of all nations that it should arouse determination, on the part of advanced and developing countries alike, to bring it to an end.

President Johnson signing the Economic Opportunity Act in 1964, designed to eliminate poverty in the United States. Formerly poverty was considered inevitable, indeed the beggar was accepted as an integral part of society. But now man takes a more rational view, and is in a position to do something about it.

In other words, man is suffering from hunger at a time when he possesses the most advanced techniques of production in history. The man in the street can verify this in his morning paper. There he reads not only of poverty in the underdeveloped countries, but of a campaign against poverty which the President of the richest nation in the world has had to launch in his own country. In our ancestors hunger aroused only feelings of compassion and charity: since they looked upon it as natural and inevitable they had no qualms of conscience. To us the problem is presented as capable of solution and therefore causes us astonishment, indignation and revulsion.

In fact there is no shirking the issue. And quite apart from the probable consequences to us ourselves, economic evolution affects us all too directly as it is – and not merely on an intellectual level – for us to permit ourselves the luxury of shrugging our shoulders. We must not only adapt our plans to the circumstances but try to improve the circumstances as much as possible. It will be said that one individual can do nothing, but this is not true of individuals in the aggregate. In various ways people can influence group decisions and, involved as we are in the contrasts and lightning changes of today, we must avoid passing judgment on current world problems in the light of past experience – like the soldiers who entered the Second World War with the aircraft and armaments of the First. We must gather further information and rationalise our attitudes, instead of coming to decisions based solely on groundless beliefs or inherited taboos, as so many do. Illogicality is more common than it would appear, even though man no longer believes in witches or the burning of heretics. Progress confines itself, apparently, to burning only the Jews (in a scientific furnace, of course) and to torturing men only for accepted crimes – such as being black in America or white in the Congo.

This book is addressed to those who want to know what is happening to us; who want to see where we are going – as far as that is possible – and who want to plan their conduct as rationally as they can. I shall therefore try to make an assessment of the

A futuristic view of Paris in 1952, from Albert Robida's *La vie électrique*, written in 1892. Although it shows imaginative inventions and no little insight into the future (a city enmeshed in electric wiring, for example), we note that it judges the future by the standards of the time.

economic forces to which we are subject, and grouping them in the three categories of population explosion, technical acceleration and social evolution. I believe that the whole of our present economic situation can in fact be explained by a combination of the factors composing these three forces. In reality, the three forces can be reduced to two, since the modern population explosion is the result of technical progress within a social setting which shows little sign of a parallel evolution. Nevertheless, the tremendous pressure exerted today on the economy and on world politics by the rapid increase in population justifies its prominence in the next chapter. This chapter will bring out the salient technical and social elements of the problem, and from these we will infer reasons for expecting a progressively more rational approach to the subject of birth in the next few years. The hope of attaining this objective, however, must not blind us to the sheer magnitude of the present problem but must spur us on to its speedy solution.

Therefore, as the foundation of the whole evolutionary process, the technical and social forces will need to be further amplified. As the famous lines from *Faust* put it, these forces can be compared with the warp and woof of that 'loom of time' at which the Spirit of the Earth works. An infinite number of threads make up the social warp and in and out of them darts the swift shuttle of technology, with such impetus that sometimes it dislocates them and has to rearrange them. I shall examine these forces in chapters 3 and 4, and try to give an idea of their characteristics and their probable effects.

It will be realised that the impact of these forces will depend on the nature of the material on which they act as well as on the milieu in which they operate. It is necessary, therefore, to make a survey of the field and to classify the social characteristics peculiar to different types of countries from the standpoint of their economic organisation. The systems currently produced by the inter-weaving of the various social warps with their technical woofs are studied in chapter 5, since the starting-point for each country's future evolution will clearly be its present situation. These systems make

XXXV
ARR^t
RUE 642
CONSTRUCTIONS
en PYROGRANIT et CRISTAL
FONDU
BANQUE

up the entire field of the world economy, and it is the interaction within this field of these previously analysed technical and social forces that we shall study. In order to determine the future evolution of each category of countries we shall make use of a method employed in physics which, after establishing the nature of a 'field of forces', states the probable path of each 'experimental body' introduced into such a field. Since these diverse systems can be regrouped into the three *ensembles* of capitalist countries, socialist countries (both on more advanced technical levels), and emergent or less developed countries, I will discuss the prospects of each of these groups in turn in chapters 6, 7 and 8. Finally I will attempt an answer to these three questions in particular: Whither capitalism? Whither socialism? Whither the emergent countries? Because these three systems are evolving interdependently, this will be equivalent to asking whether the threefold distinction will be maintained in the future or whether the three systems will converge into one or simply reveal a closer relationship than at present.

Nevertheless, this method has a flaw which cannot be disregarded. The flaw lies in making predictions on the basis of present and immediately past events – that is to say, in projecting recent history into the future. No other scientific bases exist, of course, but historical extrapolation is not enough, since the future is made up not only of foreseeable components but of imponderables. Just as there are mutations in biology, so here too the course of events may be affected by sudden changes – technical innovations, for instance, which are as yet scarcely dreamed of or new social attitudes which are still only rudimentary. Perhaps the only truly reliable assertion that can be made about the future is that it will be different from the present. Consequently it is necessary to supplement the inferences drawn from facts with what might be called an historical vision, a world view based on scientific intuition.

Strict logicians generally object to the employment of this intuitive method of cognition. But sometimes a poem reveals deeper and more universal truths than a treatise, just as sometimes a visionary can foresee the future better than an academic. Moreover, since science is always provisional, we lack criteria conclusive enough for us to be able to tell the imaginative charlatan from the intuitive genius who may well shock the scientific establishment today with assertions which are destined tomorrow to be universally admitted. The insights of a Columbus or a Galileo in the face of the theologians provide examples, often repeated in history, of the inability of 'experts' to admit a new victory of the human mind over mere dogmatic beliefs. There have always been learned officials to 'prove' that vaccination was murder, that iron ships could not float, that locomotives would skid on their rails. The scientist in fact must admit the possibility that his experience and information may later be superseded and amended. Above all, he must accept the importance of illogical attitudes for they can be a most fruitful source of intuitions which may lead to scientific discovery – though once the inspired idea has been conceived it must be subjected to the stern discipline of logic. As J. A. Schumpeter has written, with specific reference to economics, 'In every scientific venture, the thing that comes first is vision'. Without this kind of vision or creative imagination it will never be possible to glimpse what lies beyond the horizon.

2 The population explosion

Eleven thousand per hour

Some four thousand five hundred million years ago, according to modern hypotheses, a few fragments of matter broke away from the sun and began to rotate around it. Almost two thousand million years later there appeared on one of these fragments, the one we call Earth, the first manifestations of a new phenomenon: life. Gradually the living organisms grew more and more complex and diverse, until a particular species began to reveal a unique talent for dominating its environment. The exact course of events is uncertain, but it is generally agreed that a million years ago *Australopithecus* was chipping out crude stone tools and half a million years later *Pithecanthropus Pekinensis* had learnt to use fire. Man was beginning to move away from the lower animals and has since continued this advance until today he appears to want to move away from Earth itself.

Throughout this long period human beings have been multiplying, recently at such a rate that the so-called 'population explosion' has become one of the most important factors in world economics. This is how the United Nations authoritatively put the matter in its survey entitled 'The future growth of world population'. The prologue ends with these words:

> The growth of the population in the next twenty-five years has an importance far outweighing any other economic and social consideration, for it represents the very core of our existence problem.

The comment is a valid one because the population of the world is now growing by more than five thousand per hour, and this rate is increasing rapidly. According to the United Nations the average rate of growth in the last quarter of the twentieth century will be in the region of eleven thousand per hour. Each year economic expansion has to support an increasing number of people and this intensifies the size of the output necessary. Consequently our analysis of the decisive forces of the present must begin with this biological phenomenon, which is the oldest of all human phenomena.

However, the population explosion is an entirely modern factor. In prehistory it is estimated that the world population must have been somewhere between two and twenty millions (most probably in fact between five and ten millions), allowing for early man's dependence on the gathering of uncultivated food and the uncertain results of hunting and fishing. In about 9000 BC, mankind's first great technical revolution occurred when the nomadic way of life was replaced by soil cultivation and stock-rearing. This revolution of the Neolithic age permitted the concentration of population in groups such as flourished in the Nile delta and other regions of the Near East where peculiarly favourable circumstances existed.

Man was now no longer passively limited by his environment. His economic development grew and so did his number. The first cities were built and by 3000 BC the first population census had been taken. Painstaking research has enabled us to arrive at a figure of fifty-four million as the population of the Roman Empire at the death of Augustus in AD 14. A census more or less contemporary with this (AD 2), carried out in China during the Han dynasty, enables us to estimate the total world population at that time as between 200 and 250 millions.

It was a considerable advance even though it had taken several thousand years. The growth of the population had surmounted environmental restrictions, but further growth continued to be very slow. Kuczynski has calculated that one human couple at the time of Julius Caesar increasing at the moderate rate of an annual one per cent – about half the world rate today – would have given Europe a total of 700 millions by 1933, which is more than the actual total for that year. Since there were several million couples in existence at the time of Caesar, it can be seen that the rate of increase must have been considerably lower than one per cent, which is the present European rate. Huxley calculated it as an annual average of 0·07 per cent, between 850 BC and AD 1650. It must be remembered that an annual rate of one per cent, although apparently insignificant, leads in time to extraordinary results – such as those related in the story about the inventor of chess: when asked

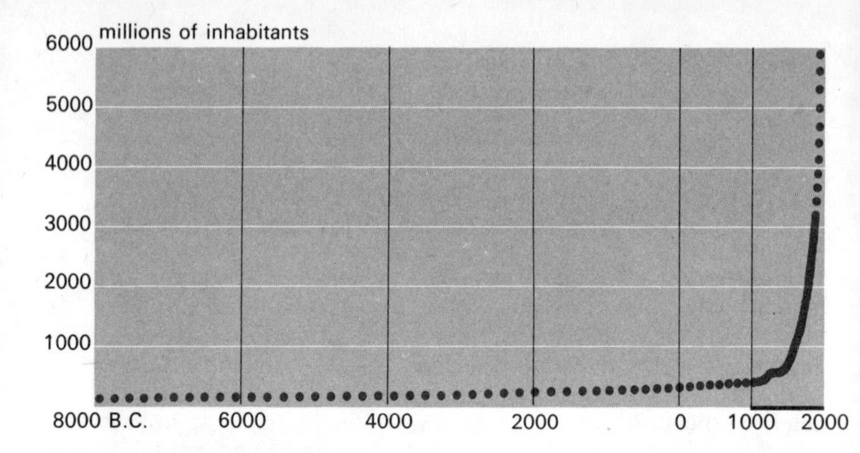

what reward he should have for his invention, demanded merely a single grain of wheat in the first square, two in the second, four in the third and so on progressively, so that in the end the Shah of Persia did not have enough wheat in his whole Kingdom to pay him. Putnam has worked out that if the annual increase of one per cent had been maintained from the Neolithic revolution there would now exist in outer space a spherical mass of human bodies several thousand light-years in diameter and by now expanding at a speed several times greater than the speed of light.

At Huxley's rate, the world population increased fairly slowly up to the mid-eighteenth century, as shown by the curve in figure 1. By then it had risen to 750 millions. But then another great wave of technical innovations appeared which, like the Neolithic revolution, also had repercussions on the population. The Industrial Revolution initiated a sharp increase in population, which started in Europe and spread throughout the rest of the world in a tidal wave that has not yet been checked, so that by 1900 the world population already exceeded one thousand five hundred million. In only a century and a half the human race had doubled. Fifty years later it had almost doubled again and in 1963 it rose to 3,135 million. According to UN forecasts it will again double before the end of the century, exceeding 6,200 million by the year 2000. Hence the use of the term 'population explosion'.

The pessimists and the optimists

If the tide of humanity were to continue to swell at the present

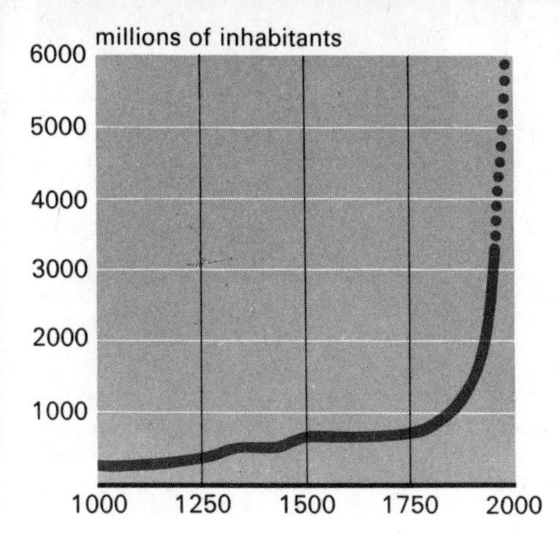

Figure 1. *The population explosion of the last two centuries.* The population explosion, which dates from the eighteenth century, is growing in intensity in our time. The present world population of 3,300 millions will double itself in thirty-five years if present trends continue.

rate, in seven hundred years, according to Brand, each person would have just over one square yard of standing-room – even supposing that all the area occupied by the oceans could be used as well. Although such a situation is inconceivable, calculations of this sort cause some authors to revive the fears of Malthus when they are faced by optimists, who rely on new techniques of production to multiply yet again the loaves and the fishes and satisfy the clamour of the ever-growing multitude.

In other eras, with more equable rates of increase, most people were only too glad to note a rise in numbers. Wars, plagues and famine wrought such havoc from time to time that instead there was a fear of depopulation and a shortage of manual labour or military personnel. Hence the Biblical dictum 'Increase and multiply' was the watchword throughout antiquity and the Middle Ages, though there were notable exceptions in men like Plato and Aristotle who appreciated the drawbacks of overcrowding in the restricted environment of the Greek cities.

In the modern European monarchies even in the seventeenth and eighteenth centuries, writers of the so called 'Mercantilist' and 'Cameralist' schools were in favour of encouraging population growth, sometimes by extreme measures such as bigamy – which was legalised in some German states after the Thirty Years' War. Population growth was valued highly as a source of military strength, as well as being regarded as a basis for economic prosperity. The first treatise on the theory of population appeared in Germany in 1740, and its grandiose title *Divine order in the evolution of the human race* now stamps its author, J.P.

Süssmilch, as an optimist. An increase in the population was particularly coveted in Spain, after losses in manpower due to the expulsion of Jews and Moors, and emigration to the Indies, as well as to the check to growth produced by large numbers of ecclesiastical celibates.

Solitary voices, like that of Giovanni Botero in the sixteenth century, were already raised in warning against a possible rapid rise in the birth rate but in general opinion was favourable to it. This optimistic view was succinctly expressed by Oliver Goldsmith when he depicted his Vicar of Wakefield as 'always of the opinion that the honourable man who married and raised a numerous family, was rendering more valuable services than those who remained bachelors and confined themselves to speculation about the problem of the population'. Even in 1786 Joseph Townsend was crying 'Population! Let's have population at all costs!' But in 1798 there appeared the *Essay on the Principle of Population as it Affects the Improvement of Society*. This was an anonymous study which sounded a clarion call among thinking people and, because of the indignant rebuttals it provoked, ended by creating a new climate of opinion. Its author was Thomas Robert Malthus. The second edition, carrying his name, came out in 1803, causing a fresh outbreak of charges against that 'enemy of the human race who had been so shameless as to get married after preaching against the evils of having a family', as Bonar recalls. But uneasiness concerning the spread of population remained deeply fixed in people's minds. Malthus became the standard-bearer of those who tried, even by means which he himself would have disclaimed, to

Far left Thomas Malthus (1766–1834). In his *Essay on the Theory of Population*, Malthus was the first to throw serious doubt on the value of population for its own sake. *Left* Lord Keynes (1883–1946). In *The General Theory of Employment, Interest and Money*, Keynes questioned the fundamental principles of economic theory by drawing attention to the real economic problems of unemployment, and by emphasising the State's role as guardian.

stem the unwanted flood of human generation. It is a curious fact that at almost the same time on the other side of the world, the Chinese Hong Liang-ki was bringing out his book *Opinions* (1793), maintaining the Malthusian doctrine that population increases faster than food production.

Nevertheless, it must be admitted that uneasiness was more acute among moralists and philosophers than among economists, who were assured by Ricardo that the level of wages would regulate the growth of population. Moreover capitalism and socialism – two ideological undercurrents that came into sharper and sharper conflict as the nineteenth century wore on – tended to shirk the issue. Liberal economists looked upon a growing population as the dynamic force behind national industry and had eyes only for technical progress as displayed in factory potential, transport facilities and commercial expansion. These were the factors which had allowed the fledgeling United States of America to grow in one century in conformity with Malthus's geometrical progression without running into difficulties. The socialists took the opposite view of this progress and ascribed the wretched state of the workers entirely to the harsh evils of the capitalist system: once these evils had been rooted out, the population could grow without restraint. Even some years ago, at the World Conference on Population held in Rome in 1954, the Soviet delegate T.V. Ryamushkin criticised the proposals for birth control as 'anti-scientific' and 'reactionary'. Economists, in fact, showed very little further interest in Malthus until Keynes sang his praises; and Keynes was stimulated more by Malthus's ideas on demand than by his principle of population. Indeed, many economists continue to regard the specific problems of population as outside their province and in no way a bar to the effectiveness of their role.

Wealthy nations and starving peoples

This attitude is no doubt due to the fact that most economists live in developed countries. For them population is what they see in the big cities or on the well-kept highways: busy folk ably and purposefully going about their normal business. But if the horizon were to be changed to the Andes, Africa or India they would find *another sort* of population. Here the people are often listless and torpid because, in the words of Lord Boyd-Orr, the first Director-General of FAO, they 'drag out their lives in chronic hunger'. Such a situation, Boyd-Orr added, is the lot of two-thirds of humanity. Apathy and indifference, if not actual stupor, is clearly the normal condition of the man who is starving.

Therefore when reference is made to the problem of world 'development', it must be borne in mind that the whole impact of this word is on the task of eliminating hunger. More than half mankind are still waiting for that elementary stage of progress: an adequate food supply. This thought was uppermost at the United Nations when it launched the Freedom from Hunger Campaign; and it is for this reason that our present population explosion is a cause for anxiety. The continuing acceleration of population growth aggravates the food scarcity still more and threatens to neutralise the efforts already made to eliminate hunger. What causes the greatest concern is that it is precisely in the least advanced continents that the population explosion is most pronounced. As can be seen from figure 2, the starving countries are the ones whose food requirements are going to show the steepest rise. The natural rate of population increase (i.e. the difference between the birth and mortality rates) is highest in the underdeveloped areas, as can be seen from table 1.

Thus while the average annual rate of increase during the next few years will be two per cent, in South America and Asia it will exceed this figure and in North America and Europe it will fall below it. Hence in the underdeveloped countries we are witnessing a pathetic race between population and food production and the outcome gives genuine cause for misgiving. It is no longer a matter of conjecture as it was for Malthus, according to whom food would increase only in arithmetical progression while population would do so in geometrical progression. Now we have concrete

Table 1. Natural population increase in the different continents, 1950–75, on a mean hypothesis. The figures represent annual rates per 1000 inhabitants.

	1950	1960	1975
Europe	11	9	8
North America	13	11	12
USSR	18	18	15
Oceania	14	14	16
Africa	14	16	17
Asia	13	17	23
South America	21	24	28
World	14	16	20

Source: United Nations

data, collected and analysed by FAO with all the impartiality and ability of their technical advisers.

How can the problem be stated accurately? To take only the quantitative aspects of feeding, without reference to the more complex question of the qualitative imbalances in the national diets of some peoples (which are nevertheless so serious as to cause deficiency diseases through, for instance, irregular intake of certain vitamins), the daily calorie needs, as calculated by the FAO, are 3,200 for a man and 2,300 for a woman, giving an average of 2,750 per head of population. Now if the countries are separated into two groups, the first comprising Asia, Africa and South America (except Argentina, Uruguay and Paraguay) and the second all the rest, it will be found that the first group consumes an average of 2,150 calories per head and the second an average of 3,060. While the first group numbers some 2,136 million inhabitants the second has only 876 million and a much lower rate of increase.

This, then, is the problem: because of the rate of population expansion we are faced with the fact that, simply to maintain the present hunger level and prevent its getting worse, food production will have to rise 100 per cent in Africa, 150 per cent in Asia and 200 per cent in South America, by the year 2000. It is clear that in maintaining such a level one cannot use terms like economic development. If the object is only to provide for the needy section

Figure 2. *Regions of the world according to the density and growth rate of the population*. The rise in population is steeper in countries with lower standards of living.

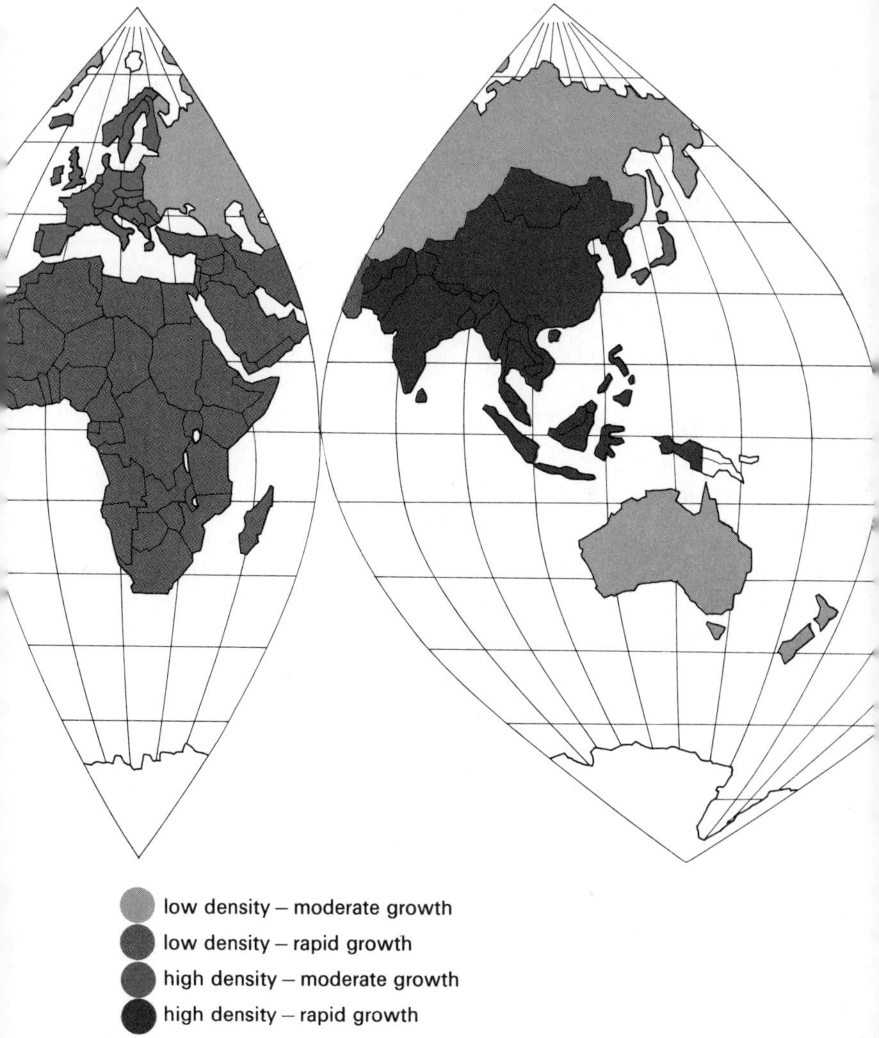

low density – moderate growth
low density – rapid growth
high density – moderate growth
high density – rapid growth

Table 2. Index of increased food production needs.
Present resources = 100.

Area of the world		1970	1980	1990	2000
Far East	Low hypothesis	148	186	233	292
	High hypothesis	207	259	324	406
Near East		154	190	240	307
Africa	Low hypothesis	128	155	189	230
	High hypothesis	143	174	212	259
South America (except the Argentine, Uruguay and Paraguay)		145	194	257	338

Source: FAO

of mankind enough food of the prescribed calorific value, quite apart from other welfare needs, FAO estimates that the requisite increases in food production will have to reach the proportions set out in table 2.

Biological forces, therefore, make it imperative that by the end of the century food production should reach between double and four times the present levels, according to area and product, if no more – and no less – than the end of starvation is to be achieved by economic development. Will technical achievement be able to meet this challenge and banish for ever the spectre of hunger, which has been man's constant companion since he first appeared on this earth?

The answer is uncertain because among the unforeseeable elements of the future there might emerge new methods of production which are impossible to guess at today. But it must be said that the experience of recent years does not, in fact, give rise to optimism.

Figure 3. *Future food requirements.* The population explosion implies a greater demand for food. In order to reach a reasonable level by the year 2000, the production of food in general will have to increase three times, that of animal products four and a half times, and that of cereals two and a half times.

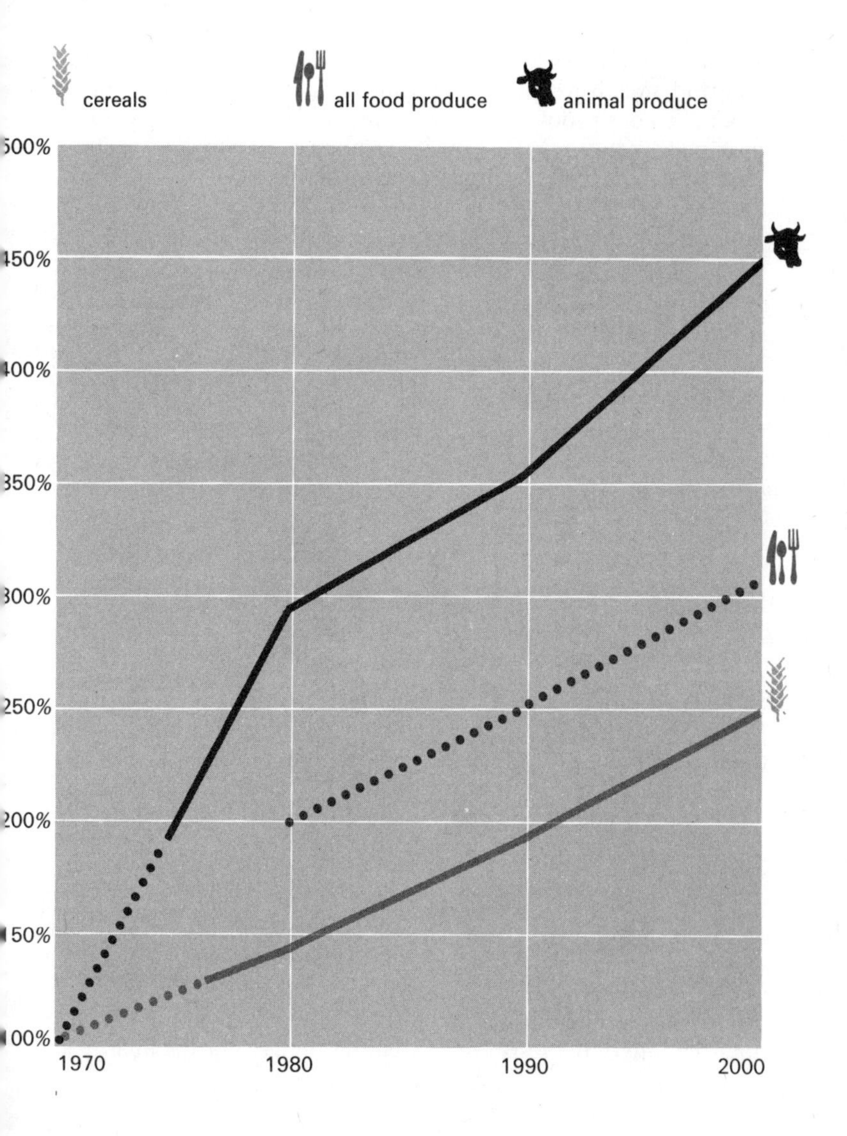

From economists belonging to each of the great camps of capitalism and socialism, to one of which the most advanced nations belong, comes proof of growing economic imbalance between rich and poor countries. A Soviet economist, L. Stepanov, stresses that while in 1950 the underdeveloped countries were receiving 12·4 per cent of world production, in 1959, according to data supplied by the United Nations, they received only 9·7 per cent. These figures can be argued one way or the other, but publications in the capitalist world are not much more encouraging. In 1960 Thorkil Kristensen, the present Secretary General of the Organisation for Economic Cooperation and Development (OECD), issued the result of investigations carried out by a group of colleagues on perspectives in world economics. According to his calculations, while net production per head up to 1980 will show an annual increase in the most advanced countries of between 1·2 and 2·5 per cent, even at a minimal assessment, in Asia it will record a drop of 0·3 per cent and in the underdeveloped countries it will increase on an average to only 0·9 per cent. On a more favourable assessment, Asia could increase to 0·7 per cent and the remaining underdeveloped area to 1·9 per cent; but the advanced countries, too, would go up to between 2·6 and 3·9 per cent, so that the disparity would be increased.

The facts are therefore alarming. But it is by no means surprising, when one considers that starving countries live in a vicious circle: they are hungry because they produce little, but they also produce little because they are hungry. This is self-evident, but the people of advanced countries, who only occasionally feel tired and disinclined to do anything at all, usually cannot imagine what it means to be in such a condition permanently. As proof of this, consider how frequently they accuse indigent peoples of being indolent and fail to notice that when the worker from an underdeveloped country emigrates to a prosperous environment and gets proper food, his working efficiency and initiative improve at once. Modern experimental studies on the effects of hunger have revealed that the longer the tests are carried out the greater the apathy and

Figure 4. *The widening gap between developed and underdeveloped countries.* According to Kristensen's estimate, the average production per head in the developed countries will increase from $945 in 1955 to $1405 (minimum hypothesis) or $2015 (maximum hypothesis). The figure for underdeveloped countries will rise only from $100 to $115 or $145. Even in the best conditions, the gap between rich and poor countries will increase by 49 per cent in twenty-five years.

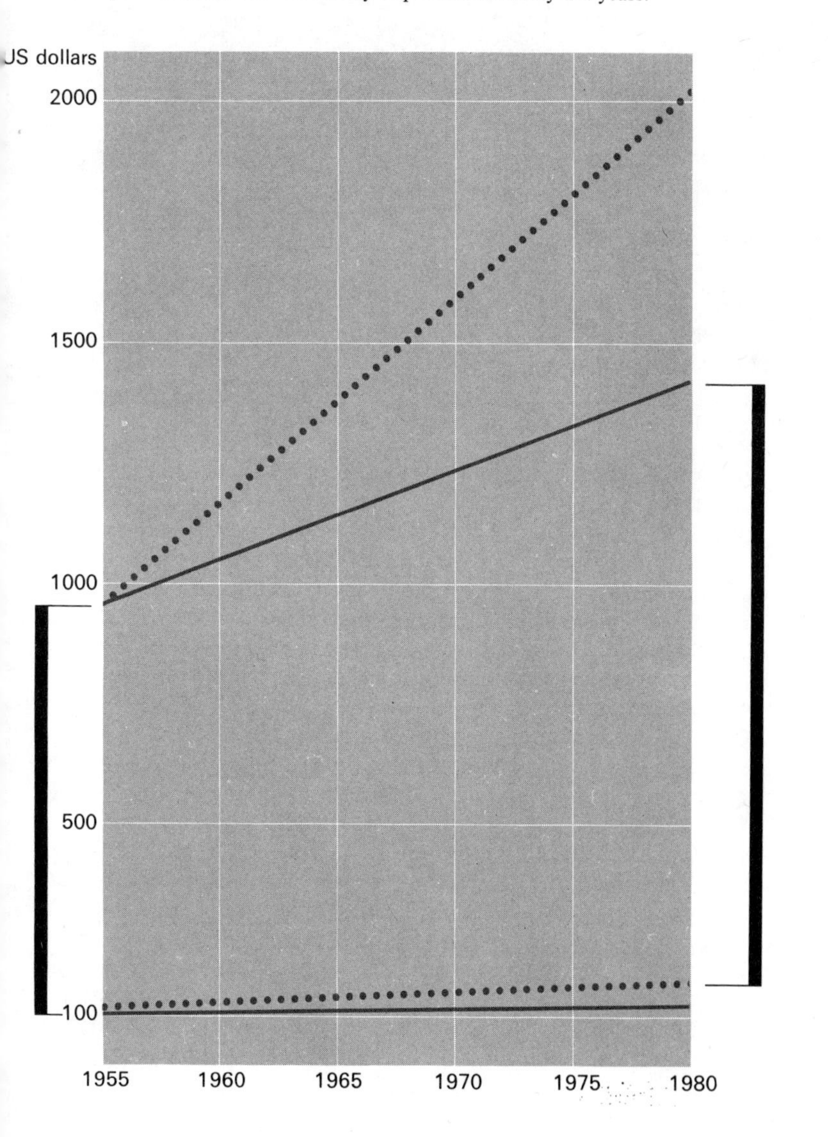

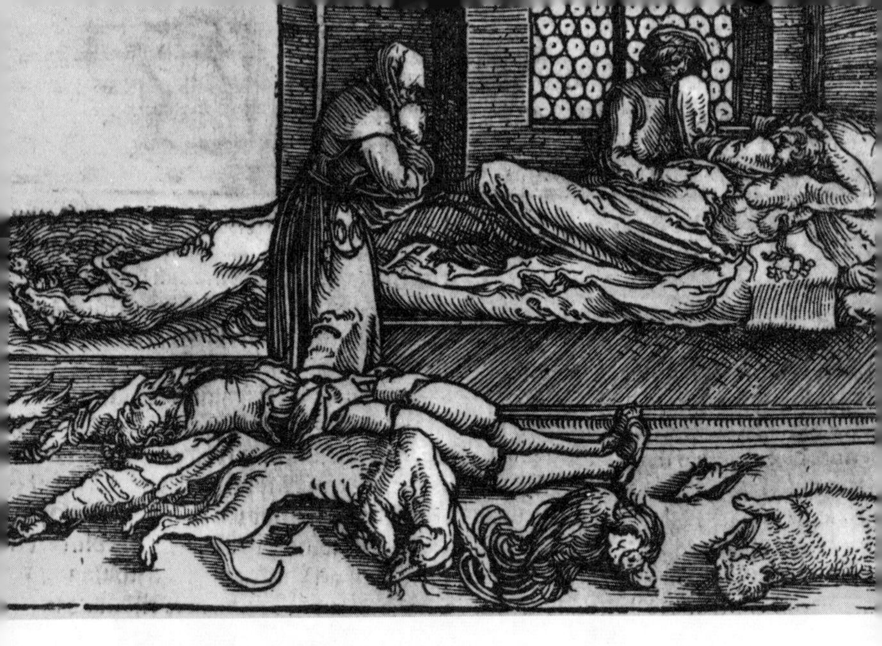

emotional depression shown by the human groups under observation. As initiative and will-power diminish, so interest is lost and it becomes impossible to concentrate on the work in hand.

Thus hunger and lack of production are mutually related. This can be illustrated with an example drawn by FAO from an article by Myron Stears in *Harper's Magazine* entitled 'The road that food built'. It refers to the construction of a highway in Costa Rica which was making poor progress until some new contractors improved the labourers' rations. Until then the workers, 70 per cent of whom came from Costa Rica and 30 per cent from the USA, were only managing to move 312 cubic yards of earth per man per day. With improved diet, and even with the proportion of Costa Ricans increasing to 88 per cent, they reached an average of 1,504 cubic yards.

It is not therefore surprising that the International Conference on Population should come to the conclusion that the rapid growth of population in an agricultural economy (which usually predominates in the underdeveloped countries) tends to lower the standard of living and can hold back economic development. The population explosion demands an increasingly higher food production on the part of a population already underfed and conse-

An illustration, c. 1520, by Hans Weiditz for Petrarch's *De Remediis* – a dramatic portrayal of the plague which decimated Europe in the fourteenth century. Before the advent of scientific medicine, disease acted as a natural curb on the population.

quently possessing only scant initiative for the increased output necessary. In spite of the optimists, the most recent experiments indicate that, under such conditions, the prospects cannot be considered encouraging. The effect on the world economy of this biological force that we are studying is to make the human possibilities of attaining economic development in these countries very doubtful indeed unless there are unforeseeable technical advances.

But do we have to resign ourselves to a reliance only on the unforeseeable? Is the population explosion a relentless uncontrollable mechanism?

The balance of life and death

To find an answer to these questions, we must make a closer analysis of the population explosion, to see if it can be checked at source. An increase in population will be correspondingly as rapid as the increase in the gap between the birth rate and the death rate. The highest birth rate figures rarely exceed an annual fifty per thousand inhabitants. The mortality rate can without any doubt exceed this during specific hazards, such as epidemics, but it is plain that on a long term reckoning it has kept below the birth rate. The slow evolution of the population over thousands of years is ample proof that on the whole mortality must have remained for a long period at a level slightly below the natural birth rate, thus bringing about a gradual excess, checked from time to time by plagues or wars which periodically increased the death rate. In the comparatively recent past the Black Death of the Middle Ages or, in Spain, the great plagues of the seventeenth century and even in 1885 the cholera outbreak which caused 120,000 deaths, are outstanding examples of this.

This situation, whereby a 'natural' compensation was maintained in the balance of life and death, began to be modified in antiquity, but with no extreme results, to judge from the scraps of evidence available. From the seventeenth century onwards we have more information thanks to the first Tables of Mortality drawn up

Two French cartoons, c. 1800, attacking Jenner's anti-smallpox vaccine. Although inoculation rid humanity of one of its greatest scourges, it was violently opposed by many at the time as 'unnatural'.

by the English 'political arithmeticians' and above all to the first true statistical counts of population. Sweden began her census in 1749. The USA followed suit in 1790 and Great Britain and France in 1801. In Spain the 'census of Count Aranda', which was the first really accurate count, dates from 1768–9, and was followed in the same century by those of Floridablanca in 1787 and of Godoy in 1797.

These documents furnish indisputable proof of the progressive decline in the mortality rate from the middle of the eighteenth century onwards. As history bears out, the cause lies in the advance of medicine and the improvement of living conditions, which have prolonged human life. Two years before the appearance of the *Essay* of Malthus, Jenner carried out the first inoculation with his anti-smallpox vaccine, which brought to an end one of the most serious plagues of humanity and gradually broke down the tremendous resistance of those opposed to all forms of innovation. Other similar advances were also playing their part and at the end of the eighteenth century the mortality rate in France had dropped to 28 per thousand and in 1830–40 to 25. In England the decline was already noticeable in 1740. The 'natural' mortality rate in Spain, too – around the 40 mark – began to decline about the middle of the eighteenth century, although in 1880–4, it still stood at 30. At about this period it was 35·7 in Russia, 38·2 in Hungary, 26·5 in Prussia, 29·1 in Italy, 23·8 in France, 18·9 in Sweden. The mortality rate went on declining at more or less the same pace in direct ratio to the spread of modernisation initiated in Europe. At the present day, only one great area of the world, Equatorial Africa, exceeds 30 per thousand. Consequently, the decrease in the mortality rate has not been a predestined biological fact, but the result of technical progress.

What about the birth rate? The ancients were already aware of how to restrict it, apart from occasional resorts to infanticide. However, they generally had no wish to apply their knowledge since, as we have seen, public opinion was in favour of population increase. The high infant mortality rate led married couples to have a

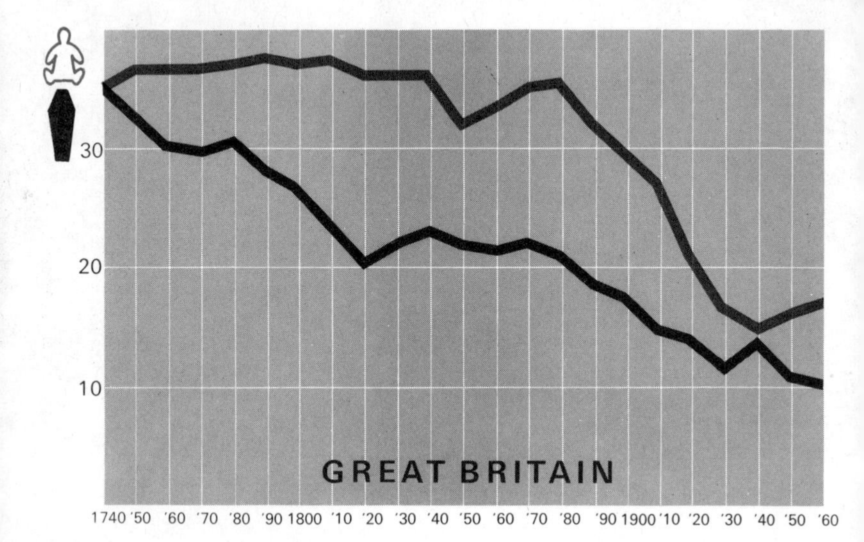

Figure 5. *The balance of life and death per thousand population*. In Great Britain, mortality fell slowly during the course of two centuries, while the birth rate remained high. In Spain, an intermediate case, this process took less than a century. In Chile, as in many new countries, the population explosion is extreme because mortality has fallen sharply in a few decades, while the birth rate has remained very high.

large number of children, so as to be sure of keeping some. Yet this attitude, which for a long time maintained the birth rate between 35 and 45 per thousand, began to undergo a change in modern times. The fall in the infant mortality rate influenced family decisions and, by the standards of the families of the Ancien Régime, which were still almost patriarchal, numbers began to be limited. Those whose ambition was to improve their lot by profiting from the opportunities afforded by the emerging middle-class world, would increasingly count the cost of rearing a large family and assess the handicaps that new babies would impose on their older brothers and sisters. At the same time, the alarm spread by Malthus awakened social considerations and the birth rate in general went on declining in modern countries to a level of around 10 or 15 per thousand, equivalent to less than half that of former times. However, the process was slower than with the mortality rate because it is more natural to apply technical achievements

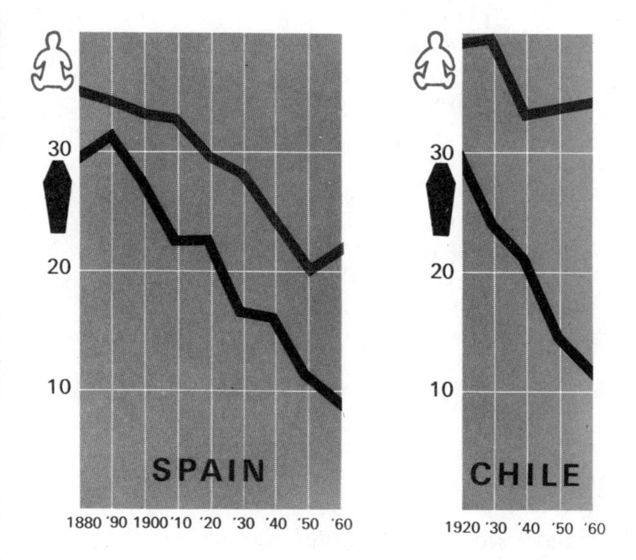

against disease and death, whereas when it is a question of controlling the birth rate, principles of a much more complex nature come into play. Therefore, in 1881–4 the birth rate was still 49·4 in Russia, 43 in Hungary, 38·8 in Prussia, 36·4 in Italy, 36 in Spain, 35·1 in England, 30·2 in Sweden, while in France it was already as low as 25·4. In Spain the annual rate of birth was never lower than 30 until 1914.

It can be seen that this imbalance between the forces of life and death, produced by technical advances, would generate a population explosion if a change came about in the relative speeds of decrease in the mortality and birth rates. When the former fell more rapidly, the population expanded considerably over a number of years. In Great Britain, for example, the birth rate was maintained at the old level for a hundred and forty years, while the mortality rate steadily fell, with the result that the population almost quadrupled from 1740 to 1880. From that year the birth rate also began to decline and the ratio of increase went on decreasing, until at the present day it has become remarkable for its absence of extremes, for although the 17·5 rate in 1960 is higher than the mortality rate of 11·5, the difference is below the world population average. With a few slight discrepancies, this has been the historical evolution of the European nations since the eighteenth century. Today almost all of them have a birth rate between 15 and 25 per thousand compared with a mortality rate of between 7 and 13 per thousand. The difference is considerably below the European rates of increase of a century ago: the explosion brought about by the beginning of modernisation has been tempered, a century and a half later, by the progress of modernisation.

But in the less advanced world the explosion continues, spreading from area to area in a chain reaction. The acceleration is even swifter than in nineteenth-century Europe because the underdeveloped countries are able to put into practice at one stroke all the medical and scientific discoveries accumulated over the years. It is true that the low economic level prevents any rapid improvement in living standards, such as the attainment of an adequate food supply; but many sanitary measures do not demand much in the way of costly supplies and even these are often defrayed by international organisations or by the advanced countries. Soap, detergents, insecticides, vaccines and antibiotics are making spectacular progress, at a reasonable cost, against infant mortality and death from disease, and biological forces are therefore causing an eruption in population. In figure 5 Chile is a case in point; and a most illuminating example is afforded by Ceylon, where the first systematic spraying of DDT against the malarial mosquito was sufficient to bring down the mortality rate from 20 to 14 in a single year, 1947. Even this figure dropped to 12 after the treatment had been continued for five years. In England nearly a century was needed to achieve the same decrease in the mortality rate. This then explains the explosion which seems likely to produce in less than two generations a total world population which will equal the sum of all human beings who have ever lived since the dawn of mankind.

One controllable force

As we have seen, this trend is posing subsistence problems, which are doubtful of solution unless something unforeseen arises. The difference between the high natural birth rate, and a mortality rate abruptly reduced by technical knowledge, is threatening to nullify all the effects being made to rescue the underdeveloped peoples from hunger. But there is one expedient already being practised by Europe: to apply a technical brake to the birth rate too. If human reason has prevailed against the 'natural' level of the mortality rate, what possible grounds can be alleged for not employing an equally rational approach to the birth rate? Of course, no justification is needed for a war against death and pain, while there is not the same ready acceptance of the use of technical weapons against the birth rate. But it must not be forgotten that though a restriction of the birth rate may check the creation of new lives, it appears in the light of the foregoing statistics about population, as a blow delivered on behalf of those already alive in the world. In the underdeveloped countries a restriction of the birth rate does not mean deciding against life. On the contrary it is a measure which gives more importance to the actual miseries of the living than to the hypothetical future life of those as yet unborn.

In my opinion there is no doubt that the choice should favour the starving living, even though it affects beings as yet non-existent, since the promise that technical progress will eventually find a way of feeding everybody is at present no more than a hope. When it is fulfilled, if ever it is, nothing will prevent a return to the natural birth rates. What I am trying to put forward here however is not my opinion but facts. And the facts today indicate clearly that the birth rate has been noticeably controlled in Europe, despite religious laws and beliefs which frequently frown on such action. As we have seen, even in countries like Spain, where the official attitude is strictly opposed to any form of voluntary control, the birth rate does not today reach half the 'natural' level. Although, generally speaking, they are lagging behind in facing up to the facts, in one or two countries the authorities are beginning to put their views into operation. Sweden is one, with the law of 1938; another is Japan with her eugenic protection law of 1948; and there are others like India, which have begun this policy subsequently. In other countries there are advisory bodies which are in operation, like the English *Family Planning Association*, affiliated to many similar organisations in the *International Planned Parenthood Federation*. Finally, some countries have tried variations in their policy, like the USSR which started by legalising abortion and instituting a campaign to popularise contraception; it later renounced this, in 1936, only to introduce further modifications, in 1944 and 1947. It can be asserted not only that a sane approach to the birth rate question is evident in a number of positive acts of this sort, but that in addition cracks are beginning to appear in those entrenched dogmatic beliefs handed down through the centuries.

Even so the problem is no simple one, and least of all in the countries where there is a pressing need for curtailing the population explosion. In India, where the birth surplus is a hundred thousand a week, the plan to encourage contraception ran into unexpected difficulties when it was decided to spread the Ogino method, because of illiteracy and lack of education among the women. Since those interested were very often unable to work out their infertile days, they were supplied with coloured beads threaded on copper wires to make the counting easier. But some of them felt embarrassed by the copper and others were opposed to touching the beads during their menstruation (believing that to do so would make them unclean) or having them near them during certain religious festivals. The most difficult part in nearly every case was to convince the women that the beads had no magical power whatsoever and that the mere fact of pushing them along the wire did not prevent pregnancy without co-operation of husband and wife. The result of the campaign was rather discouraging.

Before deriding our fellows in other continents for such stupidity, let us pause to examine how rational we ourselves have been in the past, even if the criteria prevailing at the time do invest objections with a certain aura of reason. When commenting on the unintelligent hostility towards vaccination against smallpox Cannan reports that even in 1900 one York councillor opposed certain measures to combat the infant mortality rate on the grounds that Jesus Christ said 'Suffer little children to come unto Me'. Concerning the birth rate, the European has not always held an attitude much superior to that of the women of India. In the face of this problem the pressure of dogma has in general outweighed the claims of common sense. There have been treatises as elaborate as the noted *De sancto matrimonii sacramento* (Antwerp, 1607) in which, in fifteen hundred pages, the Jesuit Tomás Sánchez deals with aspects of the theme in a wealth of detail comparable – in the view of distinguished authorities – to that of most secular literature of the period. In saying this, I am not suggesting that the Church advocates the growth of population as a paramount blessing, since, on the contrary, it extols celibacy, urges self-discipline on married couples, and rules that sexual appetites should be subordinated to the metaphysical purpose of human life. But there is no doubt whatever that the Church has greatly assisted in maintaining the taboo on the subject; hence the interest aroused by the recent discussions on the matter during the second Vatican Council.

But irrespective of attitudes, whether originated in dogma or not, the violence of the population explosion demands immediate action if irrevocable harm to the next generation is to be avoided. In Latin America the facts are clearly apparent in a population rise of 2·4 per cent per annum. This figure may not sound very impressive but it means an increase of a million inhabitants per week. The future is more serious still and the example of Chile with its 'old' birth rate and its 'new' mortality rate, is not unique. In Mexico the birth rate remained at 45·9 per thousand in 1960, while the death rate had fallen from 23·3 in 1939 to 11·7 in 1960.

In such circumstances, which are now generally prevalent in Latin America, an outlook based on dogma must give way before hard facts. Therefore, by July 1959, the Presidential Committee set

A Tamil poster portraying the misery of over-population. The future of whole nations may be determined by the success or failure of family-planning campaigns such as this.

up in the United States under the chairmanship of General William Draper to study foreign aid almost came to the point of recommending help towards a planned birth rate. Early in 1965, in his State of the Union message, President Johnson declared that he was ready to 'seek new ways of applying our knowledge in the struggle against the world population explosion'. Additional reports and inquiries confirm that this struggle is already spreading throughout Latin America where, since 1964, seventy-five different schemes for controlling the birth rate have been launched with the proper sanction of the various governments and official bodies.

Measures such as these can transform the Western hemisphere into the spearhead of a forward-looking world, and I am therefore convinced that the whole question of population is on the brink of a second transformation. If the first arose from the application of scientific progress to the mortality rate, this second revolution will result from a rational approach to the birth rate: and this does not mean an indiscriminate reduction, but a planned control. It is true that we are still a long way from the latter objective because the overthrow of taboos will not come about at once, although the information and propaganda channels of today are very much more effective than they were a century or two ago. It is equally true that we do not yet know how to control population skilfully and we thus lay ourselves open to excesses such as those of Japan, where the very effectiveness of the control of births from 1948 has brought about a rapid ageing in the population, which has merely substituted for the unproductive mouths of infants those of the elderly. Our prime concern is to modify the irrational outlook which still prevails in many areas, until millions more people are properly fed: in other words, until the dignity of the living takes precedence over consideration for the unborn. Optimistic hopes for an explosion in technical production must not check any controlling action until these hopes are in fact realised.

Without doubt this second population revolution of our time will embrace measures arising from our unprecedented scientific knowledge in the field of genetics. Its application will rationalise

දරුවන් වැඩිද ?

අඹුසැමියන්ට නොමිලේ උපදෙස්

அதிகமான பிள்ளைகளா ?

தம்பதிகளுக்கு இலவச ஆலோசனை

පවුල් සංවිධාන සංගමයෙන් විමසන්න

குடும்பக் கட்டுப்பாட்டுச் சங்கத்தைக் கலந்தாலோசியுங்கள்

23/5, හෝර්ටන් පෙදෙස, කොළඹ. 7

23/5, ஹோர்ட்டன் பிளேஸ் கொழும்பு.7

VIGILANCE

not only the numerical growth of the human race but also the quality of the population. I will do no more than mention the subject here and stress its outstanding importance, because its proper development requires expert knowledge which is lacking in the economist. I will end by affirming that at the present moment, and unless the 'second population revolution' already under way becomes more general, the flood of world population threatens to condemn two thirds of mankind to unrelieved hunger, thereby holding back its technical and social progress. The answer to this challenge lies, of course, in the advance of technical production, which depends above all on those countries already freed from the yoke of hunger and its deadening consequences. But, at the same time, the rational, humane course of action is to face up squarely to the population explosion by attempting to dam the flood before it becomes uncontrollable. Fortunately, the attitudes which were most firmly entrenched in dogma seem gradually to be weakening and it may be hoped that blind biological forces will gradually cease to be the most severe hindrance at present to any form of planned development. This has already begun in Europe, although it will obviously need a generation to establish it. A resurgence of the birth rate such as the recent 'baby boom' in the United States and other countries, can then take place – without the shadow of such grave uneasiness as disturbs the world at present. In short, I believe that in the future these biological forces will be monitored by the other two forces that we are about to examine: the technical and the social.

If mankind acts intelligently, the population explosion from now on may cease to be a problem. In my judgment the facts already point in this direction although the full effects can not be seen as yet. According to my interpretation of the present world economic situation, set out in the chapters that follow, social and technical forces form as it were the warp and woof of a tapestry of events tautly fixed upon the loom of history. I shall now deal with these social and technical forces.

3 The technical acceleration

The transformation of life

I have only to let my imagination go back forty years to my childhood to see in a flash the enormous transformation that life has undergone. I do not even need to leave my own home to realise it. To begin with, we had no television or radio. The former belonged to the science-fiction future and as for the latter, in a friend's house there was a contraption surmounted by a trumpet-shaped loudspeaker. My father, however, loathed this machine which was forever crackling with 'atmospherics', because what he liked was *music*. So we had a gramophone, which it was very tedious to have to wind up every few minutes, and a pianola. Deep down, I used to envy the caretaker who would spend all day in her cubby-hole listening to her 'crystal' with earphones on. My childish mind attributed to this invention the fact that the caretaker always knew everything; and my great longing was to buy myself some headphones and build myself a set as other boys at my school had already done. And there, too, we were certainly still using dip pens, because the fountain pen was not yet in general use, and the ballpoint was not even dreamed of.

Nor did we have a washing machine, a vacuum-cleaner or an electric iron. These things had been invented but they were not practical propositions. The washing was done as it had been for a hundred years and the dusting for a thousand. There was no refrigerator either, but there was an ice-box, which was naturally used only in summer. Because 'it wasn't healthy' we consumed few canned goods except tinned sardines, which saved me from that dreadful spoonful of cod liver oil. There were, of course, no vitamin pills and it was much more difficult to cure pneumonia without sulphanamides or antibiotics.

There were no plastics either, except bits of bakelite or ebonite on the gramophone or the light switches, unless one counts the synthetic mother-of-pearl on the spoon handles! There were no such things as plastic fabrics. Ladies' underwear made of artificial silk existed, but it had a 'common' sheen. And artificial silk

stockings were only accepted to save having to use a new pair made of real silk every day.

Horse-drawn vehicles predominated in the streets. It was a real sight to watch someone turning the handle to start a car. On very rare occasions there would be the roar of an engine overhead and everyone would look up to see an aeroplane. On Thursdays we used to go to the cinema, where a blind man would play the piano in the silent darkness. On our return home we would meet the lamplighter as he crossed from one pavement to the other to light the street lamps with his long pole tipped with a tiny flame. Finally, to turn to graver matters, even we children knew that after the first and final world conflict there would be no more wars. The proof was that things were going as well as possible. There was prosperity everywhere, except over in Russia where the revolutionary government could not last much longer now.

Doubtless the reader who belongs more or less to my generation has similar recollections. Indeed, nostalgia or amazement at the changes in our way of life are common in all recent generations. When Michelet brought out his history of the nineteenth century in 1872, he began by stressing that:

James Watt's (1736–1819) improved steam engine was produced in partnership with Matthew Boulton (1728–1809). The first engine was completed in 1774, and may be regarded as the symbol of the age.

one of the most serious and least noticed factors is that the pace of the times has completely changed, and its rate has doubled in an extraordinary manner. In one ordinary human span of seventy-two years, I have seen two great revolutions, which between them in former times would have perhaps demanded an interval of two thousand years. I was born in the middle of the great land revolution and now, before my death, I am witnessing the outbreak of the great industrial revolution.

That is to say that Michelet, like many others before him, had noticed the transformation which I want to discuss now in relation to the population explosion. Historians today are debating whether the expression 'industrial revolution' – later to be made popular by the elder Arnold Toynbee in 1884 – is the most apt. However, whatever term is used technical acceleration is unquestionably a phenomenon of the last two hundred years. Michelet, continuing the above passage, rightly emphasises that in 1798, the year of his birth, Watt and Boulton were starting to produce on a systematic scale their 'workman of iron and copper'. This was the steam engine, the dominating symbol of the age.

It is difficult to show this acceleration by a single figure, as we have done with the population growth, but its correspondence to the population increase is very clear. At first progress was extremely slow. The pace quickened in Classical Greece and more so after the Renaissance, accelerating in the eighteenth century like the population. Such a parallel is to be expected since the population explosion itself was the product of technical advance.

A few examples will give some idea of this acceleration. Norbert Wiener draws attention to the fact that the overseer of a Babylonian temple could have managed a cotton plantation in the slave states of the Deep South. Navigation is another example, for though progress was indisputably made it was very slow from the earliest craft, before 5000 BC, up to the ships of the Phoenicians or the Greeks. One of Hanno's Phoenician sailors would have felt at home two thousand years later in a caravel of Columbus; and one of Columbus's sailors, could have adapted himself to Nelson's frigates, three centuries later still. But a seaman transplanted

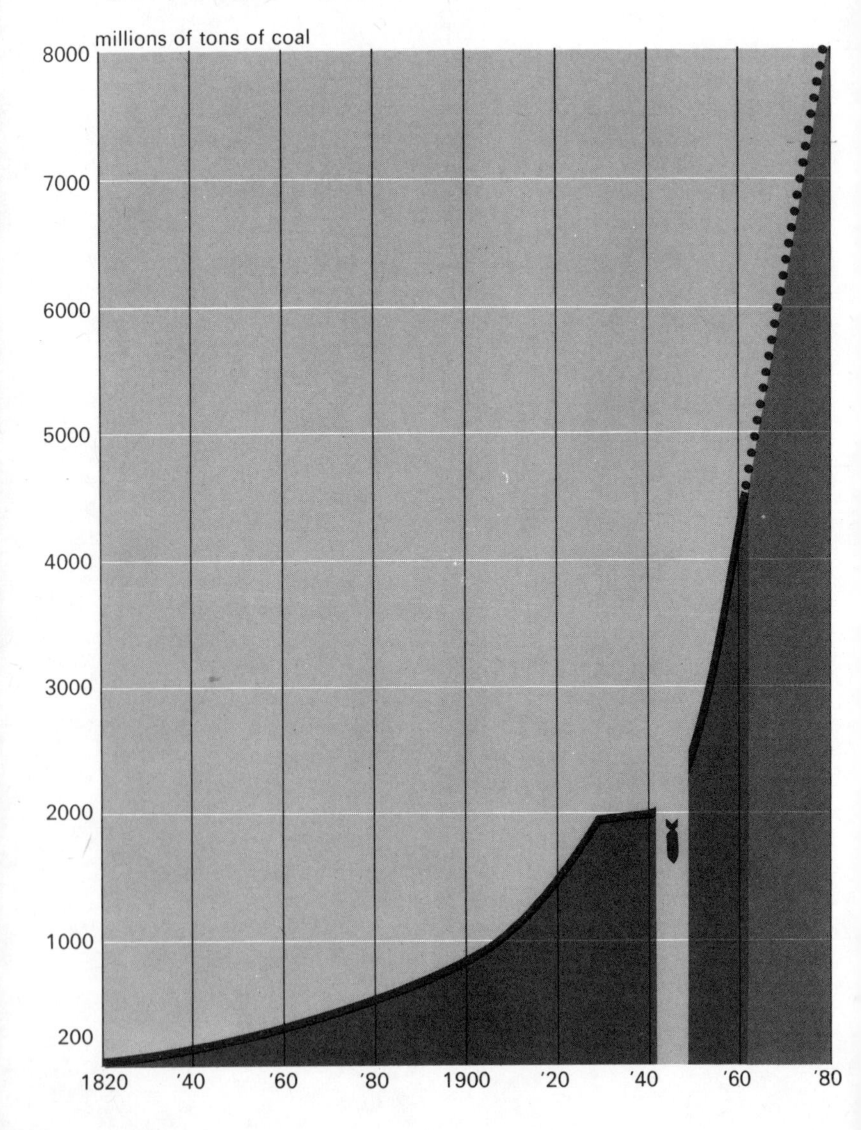

Figure 6. *The increasing consumption of energy*. A good index of technical progress is the world production of inanimate energy (coal, petroleum, natural gas and hydro-electric power) measured here as the equivalent energy in millions of tons of coal.

from the Victory to a modern aircraft carrier, would think he had been whisked into the world of magic.

Also indicative is the increase in the speeds attained by man, who until the nineteenth century could not go faster than a horse. In 1805 Paris took four days to learn of the victory at Austerlitz and, in 1830, a week to hear about Algeria. In 1865 Europe still needed twelve days to learn of Lincoln's assassination. By contrast we have the speed of present-day transport and communication methods, especially since the emergence of the aeroplane, whose development seems incredible if it is remembered that in 1903 on their first flight the Wright brothers reached only eight miles an hour.

Similarly textile manufacture remained almost static from Neolithic times until about 1490 when Leonardo da Vinci invented the shuttle. Then a century and a half elapsed before the appearance of John Kay's flying or automatic shuttle, the forerunner of all the machines which finally put an end to the thousand year-old hand weaver. Since no useful purpose is served by a random selection of examples, we will gauge technical progress by the progress of power consumption, which is generally accepted as an index of variation in the whole field of economic activity.

The available sources of energy remained almost constant from antiquity until the eighteenth century: the muscular effort of man and beast, the combustion of wood, and wind or water power. Coal had been known and used in Belgium since the end of the twelfth century, when Hulliez discovered its possibilities in a forge, but machines capable of using this fuel effectively had not yet been devised. The attitudes of the time were even less ready for it. Coal was to be distrusted by good Christians, because it was found under the earth and smelled of sulphur – two signs of Satan's abode. So it is that even after the Napoleonic wars, the entire world output of coal did not exceed fifteen million tons, as shown in figure 6.

A hundred years later, just after the First World War, this figure had gone up eighty times and it was supplemented by fifty million tons of crude oil, whose industrial production began around the middle of the nineteenth century in the United States and Roumania, together with electrical energy and natural gas. As calculated by Woytinsky, the whole of this amounted in round figures to the equivalent of 1,430 million tons of coal, almost a hundred times the figures for a century earlier. Production doubled thirty years later and today, in spite of inexact statistics about a coal-producing country as important as China, it can be said that modern sources of power are being used at an annual rate two hundred times greater than a century and a half ago. And it must not be forgotten that recently a further source of energy has been discovered, infinitely greater than coal: nuclear power.

Since these progressive figures refer to the entire world they may obscure another feature of equal importance in technical acceleration: its geographical distribution. Originating in Europe towards the middle of the nineteenth century the new technical thrust was scarcely apparent in other continents until it was introduced by Europeans themselves. A glance at maps of the different epochs suffices to show how railways – that form of transport so representative of the Industrial Revolution – first threaded their way throughout Europe, then appeared on the coasts beyond, pierced the hinterland and finally crossed the other continents. Economic historians have elaborated this process in great detail. We will simply recapitulate here the dates that Rostow allots to the periods of *take-off* in different countries, or the intervals during which the break occurred between the two types of society, the traditional and the developed: Great Britain 1783–1803; France 1830–60; USA 1845–60; Germany 1850–75; Sweden 1870–90; Japan 1875–1900; Russia 1890–1914; Canada 1895–1920; Australia, Turkey, Argentina and Mexico 1939–50 and finally India and China 1950–9. As for the overall picture at present, we have to hand a most revealing index with which to gauge the uneven growth of technical application in the various areas of the world. This yardstick is based on the annual power consumption per head of population. In 1962 the world average was just under a ton and a half of coal equivalent. The map in figure 7 shows the high level of the USA, Canada, Northern Europe, USSR and Australia, decreasing for Mediterranean Europe, some South American countries and South Africa. At present the extensive use of power associated with industrialised societies has not permeated the rest of the world. The process of diffusion still continues.

To technical acceleration and its geographical distribution can be added a further basic factor: qualitative diversification. Technical progress not only produces *more* goods and services, but constantly creates *others* that are different and were not at once available to man in his natural state. We have only to recall that a century ago the average man had no knowledge of the aeroplane, the car, electricity and the numerous applications of electronics, synthetic dyes, oil products, artificial fertilisers, artificial silk, aluminium, dynamite and the bicycle. To mention a few smaller items, there were no fountain pens, Yale locks, electric razors, zip fasteners or typewriters. Two hundred years ago there were no railways, steamships, air or gas balloons, or mechanised farming; and the textile industry and the iron smelting furnace were scarcely in their infancy. Neither was man aware of pencils, matches, mackintoshes, tinned goods, paraffin lamps or soda.

Chemistry is one of the sciences which has made such an enormous contribution to this diversification. One only has to consider the prolific network of by-products derived from coal or crude oil, or to reflect on the whole gamut of synthetic goods produced today. If we confine ourselves simply to the elements, we will recall that until Lavoisier's discoveries in 1789 only twenty-three out of all the many elements that make up the periodic table were known. Thirty-nine more were discovered between then and 1869. In the twenty years that followed a further twelve were added and from 1891 to 1900 another nine, including the four natural radioactive elements. As late as 1925 an additional five were discovered, to complete the identification of all the stable elements known to nature. Thereafter no new cycle opened until 1939, with the isolation of further elements by means of nuclear reactors, when over fourteen were discovered.

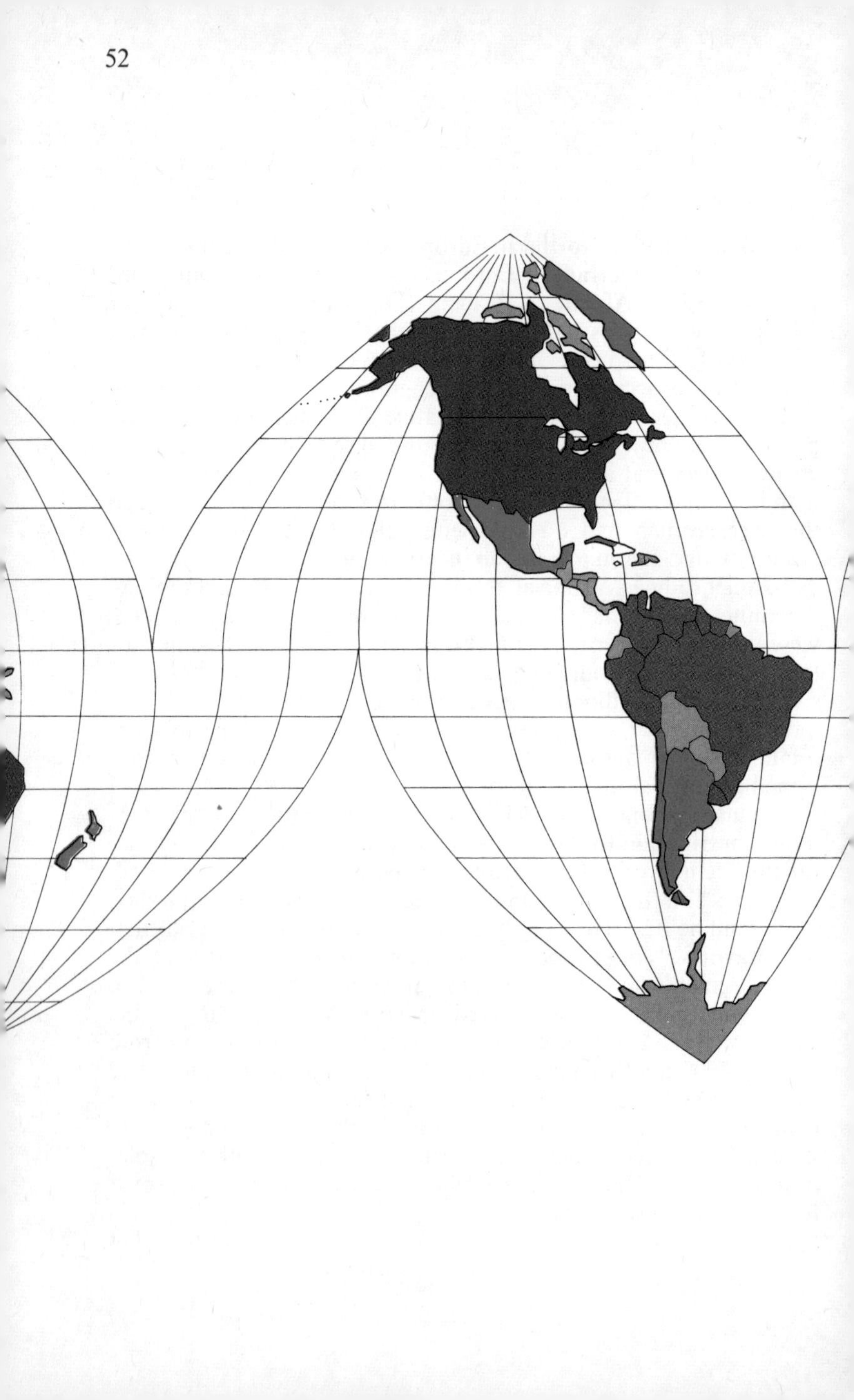

Figure 7. *The spread of technology*. The consumption of energy per head of population in each country indicates the extent to which technology has spread outward from Europe in modern times. Consumption here is measured in its equivalent in kilograms of coal per head of population for the year 1962.

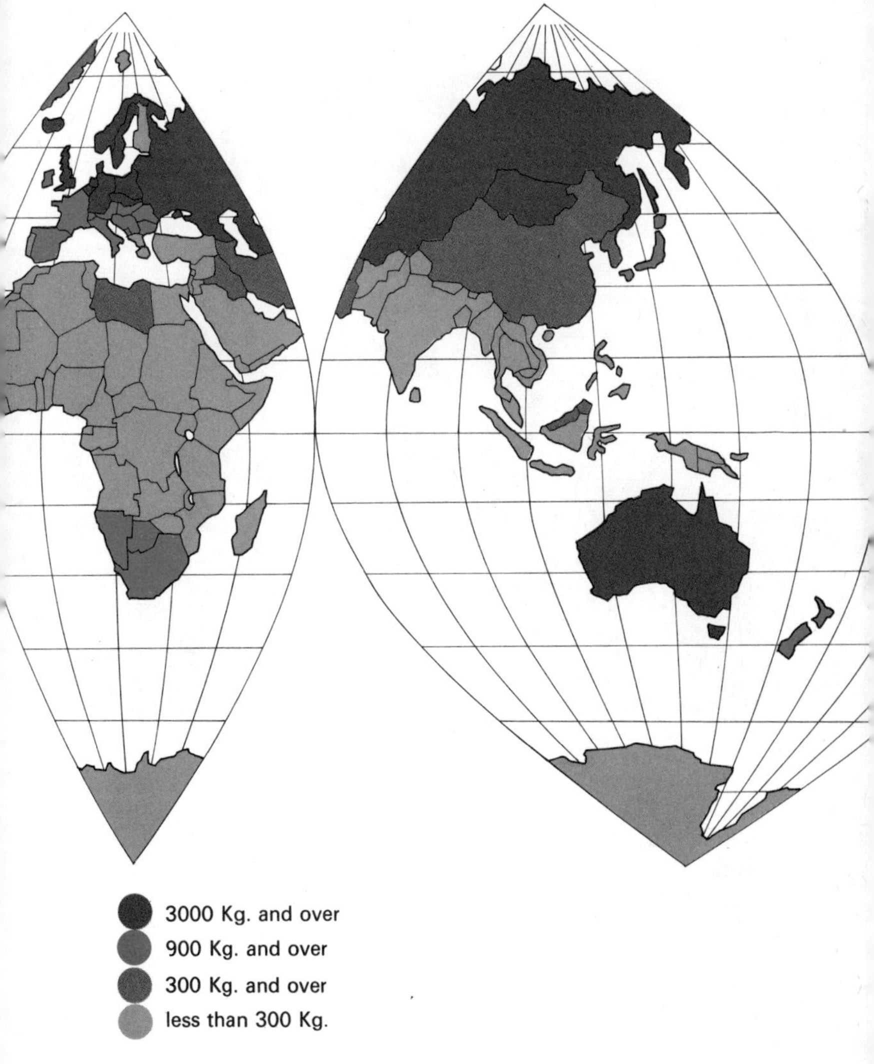

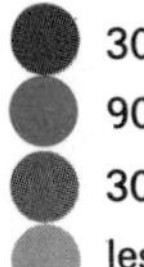

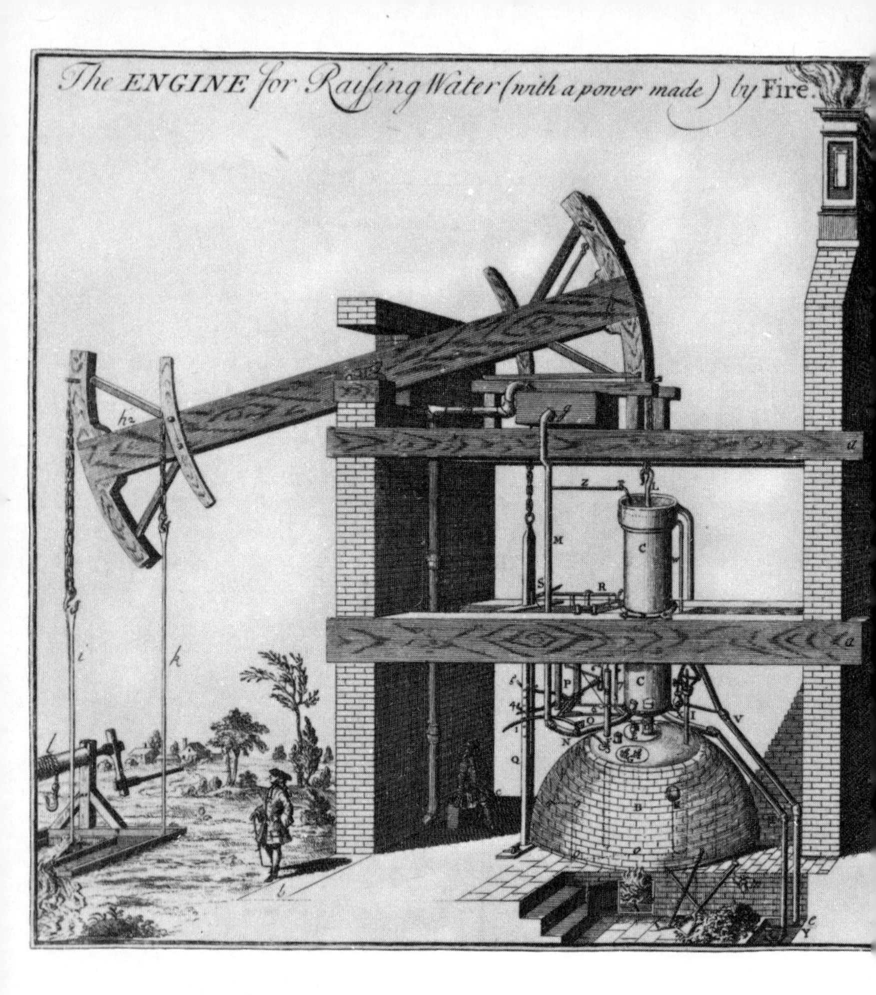

This diversification is also illustrated by developments in communication, which has a vital role in the growing dissemination of technical knowledge. Primitive man had at his disposal only his voice to transmit sound and his hands to convey pictures and signs. The invention of printing was the first great revolution. Since the nineteenth century we have had the telegraph, photography, the telephone, the phonograph, the typewriter, the cinema, radio and television. Moreover these technical processes have been combined in multiple processes of reproduction and

Beighton's engraving of Newcomen's 'atmospheric' engine (1705). Thomas Newcomen (1663–1729) set to work to find a mechanical answer to the problems of drawing water. His engine was five and a half horsepower and raised fifty gallons of water a minute from a depth of a hundred and sixty feet. It became the model for pumping engines in the mines for three quarters of a century, until improved by Watt.

diffusion so complex that today three methods of recording sound are employed: the mechanical, for the gramophone record, the optical, for the sound track in the cinema, and the magnetic, for the tape recorder. It could even be said of computers that, in fact, they 'produce' ideas, in the sense that they arrive at results which former methods found impossible to achieve, even though the process of obtaining them was known in theory. Cybernetics, the science of computers, is the modern descendant of the abaci of the East or Greece and the calculating machine of Pascal. But even if we consider this field as the preserve of the scientist, the so-called mass media so profoundly affect the man in the street that they are rightly regarded as the real prime movers in the social transformation of our age. Since technical progress is a basic factor in economic advance, these instruments, used to promote the other aspects of technology and introduce them both to the individual and to the masses, will have a decisive effect on future development.

To sum up, life up to two hundred years ago bore a much closer resemblance to that of the Greeks and Romans than to ours today. But although two hundred years exceed the life span of man, they are a mere trifle in history and do not even exceed the effective life of a normal machine. In fact, one of the earliest steam-engines, before the improvements brought in by Watt, was Newcomen's so-called 'atmospheric' engine, designed in 1705. The last engine built by this engineer's own hands to raise up water was still in service as recently as 1934 and to this day is to be seen in sound condition at Barnsley in Yorkshire, with its huge cylinder over nine feet in height, a venerable witness to the whole revolutionary process described above.

Acceleration, dissemination of ideas, inexhaustible diversification. What is this force of technical progress? What are its origins? How does it affect production and economic development? To answer these questions we must widen the field of observation, as we did in the treatment of population. We shall then understand why a process which crawled at a snail's pace for thousands of years suddenly moved into top gear.

The slow incubation of technological progress

I make no attempt here to summarise something as immense as the history of technical achievement, but it is absolutely essential to stress that both it and the spirit that inspires it are the product of modern times. Before the Renaissance technical experts did not exist. Such a concept requires a mobile society, like ours, in which sudden changes are accepted readily, in which the spur of initiative and the desire for financial gain are considered part of man's nature, where men uproot themselves without a pang, change jobs with ease and jump from one brand of food or clothing to another – a kind of society, in fact, which never pauses to reflect that such attitudes are by no means part and parcel of the nature of man but the result of centuries of training in the practice of thinking on one's own account. It is beyond dispute that mutations do not predominate in Nature herself, as economists are reminded in Marshall's famous *Principles*, one of their basic textbooks, where the opening theme is *natura non facit saltum.* No, the changes in Nature are accomplished slowly, because even her mutations need time to spread and establish themselves. Consequently, while man's natural habitat was the arbiter of his world there existed artisans and craftsmen but no true technical experts; there were sorcerers and wise men, but no engineers. In each case the one is separated from the other by the gulf dividing a stubborn rejection of all that is new from an enthusiasm inspired by that newness. Many centuries had to elapse before the gulf was bridged, as if it were too painful a process for our brains to have to learn to go outside the experience of our earliest childhood. This was such a laborious feat that even a man as modern in outlook as Galileo held that Nature can be conquered by conforming to her rigours (*natura parendo vincitur*). In this sentiment he revealed his allegiance to both worlds: to the modern in that he yearned to conquer, to the old because he was still subservient.

The traditional attitude, with its resistance to change, can still be detected in the rural districts of some truly advanced societies.

Plainly, it is dangerous to generalise. Ellul warns us, for example, against the oversimplified notion of a world of antiquity split into two mentalities: the one passive and Oriental, the other active and European. In reality the East was the source of all the numerous discoveries between the Roman era and the Crusades, embracing the centuries of Hispano-Moorish contact on Córdoba and Toledo, to whose college of translators Western progress owes so much. However, without risking the charge of oversimplifying, it can be stated that although Greece was the cradle of reason, she was herself much more academic and theoretical than technical and practical. Again, despite their realistic and enterprising outlook the outstanding achievement of the Romans was more in the sphere of social organisation – certainly very important – than in the practical application of the knowledge they had already acquired. Even a rather exceptional case among the ancients, such as the constructive genius Archimedes, 'held as base and worldly' according to Plutarch 'the practice of mechanical engineering and especially scorned any art that was prompted by necessity'. Similarly, to Cicero, nothing noble could come from a shop or a work-bench.

This disdain persisted for several hundred years among the upper classes of Europe. It was not the lack of eminent inventors that delayed progress but the absence of any community interest in changing the way of life. Clear proof of this lies in the importance of the discoveries at the School of Alexandria, where the institution of the *Museum*, about 280 BC, ushered in two hundred years of quite astonishing progress in mathematics, astronomy and mechanics. Although a native of Syracuse, Archimedes himself was educated at the *Museum* and created or perfected systems of levers and pulleys, as well as the water-screw which bears his name. Another Alexandrian of the third century BC, Hero the Elder, was a tireless creator, whose genius reminds one of Leonardo's. He invented the *aeolipyla* – a primitive steam-engine – the *hodometer* – the forerunner of the taximeter – an automatic dispenser for liquids, which was operated by a coin like those which now deliver cold drinks (though it is noteworthy that the Alexandrians used it

An engraving of one of the inventions of Hero of Alexandria. In the third century BC society was not prepared for an invention of this type, and like so many others originating at the *Museum*, it was considered little more than a toy.

for the purpose of administering purifying waters in their temples), and a miraculous shrine so contrived that as the fire was being kindled on the altar, the door to the sacred precinct opened of its own accord. These and numerous other discoveries had scarcely any general circulation and remained merely objects of wonder or amusement.

Because of its disavowal of all material things, Christianity at its outset was plainly opposed to technical matters, giving the Emperor Julian reason to blame it for the decline of productive labour. Even in the fifteenth century the economic ethics of the Church prevailed, embodied in the principle that though man can engage in business pursuits without thereby incurring sin he cannot ever be truly acceptable in the eyes of God while so doing. By its condemnation of slavery, however, Christianity removed one of the factors which had most contributed to the relative unimportance of technical progress till then: cheap labour. The concept of the dignity of human labour made gradual headway among Christians, diminishing the old antagonism to manual occupations. The monasteries were centres for the spread of learning and enlightenment, with such interesting men of science among their inmates as Roger Bacon and Albertus Magnus. There is a story told about the latter that he was successful in making a true *robot* capable of opening the door for visitors and carrying out other minor duties. One day the poor automaton was smashed to pieces by St Thomas Aquinas, who was seized by a fit of violent rage when this spawn of the devil came near him. This incident did not deter St Thomas from furthering the rationalisation of thought in his turn by basing his Scholastic doctrine on Aristotelian principles.

Thus a few figures appeared like volcanic islands amidst the sluggish waters of a society resistant to change and firmly set in tradition and dogma. Notwithstanding the ascetic indifference of the Middle Ages, the embryo of a new attitude which was to sweep Europe towards a technical, and therefore a changed, way of life, was slowly taking shape. According to Wiener there were three decisive discoveries which determined the advance in this direction:

the compass, gunpowder and printing. The compass undoubtedly opened the door to the great geographical discoveries, gunpowder gave access to the hitherto impregnable castles which were the backbone of feudal society, and more important still, printing hurled the book like a battering-ram at minds hidebound by convention. The era initiated by Johann Gutenberg was almost a repetition of the Alexandrian epoch. Archimedes and Hero are paralleled by the new era's remarkable genius Leonardo, who appears to have invented or anticipated everything in existence. Men began to believe in themselves and their power. The Church continued to inveigh against overweening pride to no avail, for in the flourishing Italian cities admiration was accorded to subjective *virtu*, the power to achieve great deeds whether in an ethical sense or not: with Leonardo, appeared Machiavelli.

Reasoning was beginning to shake off the fetters of dogma, though they still controlled the beliefs of the establishment. A singular personage, part alchemist part chemist, who abbreviated to Paracelsus his long name of Philippus Aureolus Theophrastus Bombastus Von Hohenheim, expressed the new outlook lucidly when he said in 1536:

It is God's will that we do not confine ourselves to the acceptance of an object as we are given it but go into the reasons for its creation.

After Giordano Bruno we come to Galileo and Descartes, who may be regarded as the first modern men. In the judgment of Ortega y Gasset it was from about 1400 that man first began to abandon his dependence on Christianity. Thomism began to be outmoded, and the key words in vogue were these: *reformatio, renasci, renovatio*. Reform, rebirth, revival. As Alfred von Martin concludes, in his *Sociology of the Renaissance*, the old social conditions with no rational basis gave way to a new order founded on system.

Once this stage was reached all was ready for the floodgates to open, and with the year 1600 a veritable torrent of new ideas was let forth, whose full impact was not to be realised until later on. A fresh intellectual attitude was forming which soon became widespread throughout Europe. Any handbook on the history of science or technology sets out the following milestones: Kepler's laws and the theory of Copernicus, Jansen's microscope and Lippershey's telescope, Galileo's pendulum and Torricelli's barometer. Napier's logarithms and Pascal's theory of probability, the differential calculus arrived at independently by Leibnitz and Newton, and, capping them all, Newton's laws of motion, which in 1687 established the theory of the universe that was accepted until the beginning of our own century. Man's relationship to the cosmos was no longer myth or dogma but a statement in the form of an equation. The slow process of incubation was over. The world as we know it had been born.

A mechanised world

In this stream of events several dates could be isolated as the starting-points of the technical era. The one just quoted for Newton's *Principles of Mathematics* could be used, or 1751, when the *Encyclopédie Française* appeared, since its spirit is so representative of the age. However, as economic development is our major concern, we will choose 1782, when Watt finally perfected his steam-engine, which was to become the symbol of progress and European wealth for more than a century. This machine marked the advent of the mineral fuel age in which man began to consume the forests which had been submerged by geological processes. Thousands of years of solar activity and carbonisation reached modern times in the concentrated form of coal, offering an unprecedented source of mechanical power. A comparable leap forward in the history of power will not be found until our own day, when by nuclear fission energy is drawn in a split second from the tiny solar system of the atom.

Whichever date is preferred, it was in the eighteenth century that the technical dam burst under the accumulated pressure of several factors; the long incubation described above, geographical discoveries, the gold from the Indies which revolutionised the European economy, the flexibility of society and the erosion of the old dogmatic notions. I am not going to give a detailed analysis of the process but it is important to determine the basic nature of industrialisation. There can be no proper understanding of this phenomenon unless it is clearly seen that its very essence consists in seeking the maximum rationalisation of behaviour. The technologist does not accept traditional standards or things as they are. To quote Paracelsus again, the technical attitude obliges us to understand why:

> the wool is on the sheep and the bristles are on the hog, so that we can assign each thing to its rightful place, and dress each dish to bring out the maximum flavour and fashion dwellings for the winter and roofing tiles to ward off the rain.

By dignifying labour and regulating monastic administration, the medieval Church made such outstanding contributions to industrial advance that Sombart could state that the true instigators

Fig. 1.
Fig. 2.

Two illustrations from Diderot's *Encyclopédie Française* showing the art of glass-blowing. The rational spirit of the time led not only to technical progress but also to the exact recording of it. The *Encyclopédie* was intended as a compendium of human knowledge.

of capitalist principles were members of the Benedictine order (though this of course was not their intention). With *ora et labora* as their watchword, their administration and their book-keeping were appropriate to lives regulated by the strict tempo of monastic hours. It is not surprising that the monk Gerbert, afterwards Pope Sylvester II, should be credited with the invention of the weight clock at the end of the tenth century. Since this type of clock had a prototype in the invention of Hero of Alexandria, this story is probably untrue. But for that very reason it is all the more significant. Such a timekeeping device was fundamental to the growing technical world – which already knew of its existence before 1335, since there was a weight clock at St Paul's Cathedral in London in 1298 for example, and another in Beauvais. The division of the hour into minutes and seconds had already become general by about 1345; and when by the end of the fifteenth century a Nuremberg clockmaker invented the first watches for hanging around the neck, the most astonishing rationalisation ever introduced into the natural world by a technical society was complete. Nothing less than the whole realm of time – the experience, so fleeting, of joy, so heart-rending of melancholy, and the seasonal changes of days growing longer and nights drawing in, had been converted into the mechanical slicing, the rhythmic ticking, of each second. If this mechanical time, as indifferent to nature as to our own emotions, were to be taken from us today, the whole industrialised world would collapse about our ears. Mass production, time-tables, the co-ordination of all our planned movements, the entire organisation of our life within the community would return to the vagueness of natural time, with no rationalisation. This vagueness had little effect on the old traditional society. It was scarcely felt as a nuisance when, as Marc Bloch relates, a tribunal required to give a decision on the expiration of a certain payment date, had to go into lengthy deliberations before pronouncing on whether the last quarter of the day had or had not elapsed. But with the mechanical clock we are reminded twenty-four times a day from the towers of every city that something valuable is slipping away from us, minted exactly into hours and minutes as gold is into coins. The mutual relationship of time and money eventually became axiomatic. Already in 1678 the stern spirit of puritanism speaks through the mouth of the preacher Richard Baxter when he thus exhorts the faithful:

To redeem time is to take heed that it be not squandered in vain, but let each minute be used as a thing of great value to be fully expended in the course of duty.

Later on, with his famous *Time is money*, Benjamin Franklin in 1748 was to coin the slogan that once and for all made time an object of veneration in the offices and factories of the capitalist society.

In his celebrated *Protestant Ethics and the Spirit of Capitalism* Max Weber in 1905 launched a dissertation which was at once well argued and fruitful; and in his *General Economic History* he defines the dominant characteristic of the industrialised world thus:

In short what capitalism created was the durable and rational accounting system, rational industry, rational Law; to all of this should be added *rational ideology, the rationalisation of life, rational ethics in economics.*

These italics are Weber's own and von Martin supports his view with a vivid example of systematic rationalisation when he tells us that in an account-book of the Venetian Jacobo Loredano he came across an entry which read:

Duke Foscari: my debtor for the death of my father and my uncle.

Entered on the appropriate line on the opposite page is the record of receipt of payment when Loredano had carried out his vengeance on the Duke and his son – a *vendetta*, all properly accounted and submitted to rational audit!

Rationalisation is indeed the core of the industrialised world so that nearly all the other characteristics usually associated with that world can be inferred from it. Take as an example the principle of moral neutrality in technology, which the enemies of progress find so difficult to accept. Down through the ages there has been the constant accusation that technical innovations are 'the inventions of the devil' or 'the offspring of evil'. This attitude is derived from the Book of Genesis, where the invention of the practical arts is attributed to the three sons of Lamech, a direct descendant of Cain the accursed: Jabal, the progenitor of all tent-dwellers and flock-rearers, Jubal, of all harpists and players upon the organ, and Tubalcain, the father of all metal workers and coppersmiths. This is neither the time nor the place for an inquiry into the real motives for such a devious interpretation, which is analogous to the ascription of technical feats to cripples like Hephaestus and Wieland, or men condemned to punishment like Icarus and Prometheus. Despite such arguments the fact is that technical achievement in itself is neither good nor bad and cannot therefore be blamed for the feeling we sometimes get that we are living in a world where objects have the upper hand.

It is true that to a certain degree a kind of dehumanisation, a callousing, of our environment has been brought about; not by any evil design of the objects themselves, but from another effect of the technical habit, arising from its rationalising and unifying tendencies. The technical mind seeks efficiency above all else and once achieved efficiency comes to be looked for in everything. If during the construction of a modern highway in an underdeveloped country, it is found that traditional customs are causing a cut in the number of working days or reducing output, these customs have to be subjected to rational standards. It is the unifying tendency of the technical attitude that demands this, for it resists an assault on the efficiency criterion and prevents its rejection for another point of view. Thus rationalisation is extended, even to our own amusements, but the fault does not lie with the technical environment. If material efficiency were not considered the paramount force it is other forms of behaviour would prevail, as they did in classical Alexandria or in China, where the compass, gunpowder and printing were known without their application becoming widespread, as they did in Europe. The Chinese compass did not encourage exploration in a people content with their own environment; gunpowder was reserved for firework displays at the great festivals; and printing was accounted a crude and paltry art compared with the high regard in which penmanship was held in the Celestial Empire.

Technical progress is, first and foremost, a process of rationalisation. The industrialised world thus runs counter to the natural world. It is this principle that Ortega y Gasset had in mind when he defined industrialisation as 'the reform that man thrusts upon Nature in consequence of the fulfilment of his needs'. Ortega adds:

These needs are thrust upon man by Nature, so he responds in his turn by bringing about a transformation in Nature.

The conditions are thus reversed and since man owes much in his own make-up to Nature, the effects of technology rebound on their instigator and thus the feeling is born of being the slave of his own handiwork. For rationalised uniformity is undoubtedly making ever-increasing inroads on our whole environment. It is hardly surprising that Karl Jaspers emphasises the contrast between our world and the other great 'axial' epoch in history, which, long before our time, produced within the space of a few centuries a large proportion of the founders of the great religions and moral systems: Confucius and Lao-Tse, Buddha, Zoroaster, the Prophets, Homer and the outstanding classical thinkers.

Even two or three hundred years ago, while the technical eruption was in full spate, its originators seemed to behave in accordance with impulses rooted in the natural world before their time. Darby, the famous ironfounder who introduced the use of coke as a substitute for coal in blast furnaces (1709), was guided in his discoveries by his Quaker convictions, according to which God must have had some purpose in mind in placing coal next to iron in the Birmingham area. It was thus difficult for men to abandon the old world and stride into an era where technical forces were decisively in the ascendant.

The growth of desires

We can now collate a number of facts to improve our knowledge of these technical forces and so assess their future consequences and direction.

In the first place we have seen how there emerged in Greece in the midst of a world of traditional societies an increasing appreciation of *reason* which, after fleeting eclipses and temporary setbacks, established itself for all practical purposes in Europe at the start of the modern era. The development of fundamental principles and attitudes based on reason related to experience – to science, philosophy, economics, politics – produced, from the eighteenth century on, an *acceleration* in the practical applications, which increased the range of human power over nature.

This quantitative acceleration has been further increased by *geographical distribution* and by *qualitative diversification*, which has stimulated the production of a variety of manufactured goods which have found their way, prompted by reason, into every sphere of human life. Thus a double process is at work to gear our era to the technical drive: there is the process by which more and more traditional societies are incorporated into the modern world and the other by which progressive rationalisation is applied to certain aspects of life, which until now have remained outside the influence of technical advance. It is undoubtedly true that in other continents, and in certain rural areas of Europe, there remain some human communities where life has only a fleeting and superficial contact with the modern world. A century ago Japan, and sixty years ago China, both deliberately shut themselves off from technical innovations. It is also a fact that even in our own world – since reality is more complex than the ardent system-monger would like – there are signs that technical progress tends to keep traditional industries in being: for example rural electrification has allowed the one-man workshop to continue, when otherwise it would have been forced out of existence by competition. Phenomena such as these, anachronistic in some cases and anticipatory in others, have no real effect on the general advance of the tide of industrialisation. Following the ascendancy of the magician came the era of the wise man or the philosopher and today we dwell in the age of the engineer, or rather of the organiser. When Stalin used to address the artists of the Soviet Union by styling them 'engineers of the soul' he was simply reflecting this reality in a vivid turn of phrase.

The transformation of our environment is an effect of this advance, causing the appearance of what Dessauer calls a *fourth kingdom* among the three classic kingdoms of Nature. Besides the animal, vegetable and mineral environments in which our lives had moved exclusively till now, we come across our own creations, sometimes with regret, sometimes with gratitude. It is not solely a matter of machines, although the term 'mechanisation of life' is the one most generally applied to all that is detestable in the transformation, but also of the effects of chemistry and biology, psychology and social science, which have begun to probe man himself and to learn to sway his motives through communications and propaganda. Again, the notion of the worker as the slave of the machine is already out of date, for cybernetic automation is beginning to take its place. Instead man today feels that his nature is being subjected to other more subtle enslavements and this feeling has not yet been clearly defined.

An outstanding example of this is afforded by our frequent impression that the powerful technical media of propaganda and diffusion mentioned in previous paragraphs are conditioning our ideas (and do we not already have *air*-conditioning in our houses?). From the standpoint of economics this situation must be expressly emphasised because while the progress of production techniques can be clearly observed, many people do not realise that the real expedient of the modern economy is not so much the capacity for output as the techniques of consumer incentive. A large modern undertaking does not confine its production to goods for a given market but in addition develops a demand for those goods by creating its own consumers. Today the inclinations of the masses are cleverly manipulated by advertising and public relations experts. With the aid of psychology, they exploit the most secret emotions of the individual – sex, desire for status, loneliness – selling motor-cars by associating them with a sense of power and sexual drive, and face-creams with an assurance of beauty. According to Vance Packard, the president of the American Public Relations Society in an address to his colleagues was able to state that 'the material which we work on is the fabric of human minds'. And to quote an advertising directive:

The makers of cosmetics do not sell lanolin, but hope ... We no longer eat oranges, but vitality; we do not buy a motor-car but status.

The consumer's freedom of choice has thus remained severely restricted not only as regards consumer goods, but also as regards his aesthetic experience, his political ideology, and even his religious beliefs. There are techniques for 'launching' a painter or a novelist as there are for engineering a favourable referendum – much more subtle methods than the old scenes of electioneering violence. Even the churches have to think about keeping up with the times and taking public relations into account. What started as an attempt to understand the facts in terms of sociology and psychology has gone beyond the realm of pure science. It has produced a set of techniques by which we all at times feel indefinably restricted. We are constrained to demand 'voluntarily' soap X or candidate Y.

Nevertheless since this conditioning is part of the nature of things, it is not harmful in itself, however enduring and influential it is shown to be in modern experience. It is not 'fiendish'; nor has it intentions of its own. To describe it as either good or bad has very little meaning, because its value can only be assessed in terms of how effective it is, and those who abide by ethical standards are always subjective. It is simply a tool and if its use increasingly pervades our lives it is because rationalisation has brought about an automated society. Once we accept this we must inevitably follow the most rational line in any field of behaviour, and must consequently help in spreading the technical influence of rationalisation. We ourselves are the ones who bring technology into our lives: and it is not technology which bears down fatefully upon us. I shall not discuss here whether we are right or wrong in doing so: I only wish to emphasise something comparable with my statement about the population explosion: namely, that if here too we are in the throes of an uncontrollable hurricane, its violence is fed by our own actions, not by some irresistible law of the universe. Simply practising the contemplative attitude of the yogi in front of the powerful mechanical equipment used in road construction would be enough to induce utter indifference to it and thus avoid the characteristic attitude of the conditioned devotee of technology.

It must however be noted that personal denial of rationalisation is much easier for the philosopher than for the economist, or for the individual than for the community. Since nobody approves of hunger, we all advocate development, thus putting the highest value on production efficiency and subjecting our behaviour patterns to the criterion of technical achievement. That is why man, or at least the economist, submits voluntarily to an enslavement which today in part displeases him and in part makes him afraid of an extremely uncertain future.

The double edge of technical achievement

Technical achievement is two-edged for the simple reason that we do not know where it is leading us. Will the tide end up by covering the whole planet and totally engulfing us? Will it be too late when we finally try to stem it?

The previous chapter on the prospects of the population explosion dealt with similar fears by stating that the problem could be shelved for the present even though the pressure of population is at a more serious level than is desirable. But there is no complete answer in this case, because the solution does not depend entirely on the factors already examined. It depends even more on human decisions, which are based on social attitudes towards the problem.

Of course one can understand the scepticism of the many people who doubt the possibility of adopting anti-technical decisions or relinquishing the material benefits gained as a result of increasing rationalisation. When we feel sometimes that we are the victims of machines, of the treadmill of city life or of the clamorous insistence of propaganda, it is natural to think that if we have let things get so far already it will become increasingly difficult to hope for any reaction against them.

When we are confronted by the techniques of manipulating incentive and demand, we become still more doubtful, especially if we take for granted that those using such techniques would prefer to retain all rationalising tendencies. Have we not then gone too far already to be able to escape the inrushing tide? The problem has an important bearing on our proposal to look into the future.

I wish to emphasise again that as long as a vast empire of hunger still holds sway, this question does not make sense from the economist's point of view. Hunger demands development and development entails technology. If Europe had not opted for a more efficient and productive procedure three or four centuries ago, hunger and epidemics would have gone on ravaging the world as they did a thousand years back. However, granting this, is it not just worth asking whether the European formula is the only possible method? The underdeveloped countries have the advantage of being able to copy European technology and although this advantage doubles the acceleration of the whole process – for it rapidly decreases the mortality rate – it also brings into sharper focus both the benefits and the drawbacks of rationalisation. In the seventeenth century the burgesses of the City of London were financing the experiments of the newly founded *Royal Society*, while King Charles II, according to his courtiers, was laughing uproariously at those gentlemen who claimed they could weigh air. The merchants were putting their trust in science, thinking, quite rightly, that those experiments would explode the irrational ideologies from which royal power drew its strength. They did not visualise, however, that in the long run the same science would bring them in subjection to other social groups. The emergent countries can look at themselves in both sides of our mirror; the one shows them the benefits attained by technology and the other warns them of its attendant risks. Will it necessarily prove impossible to unearth a formula by which the latter can be reduced

Scene from *Modern Times*.

without too much of the former being lost?

We shall go more deeply into this possibility later on but in any case the answer to our question depends on community decisions. Proof of the gathering speed of the technical shuttle, as it moves on the loom of history, is not enough. We have also to consider the warp with which the threads of the woof are interwoven. In other words, we must examine the structure of the societies which put decisions, whether of a technological nature or no, into effect. Therefore in the next chapter we shall examine the forces which control society.

4 Social change

An abrupt awakening

The last day of December 1899 was a Sunday. In many houses in Britain the scene was identical: an English gentleman was reading the last issue of *The Times* for the century that was drawing to a close. Perhaps, prominently displayed in some illustrated magazine, lying open on an occasional table near the great wing-chair, could be seen the plump figure of Her Majesty Queen Victoria, now in the sixty-third year of her happy and glorious reign.

In our unstable and transitory world, could anything be imagined more solid and secure than an English Victorian, the subject of a monarch whose power showed no signs of decline, reading the most imperturbable newspaper in the world, in the privacy of the home that was his castle, with his feet warmed by the source *par excellence* of kinetic energy, all-powerful coal? Tibor Mende has included the editorial of that number of *The Times* in a book. It is true that the Boer War was raging, but no Englishman doubted its successful outcome. As for the rest, the world was as calm as a millpond whose tiny ripples even served to add a touch of genteel interest to the serenity of the scene. In Great Britain the economy could not have been going better. To crown everything, in the words of the writer of the leading article, 'The summer had been *almost too* glorious'. Undoubtedly, as in Browning's poem, the world beneath the sky was perfect.

The English world, of course; and the European world, in general. For Europe was then at the zenith of its power. Before two years had passed the Queen whose reign seemed never-ending would be dead. Before fourteen had passed another seemingly everlasting monarch, Franz-Josef I, Emperor of Austria-Hungary since 1844, would have suffered the grievous fate of seeing his world collapse about his ears before he met his own end. But on that last Sunday of the century, the European horizon appeared untroubled. Nearly half a century later an economist, Wilhelm Röpke, would express the same nostalgia for it as Talleyrand did for the Ancien Régime when he stated that he who had not known it had not lived. In the opening paragraphs of his book, *The International Community*, Röpke writes:

The author of this book belongs to that generation, which, in its youth, could still breathe the radiant twilight of the Western world's long day of happiness which lasted from the Congress of Vienna to August 1914: that glowing span of which those who have only known the present polar night of history can form no true idea.

Röpke published his book in 1945, when the Second World War had already roused from their golden slumber those Europeans who had not learned by experience from the First. In the period between the Wars, the 'Great Depression' of 1929 had brought a distant rumble of the instability of the world. But on that *fin-de-siècle* Sunday scarcely anybody would have detected the clairvoyance of a passage like the following, written in 1885 by the German economist von Neumann-Spallart:

It can be stated that today the economic supremacy of Great Britain is on the decline. The centre of gravity of material prosperity which has been stationary in the British Isles for the last two hundred years, is gradually moving towards the continent of Europe. Simultaneous with this, another movement can be discerned: a large proportion of the cultural force of Europe is passing to other continents, especially to North America. This twin-pronged course gives a glimpse of the future centre of world commerce: on the shores of the Atlantic between NW Europe and the Eastern sea-board of North America.

Certainly by 1899 the zenith of Europe had lasted more than a century and it was no surprise that Europeans had come to regard its continuance as being as natural as the cycle of the seasons. Europe had created technology and it had given her control of the world. When those frock-coated gentlemen looked at a map, showing the sea-routes marked on the blue oceans and the railway networks criss-crossing the continents, they were witnessing their overlordship in that vast web, which carried food and raw materials from the whole world to Europe's mighty heart, whose technological throb pumped out in return a life-blood of capital and manufactured goods (figure 8). The process had been going on ever since the Spanish and Portuguese navigators had encircled the globe in the sixteenth and seventeenth centuries. In the eighteenth century this idea had already been expressed by a true Spaniard, yet a true European, whose posthumous work, *Letters from Morocco*, has affinities with Montesquieu's *Lettres persanes* and Goldsmith's *Citizen of the World*. In one letter, Don José de Cadalso writes:

How does the wealthy man of this century spend his income? He is awakened by two periwigged and liveried valets-de-chambre; he drinks exquisite Mocha coffee from a cup imported from China via London; he arrays himself in a shirt of finest Dutch cambric and a very elegant French dressing-gown woven in Lyons; he reads a book calf-bound in Paris . . . he dines off plate designed either in Paris or London . . .

The same idea was expressed by Keynes in his famous work *The Economic Consequences of the Peace*, 1919, even after the first violent awakening of Europe by the howitzers of what was then called The Great War – because it was not then known that in historical retrospect it was only going to be the *First* World War.

Keynes, however, was already aware of the end of European hegemony, when he exclaimed:

What an extraordinary episode in the economic progress of Man was that age that came to an end in August 1914!

The statistics, indeed, speak volumes. In 1890 the USA drew level with Great Britain in iron and steel production. In 1906 she exceeded Britain's coal output. Coal and iron, the nerve and sinew of the heart of the European world, were now vitalising other countries which were soon to be self-supporting. In 1913 Imperial Russia equalled the considerable iron and steel output of France.

Thus the two new poles of the world political field were beginning to emerge, but they would still require time to consolidate. In 1917 Czarist Russia collapsed and after long years of internal struggle and reconstruction in accordance with new ideals, the USSR was born in 1923. It was to withdraw within its own sphere, although it would radiate a powerful transforming influence as the 'fatherland of the proletariat'. In the USA the Republican victory in 1920 meant a revision of Wilson's policy by a return to an isolationism

which prevented American's representation at the League of Nations, though the League had come into being at the suggestion of the American President himself. In reality, without its affecting their former influence, the two great world powers did not become the guiding-lights of their respective camps until the Second World War, from which human society emerged considerably altered.

Europe, in fact, was no longer the heart of the world. The war cut her in two with the Iron Curtain, and profoundly unsettled her economy, so that she had to depend on North American aid for her initial reconstruction, provoking a series of declarations of independence. From Indonesia to Palestine, the European flags that had fluttered over Asiatic lands since the fifteenth century had to be hauled down in the space of a few years. In 1960, the second wave of grants of independence, this time to the former African colonies, completed the liquidation of the European overseas possessions. In the meantime the Soviet Union and the USA were increasingly extending their spheres of influence, although in a non-colonial form.

The world situation had undergone a complete transformation. Up to 1914 Europe had dominated the stage like a *prima donna*, captivating the audience in that opera house, all velvet and gold, in which modern history up to 1914 was being staged. Even if the

Figure 8. *The world economy in 1900.* At the end of the nineteenth century the world economy was based on Europe. Shipping lines surrounded the continents like a circulatory system, bringing food and raw materials to the European heart in return for capital and manufactured goods.

diva, as is frequently the case, was rather on the mature side and scarcely sylph-like, her brilliant past and her artistic flair still allowed her to queen it in the centre of the stage. But in 1945 it was not she who was given the major role, for that was now shared by two rival artistes: a tenor and a baritone: that is to say, the 'good' and the 'bad' – the USA and the USSR, to whom both adjectives are applied, according to our viewpoint geographically. Europe slowly unwound as she was wooed tempestuously by both of them, while she gradually recovered her breath in case a star part should come her way again.

Such is the construction that many people still put on the present situation, but even this has already changed. This bipartite structure, in which the nations are polarised around either the USA or the USSR, has lasted for less time than the European hegemony. In this respect it betrays the same rate of acceleration as that already stressed in the fields of population and technology. In the opera of the old European theatre there were always other characters (the chorus of warriors, rustics or intriguers grouped in the background), but nobody ever took them into account. What is taking place before our very eyes is in fact the amazing transformation of the chorus. Their words are no mere echo of the principals for they have songs of their own and on occasion they are listened to more than those of Europe and the other two. Moreover, from among this chorus new personalities are starting to emerge. At the Moscow Conference in November 1957, to mark the fortieth anniversary of the Communist revolution, China was admitted for the first time on an equal footing as a great power. In March 1963, *Red Flag*, the organ of the Chinese Communist Party, declared that its ideological dispute with the USSR (the struggle between the authentic Marxism of Mao Tse-tung and the revisionism of Khruschev), was the third great controversy in the history of Marxism. China is undoubtedly the most important among the personalities to have sprung up from the old subdued chorus, but not the only one by any means.

Thus increasingly rapid changes have continued to take place in the centre of gravity of the world organisation, although the Western nations, who have remained sitting in their old opera house, are often unwilling to admit it. After 1918 Europeans believed that the war had denoted only a temporary fit of insanity; they made up their minds that it would be the last, firmly believing in the slogan of President Harding that the solution lay in getting back to 'normalcy'. The economic prosperity of the 'twenties seemed to prove them right but the slump dispelled their illusions. In spite of this, President Hoover's slogan in the face of the Depression was that *prosperity is just around the corner*. The Western *bloc* still had not learned their lesson and when their delegates met in 1944 at Bretton Woods to organise the world economy in the wake of victory, they framed the International Monetary Fund. This provided such inadequate restrictions on the fluctuation of the rates of exchange that scarcely six months after fixing the official standards the French franc had to overstep the limits imposed by the Fund and was soon to be followed by the pound sterling and other currencies. The world economic scene had changed so much that it did not allow these currencies to continue along the course planned by the experts, whose mental outlook was still based on the pre-war situation.

It must be clearly understood that the two world wars were not momentary whirlpools in the midst of a placid stream. Nor was the Great Depression a fleeting slump. Wars and slumps were only superficial, though very violent, manifestations of deep-rooted changes, just as the explosive character of a volcanic eruption draws attention to continual subterranean activity. We are living through a stage which, when seen through the eyes of the future, will be easily recognised as a lengthy process of readjustment between two world balances. An alignment is taking place between a world based on an exclusively European industrialisation dominating an entirely traditional community and a new order which will have to be founded on the economic development of the whole of the community. Hence the rapid change from one situation to another, the acceleration of each process and the brevity of the hegemony of the USA and the USSR in their respective camps. Hence, too, the increasingly prominent emergence of the new countries, which in the old opera had only subordinate roles in the chorus.

In other words it could be said that during the one hundred and fifty years of the technical and population advances, the social warp on the loom of history has not been noticeably altered, except along the narrow border corresponding to the European section of the community, across and through whose threads the shuttle of technology has been constantly moving. However, as we have seen, through the veering of the world centre of gravity, this situation is already being modified. The geographical diffusion of technology, referred to in an earlier chapter, is creating incentives and trends by promoting the modernisation of non-European communities. In brief, just as the trend towards a reduction in the birth and mortality rates is now being repeated in the other continents, and just as technology is taking deeper root in their soil, so the social transformation which Europe underwent in the modern era is being re-enacted.

Yet the European technical acceleration was pre-eminently a social evolution, related as we have seen to a set design of human organisation: that of capitalism. The readjustment of the world in our age is directed on all fronts by those forces of social transformation which sometimes show themselves in outbursts of revolution, but which, even in periods of calm, go on fermenting underground in the depths of the community attitude.

Technology and society

Perhaps my assertion that technology has given rise to the trends which are transforming the non-European world provokes immediate anti-Marxist opposition: for it is now acknowledged that this is the thesis of historical determinism. It is worth while pausing at this point because it is important to understand this controversial statement.

First and foremost let us stop being 'anti-Marxists'. This is something as anachronistic as being anti-Cartesian, since the influence of Descartes reaches out to every one of us, although nobody today remembers his erroneous theory of whirlpools to explain the movement of the planets. A present-day economist may very well not be a Marxist but he cannot be 'anti-Marxist', because if some of Marx's statements are indeed false or debatable, his ideas taken as a whole permeate even the least socialist inclined of today's economic systems. If it were not for what is ingrained in mental habit, and material gain, nobody would now deny the influence of Marx on the world economy. The role attributable to technology as a determining factor in social organisation would not then arouse 'ideological' clashes. It is a fundamental question for us, for on it depends our opinion as to the predominating factors among the different forces that we are examining.

It is a well-known fact that historical materialism upholds the view that the economy governs the other aspects of social life. When Engels stood before Marx's newly-built tomb in 1883, to deliver a moving farewell, he could ascribe to him the great discovery that:

> the production of the immediate material means of subsistence and consequently the degree of economic development attained by a given people or during a given epoch form the foundation upon which the state institutions, the legal conceptions, the ideas on art, and even on religion, of the people concerned have been evolved.

Therefore, since the decisive role in this production belongs to the forces of output capacity, which ultimately depends on man with his tools and his technology, the latter is the essential factor determining all the characteristics of the life of a society. The modern *Manual of Political Economy*, edited by the Academy of Sciences of the USSR, puts it very clearly when it states that:

> production development springs from changes wrought in the forces of output capacity and mainly from changes in, and development of, capital equipment, and geared to these are the corresponding changes which operate in the field of production relations

and which knit men together socially to achieve economic efficiency.

In other words, to use an example as well known as it is expressive, the thesis states that just as the technical achievement of the water-mill created feudal society, so too was the latter destroyed by the steam-engine, which corresponds to capitalist society.

Marx, of course, never made the assertion that technical and economic considerations arbitrarily determine *all* the rest. This representation is an exaggerated caricature invented by anti-Marxists the better to deny the thesis. The position was made clear by Plekhanov when he wrote that it is not claimed out of hand that the minuet was the direct result of the economy of the eighteenth century in France, but it can be stated that in their general outlines the cultural values with which that kind of music is in accord are conditioned by the social organisation resulting from the economic situation. Furthermore, certain Marxist writers even distinguish within the social framework between a 'superstructure' directly determined by the method of production and a higher 'social conscience', which is less directly determined and which in its turn influences the other components. With such modifications as these, the idea that the economy, as the organisation of production and the circulation of goods, constitutes the bedrock of the other institutions in the society and their historical evolution, is a conception now admitted by those who are not Marxists, such as Schumpeter and Karl Popper.

Nevertheless, it cannot be deduced from this that technology is the motive force or, as the Thomists would say, the 'first principle' of history. As we indicated in the previous chapter Alexandria already possessed the elements capable of touching off the powder trail of the technical explosion, and yet this trail did not burst forth until nearly two thousand years later. Similarly, we noticed that at the height of the Middle Ages, an Aristotelian rationalism was hardening within the stagnant waters of dogma, while at the same time in the monasteries the germ of an organisation appeared, to found the subsequent elements of the capitalism of the future, whenever geographical and cultural discoveries should inspire the outbreak of the Renaissance.

Was Max Weber right then when he put forward the opposite theory to Marx, viz. that technology and economics are simply the outcome of ideology? We have seen that Weber framed this theory when dealing with this very matter, the origin of capitalism. He explained it as the Puritan and Calvinistic spirit of rationalism springing from the Reformation. However, pre-Lutheran capitalists are legion and post-Weber historians are only partially convinced by this theory, concentrating more on gathering concrete facts about the evolution of prices and population than on speculation about the 'spirit of the times'. In fact, an argument over whether the economy determines ideology or vice-versa is rather like a return to the old medieval debate whether the hands feed the stomach, or the stomach supplies strength to the hands. Technical production and ideology are neither cause nor effect. Both are facets of the general process of evolution, which, since it affects every avenue of community development, carries them along with it too. The loom of history supplies the shuttle which moves the technical woof and thus gradually develops the social warp as it passes through; neither owes allegiance to the other. Both continually interweave with each other as time goes on. If at times the so-called technical innovation flourishes first, while at others it is a mere offshoot of a social situation already geared to its arrival, we are liable in each case to vary our mental image of what we estimate as cause and what as effect.

In the special problem which is our concern here Marx was right, for as he contemplated his mid-nineteenth century world, he saw that technical forces were making a new mould for the social structure. The technical application of steam was herding society within iron rails, diminishing the importance of the old country aristocracies in favour of industrial magnates and transforming rural life into the urban existence of the proletariat. It may be equally possible, by going back into history, to show that this situation had its origin in a previous attitude. What is important for our lives today is the deluge of applied technology for it determines the shape of our houses, the preparation of our food, the kind of amusements we enjoy and the direction of our studies. Keen observers have blamed modern technology for the decline in moral standards and other 'evils' of our time, so that though they may consider themselves rabid anti-Marxists they are really proving Marx right. As far as our era is concerned Marx is entirely in the right, for technology conditions social life, although this, in turn, stimulates or resists technical evolution.

How can one doubt the effects of technology in Europe where we are witnessing the swift accomplishment of schemes for European integration after long years of Utopian theorising? If the idea of European union has existed in embryo since the Middle Ages, though it is only now beginning to be put into effect, we must admit that it is not the outcome of the finesse of present-day diplomacy. It is not difficult to see the decisive importance of technical progress in the acceleration of the process of integration. Nuclear power, modern armaments, the enormous scale of modern mass-production for whose absorption a vast market area is indispensable, and analogous factors, demand organisations greater than the existing countries of Europe. Just as the little feudal states proved inadequate to meet the new conditions of life at the outset of the modern epoch, so the 'great' nations of Europe have found themselves too small. For this reason six of them have found it necessary to unite as the European Economic Community. For the same reason Great Britain – half a century ago the head of a world Empire – stated in 1957 that she lacked the means to embark upon the launching of satellites like *Sputnik*, which had recently been put into orbit by the Soviet Union.

The Marxist theory is certainly true of Europe today, and it is all the more applicable to the non-European world. At this point we can return to the argument that prompted this necessary digression, for in order to understand our present position it is essential for us to realise how the technical influence of transport and communications has brought about the clash of civilisations which is unsettling the underdeveloped countries much more violently than the political revolutions disturbed Europe. Ships and aircraft, radio and television, the latest capital goods and the modern city: when such wonders as these are introduced into age-old societies or exhibited to visitors from them the mind experiences such an indescribable shock that every kind of subjective trauma and social upset is unleashed. Hunger excites a yearning for effective employment and this yearning leads to a craving for technical importations. Communities with an organisation similar to that of pre-capitalist Europe suddenly feel the urge to leap into the twentieth century, where only affluent societies dwell. Since this urge can be only partially satisfied, and at a speed which varies according to the level of life in the community, contradictions abound and dissensions are heightened to fever pitch. Despite the Cromwells and the Robespierres, Europe was able to evolve with relatively short peak periods of violence because technical means, such as steam, electricity, the aeroplane or the atom, developed in sequence, giving plenty of time for mental attitudes to adjust themselves to each in turn. The new generations of Asia or Africa, however, have everything spread out before their gaze at the same time, as before a child in an enormous toy shop; they are thus suffering simultaneously the pangs of craving and frustration, which are the cause of the dramatic explosions of our time.

I have previously mentioned that we are experiencing a crisis of social adjustment between two historical balances. In this crisis the first collision of economic forces appeared as a stage in the market alignment among the 'Great Powers'. It is now a collision between the demands of the hungry peoples and the resources available: a clash between want and development. What is really necessary is the immediate spread of technology among all peoples by the wave of a magic wand. This, of course, is not possible: hence the state of tension in these peoples as they hover between plans and feasible action; hence also the state of tension in each individual as he is torn between the world in which he was born and the world in which he would like to live. These tensions, expressed briefly, are merely the crises inherent in the modernisation of old social structures. In other words they represent transformations in the social warp. We must now consider the nature of these societies that are in a state of ferment.

Traditional economies

The power of technology to transform life is constantly displayed before the gaze of those traditional societies eking out a bare existence in the world. But technological means can be introduced only when the atmosphere is favourable: otherwise they will remain mere curiosities, as they did in Alexandria and China. Modern ethnological experts have constantly stressed the need for a receptive social attitude. Such an authority as Raymond Firth, when addressing the International Congress of UNESCO in Paris in 1954, mentioned this matter of the environments that prepare the way for modernisation and made specific reference to the peoples of SW Asia:

> Although it is technical progress which has set the wheels of social evolution in motion, it can be asserted that such a progress would not have been possible if those, at least in certain social circles, who welcomed the chance of greater benefits, had not come to terms with it and accepted it. This means that the determining factor was not really technology proper, but the dawning consciousness of the possibility of obtaining higher incomes by using it and the resources available. Even an understanding of the service provided by the new techniques or methods is not enough; what is needed in addition is a readiness to submit oneself (or all the others if one is in a managerial capacity) to a new discipline, by giving up some of the freedoms that have been enjoyed hitherto. Social evolution is the outcome of human decisions.

In short, it is human decisions that admit technology and these decisions depend to a very large extent on the social attitude to various problems. Eighty years have gone by now since Unamuno remarked that the mere existence of the plough with the mould-board was not enough to ensure its universal adoption, for while some nations will adopt it and substitute it for the traditional plough, others will daub it all over and set it up as an idol, in the belief that the act of worship will induce it to achieve the same results as if it were applied to the tasks of cultivation. This difference in outlook appears as a series of stages in historical evolution, and it is essential to understand the characteristics of these traditional economies so divergent from our own. Otherwise we shall fall into the same error as so many Western economists who, forgetting the importance of the attitudes in force in those societies, believe that development must inevitably result from investment, which merely gives the underdeveloped countries an injection of technical innovations and capital goods.

This was the belief of the first post-war Labour government in Britain, for example, when it launched the famous ground-nut scheme in East Africa. The aim was to extend the cultivation of the ground-nut over more than thirteen thousand square miles of virgin land, so as to relieve the shortage of fats. From the economic and agricultural points of view the scheme was planned down to the last detail, and yet it failed. Above all, this failure was due to a complete disregard of the mentality of the native labour force who, though perfectly capable of handling tractors and other farm machinery, showed not the slightest interest in a steady job. Once they had earned enough money they went back to their villages to enjoy it and there they stayed until they needed some more. Therefore it is essential to bear in mind the factors which decide the courses of action in those economies usually classed as 'Third World'. This residual term is not the most appropriate for nations that are emerging in the heart of world development, for they are the protagonists in the fierce struggle going on at the moment.

What is the nature of these collective or community warps? First and foremost, the behaviour of such communities is almost always inspired by a traditional understanding of life. The traditional world takes its shape in accordance with the outward face of nature, as it is expounded in myths backed up by tradition or belief in truths revealed in a supernatural way; but the modern view of the world is highly scientific and rational.

In just the same way human decisions within the traditional

society are not bound by previous logical and objective reasoning but rather by custom. The peasant tills his land in a certain way because 'it's always been done like this'. The school-teacher repeats the 'wisdom of the ancients' to his charges. The woman is made ready for motherhood with a ritual display of forewarnings which are 'the quintessence of life'. Nobody will give a rational explanation, for example, of why women cannot eat eggs – an embargo in force until very recently in the central areas of the Congo, where any husband could divorce his wife, and claim the cattle forming her dowry, if he caught her out in such a monstrous crime! Traditional man, in short, looks upon the legacy of the past as inviolable even in the everyday circumstances of his life. Modern man, on the other hand, is constantly transforming his environment to suit his liking.

Linked to this veneration of tradition is a strict hierarchy of the various social levels, sometimes as rigid as the caste system in which movement from one to another is impossible. The authority vested in the upper levels is justified on the grounds of tradition and, as on most of the other levels, particular offices or occupations are often passed down in the same family from generation to generation. Consequently tradition and hierarchical authority are the backbone of these economies and basic decisions spring from them and take their direction from them.

As is only to be expected, any innovation meets with disapproval and is viewed almost as an attempt against the 'social order'; it is just the reverse in modern societies, where individual initiative and an inventive turn of mind are admired. So a society built around the craftsman, rather than the technician, prevails, traditional methods are perpetuated in strict conformity with the pattern laid down in the past and no changes inspired by rational criticism are tolerated. The economy's main prop is a barely rationalised agriculture, with a wretchedly low yield as a result, and this usually accounts for two-thirds of the labour force. Hence the low income level per head, over twenty times smaller in the poorer countries than in the advanced, the vicious circle of hunger and the imperative need for development.

This explains another typical characteristic of such economies: their *dualism*. This term is applied to the coexistence, even within the traditional milieu, of sharply divergent patterns of life – as, for instance, in the contrast between town and country. In the town, the power is in the hands of the authorities, the great property owners, officials, tradesmen and shopkeepers. In the country dwell peasants and skeleton departments representing urban headquarters: local authorities, government officials, the teacher and the small tradesman. The variations in this arrangement can be considerable; but as soon as the smallest urban nucleus appears, a dualism inevitably arises between these patterns of life, which are bound together and yet distinct.

This primary dualism is subject today to other influences through the violent impact made on such primitive societies by the appearance of up-to-date capital goods. It may be said that in the present standardised world there no longer exist strictly traditional societies of any importance. External influence, whether or not through colonisation, promotes, side by side with a subsistence level agriculture dating back a thousand years, another system of cultivation run on commercial lines and directed at the export market. Of such a kind are the huge plantations employing the most modern technical methods with heavy financial backing from the West. At the same time modern buildings are seen to arise in the poorer districts. A huge factory or a mining plant goes up next to the craftsman's workshop, a new university next to the village school, a modern sports stadium alongside traditional pastimes. In brief, the so-called dualism becomes a heterogeneous complex of differing conditions and growing social and psychological contradictions.

When this occurs, transformation is already on the way and a transitory stage has begun in which it is only a matter of time before a more modern economy takes over. However, until this period of particularly sudden ferment is reached – a period much more violent and rapid than the corresponding period in European evolution – these economies have considerable stability. Over two thousand years ago conditions were as they are now and descriptions of them, such as Strabo's of India in the first century AD, continue to be perfectly valid. Some reformers, whose zeal leads to over-simplification when they are confronted with such a complete lack of movement (astonishing to us who are conditioned to constant innovations) tend to believe that such a fossilised state is due to the armed repression by which some despots crush whole peoples. Nothing is further from the truth, since stability is chiefly the result of the unqualified veneration that the population has for the existing 'order of things', accepting it as an unchangeable 'decree of nature'. The people live in a natural environment, of harvests and hail-storms, good and bad seasons of nature. They feel that the sending of rain or earthquake lies in the hands of superior powers and by extension they believe that these inscrutable forces have also designed the social warp, which is therefore immutable. The insignificant lives of the people are in the power of the gods and those whom the gods invested with their authority in the dawn of time, whether Pharaoh or the Son of Heaven. The decisions of those in authority thus come with supreme wisdom and to rebel would be a sin, as the priests are always telling them. In short, far from being confronted by an oppressed race, we find before us a people who even fear the possibility of a change because, though it might bring a dubious improvement, it would entail an overwhelming psychological effort for them to adapt themselves to it. Moreover, the lives that these races lead, sunk in their penury, at least offer a profound inner security, a freedom from the hard task of carrying out the responsibilities of liberty according to conscience.

It is true that at the transitional stage which we have now reached, the *status quo* has often been maintained by force. Yet this has been simply because mental outlooks had already begun to change and the decisions of the upper hierarchies had been called in question. While the traditional attitude lasts, Bert Hoselitz's explanation holds good; for he states plainly that what is

Scene at Djakarta, capital of Indonesia. The new rises behind the old – but the old lives on too.

fundamental in these societies is:

> the fact that traditionalism does not merely consist of the acceptance of traditional norms because they appear to aid in the solution of current problems, but rather in the appeal to traditional norms because of their antiquity and the alleged sacredness or ideological superiority of these norms. Traditionalism thus implies an ideology: it is the exaltation of tradition for the sake of tradition.

This bowing to tradition simply because it is tradition contrasts vividly with behaviour inspired by a rational analysis of situations and problems. We can thus pick out two types of social weave on the loom of history: one where the lines of the pattern are above all determined by the technical and rational woof and another where these proceed from the texture and arrangement of the threads in the thousand-year-old warp. It is obvious that between the two of them there are combinations leaning more towards one influence than the other. Yet generally when technology is the dominant force, as is usually the case today, it will be largely responsible for the increasing number of innovations and the modernisation of the environment, involving man in the production of commodities for man, converting the desert or jungle confines of his life into asphalt and reducing his natural milieu to little more than a stunted tree in a tiny yard or a patch of sky visible only when he cranes his neck to peer between the cliffs of concrete. In the traditional society, the innovations of the encroaching technical thread are lost among the sturdy and unchanging fibres of the warp. The weave is constant, the years follow each other bringing the cycle of seasons, children are born according to the laws of natural fertility, only to pass away prematurely in adolescence at the dictates of the natural mortality rate. Men repeat their unchanging lives, each one accepting the state to which he was born as the tree accepts the rocky soil to which the wind happened to carry the seed, and with the same vegetable passivity subordinate their actions to the dictates of what they consider the natural order of heaven and earth.

The dynamic breach

This traditional stability seems nowadays to be continually threatened by a dynamism bringing in its wake the stresses of modern life. These disturbances are caused by various factors and agencies, but they can be classified as endogenous or exogenous, according to whether they originate within the society or are the result of pressures from without.

Endogenous factors alone were responsible for the evolution of Europe and they all contributed in their different ways to bringing about one result: the infusion of rationalism into the stagnant waters of custom. It had to be a very slow process as we saw when we considered the first appearance of the technical habit. We know nothing of the first human animals, Promethean to us now, who felt the first stirring within their minds – the impact of the first 'Why?'. Why should I scratch the earth with my hands like all the others if I can use a stick? Why do they all say that this fruit cannot be eaten? And so on, with endless questions posed by the realities of life.

In the Athens museum there is a statuette from the Cyclades which has preserved for us for three or four thousand years the figure of a dauntless thinker, his whole being, as it were, tautly frozen with the tense effort of self-interrogation. The chiselling is crude; it does not have the perfection of Michelangelo's *Penseroso* nor the placid nudity of Rodin's *Thinker*. Yet this very lack of polish is perhaps more in character with the idea of the intellectual emerging from petrified nature. We have here a striking image of those first reasoning men who were no doubt few in number and would probably have suffered for their presumption had they uttered their thoughts. Yet in the Ionia of the seventh century BC they were the nucleus of a School, the life-blood of a city. Three hundred years later Aristotle formulated the logic which has held good for two thousand years. The story of the outstanding innovators and their influence, with all the subsequent effects of misconceptions, is too well-known for us to repeat here. These men were the founders of custom and tradition.

Paradoxically, its own exponents would on occasion put tradition on trial before the tribunal of rational criticism, as when two dogmas or two authorities were in opposition, each claiming to be right. Pharaoh's brother, for instance, when aspiring to the throne, would try to enlist support by calling into question the legality of the reigning monarch's claim, pointing perhaps to some flaw in the coronation ceremony or the patronage of certain gods and goddesses: in other words, denying before the people as many sacred and inviolable principles as possible in order to cheapen in their eyes the mystic aura surrounding the solemn rites. Certain periods of crisis, such as famine, drove desperate peoples to throw aside all restraint by rebelling against the abuse of authority; though always quelled, these revolts left a fairly permanent mark. In short, the combined effect of innovators, clashes between aspirants to power and periodic crises began to mould primitive myths into a pattern of progressive rationalisation. It was this pattern, which in spite of setbacks gradually brought about a new texture in the fibres of the social warp. In this manner the impetus continued from the man of the Cyclades statuette and his still more primitive ancestor to the European of modern times. By way of example, Hagen has made a sociological study of English history, showing how reverence for the established social order which existed in 1087 was gradually shaken off during the first cycle ending in 1422; the tempo was then quickened during the next cycle of only one hundred and fifty years which ended with the Stuarts.

In the case of traditional economies which survive today, these factors are further heightened by exogenous influences with all their enormous power of acceleration. When the Spaniards, and later other Europeans, transplanted their own social organisation into American soil, the natives found the printing press suddenly installed in their Neolithic surroundings, and in one bound proceeded from myth to syllogism. Europe continued the spread of rationalism (and, of course, the economy of exploitation, but a rational one) throughout the remaining continents, up to the nineteenth century. It goes without saying that there was stubborn resistance and that for millions of men the traditional way of life still remains the prevailing thread in the collective warp. Nevertheless the mirage of economic development beckons all these countries and this mirage will not become reality without increased productivity, that is to say, without the application of technology by a rationalised society. The urgent pace of the technical shuttle is tearing the threads of the ancient warps, and their transformation is inevitable. Otherwise they will be rejected like other human groups who already belong to the past.

The transformation of the economic structure, hastened by the spread of technical knowledge, is a process that is going on before our eyes and will not be denied. It is, however, very difficult to assess its quantity, even by using an index as representative as that used for technical acceleration in the previous chapter: the power consumption per head. Some sociologists have attempted to formulate their long-term analyses of this evolution on some sort of an objective basis. Thus we are indebted to Sorokin, an author of considerable experience in the field of social dynamism, for some figures which give a partial assessment at least, although they only refer to the eight main European nations taken as a whole. Basing his study on a classification of over one hundred thousand pictures and sculptures from the cultural output of the area under discussion, Sorokin compares the number of those whose motif is religious with those whose theme is secular. If, as seems reasonable, such data can be accepted – at least in part – as an index of the majority feeling aroused by dogma and rationalism respectively, the trend of evolution is seen to be marked. Before the tenth century, medieval works of art were 81·9 per cent religious and therefore just under a fifth were secular. Between the tenth and fourteenth centuries the gap was wider still, but the proportion of religious themes dropped to 64·7 per cent in the fifteenth when the attitude characterising Europe today was in its infancy. In the seventeenth it barely exceeded half (50·2 per cent), and in the eighteenth it fell below a quarter (24·1 per cent). Finally in the nineteenth it plunged to 10 per cent and the twentieth has not yet reached 4 per cent for works on sacred subjects, either on canvas or in sculpture. Secular themes stand at present at 96·1 per cent.

This rationalisation of outlook, which the above figures of course only imperfectly reflect, has a special bearing on the social mobility which is such an important feature of the kind of dynamism that economic development demands. This growing mobility can be measured to a certain extent, but one need only glance at historical evolution to realise that the gulf between the extremes of the social scale have been rapidly narrowing. In many ancient societies the monarch was a divine being, far above mere mortals and consequently quite out of reach of the slave, who was not even considered human. Yet the god-king developed first into a ruler by divine right and then into a constitutional monarch, by degrees yielding his position to heads of state, who are not hereditary or even life-holders of the post. For his part, the slave moved up with serfdom to human status, though he still belonged to his lord; he then became a labourer with constantly increasing skills. Today the remains of class distinction are very often preserved in the social conventions, but social mobility does not have to contend with such insurmountable obstacles as, for instance, the caste system in India or the feudal institution of nobility. Scientific progress in haematology has exploded the myth of blue blood!

A comparable mobility is seen on the geographical plane since people are much less tied to the areas where they were born and it is much easier to decide to move house. An important corollary of this increasing mobility is the growing urban concentration in some of the new countries, notably in South America. This increases the dynamisms of social transformation, for when men are uprooted lock, stock and barrel from their traditional environment in the country and plunged into the modernity of city life, they are much more susceptible to mental changes.

The distribution by occupations of the active population is likewise significant. Civilisation carries with it, for instance, an

Man's view of the beyond.
Below Early sixteenth-century woodcut.
Right View from a Gemini rocket.

increasing absorption of labour by modern services – commerce, banking, transport, the professions. The sociological importance of this lies in the fact that it increases the number of trained as opposed to unskilled workers. It was this distinction between 'white-collar workers' and the proletariat which affected the nature of the social conflicts so much in evidence during the last hundred years. However, since it is impossible to make a complete analysis of the social evolution in terms of the population structure, and since traditional societies are predominantly agricultural, we can accept as an index of the evolution towards a modern, technical environment the progressive decline in the numbers of workers engaged on the land.

In *The Conditions of Economic Progress*, Colin Clark has compiled a copious dossier of facts for various countries over long periods. We can see, for instance, that in Great Britain the percentage of the population actively engaged in agriculture went down from 23·1 in 1841 to 4·5 in 1951, and in France from 43 in 1866 to 17·4 in 1951. Other countries show a similar progressive decrease, but it is most interesting to note the present-day difference between the most and least advanced countries. Along with the percentage quoted for Great Britain we find for an intermediate country like Spain 69 in 1887 and 41·3 in 1960, while for the least advanced like Thailand or Pakistan the figure was over 70 per cent in 1950. More reliable information is to hand for the present period in the figures

Figure 9. *Urbanisation in Latin America.* The chart shows population density in Latin America. The rectangles are drawn in proportion to the total population of the country; the red parts represent urban population, the blank spaces rural population.

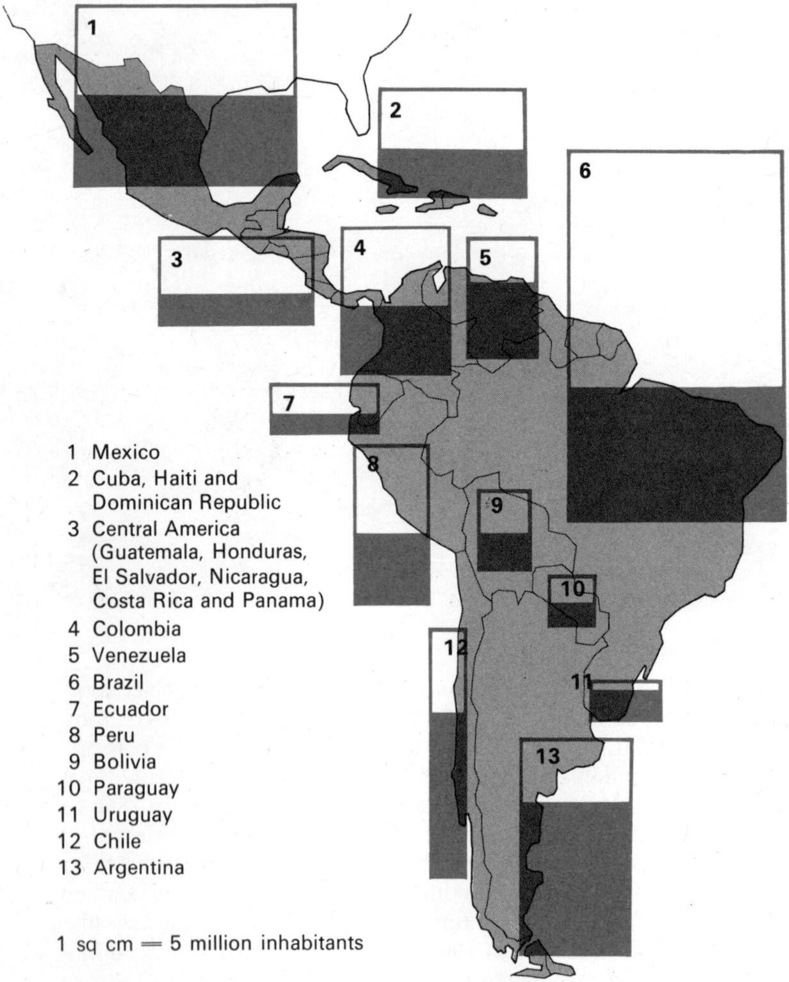

1 Mexico
2 Cuba, Haiti and Dominican Republic
3 Central America (Guatemala, Honduras, El Salvador, Nicaragua, Costa Rica and Panama)
4 Colombia
5 Venezuela
6 Brazil
7 Ecuador
8 Peru
9 Bolivia
10 Paraguay
11 Uruguay
12 Chile
13 Argentina

1 sq cm = 5 million inhabitants

furnished by the *Yearbook of Labour Statistics*, published by the International Labour Office, of Geneva. Using these, a phenomenon can be gauged which varies in intensity from country to country, but which operates over the whole globe as a fundamental law of social organisation, namely that the more modernised a society, the lower the percentage of the population engaged in agriculture.

To conclude these remarks, we have found that the social warp, our theme in this chapter, as with biology and technology, is affected by forces which are today taking the same course that they took in Europe in the past, but thanks to European influence their tempo is much swifter. The trend of these forces is towards modernising the warp of social structures, and together with the population explosion and the technical acceleration, they constitute the factors which unite to cause that dynamism that is driving us along the course of our present-day economy. Now that we are familiar with these, our next task will be to examine how they are woven into our everyday life, so that we can understand the field of forces which surrounds us.

5 The resulting systems

Yang and Yin

The history of the water-mill, as related by Marc Bloch, is an excellent illustration of some of the ideas we have put forward.

The water-mill was probably invented in Europe, just before the Christian Era, as an adaptation of the water-wheels used by Eastern gardeners for irrigation. It was a most useful mechanical device, but it evoked scarcely any interest. There is an obvious explanation. Why should a society bother itself about the construction of water-mills when it counted slavery among its institutions? The milling of grain was carried out by cheap labour. The structure of society made the application and spread of the invention unnecessary.

Social values evolved, however, and slavery disappeared. Its disappearance was partly a practical contingency: the wars of the Romans culminated less and less often in the victorious annexation of new territories and the triumphal parade of captured slaves. It was in part also due to religious influence, since Christians were forbidden the practice of enslavement and in any case the sources of supply were drying up, as more and more barbaric tribes turned Christian. Consequently mills proliferated and not 'for jocund water-nymphs to grant repose to weary serfs', as one poet of antiquity put it, but simply because the human machine had now become much more expensive. Since the nymphs were cheaper they balanced the installation costs.

Indigent families with limited consumer demand continued to make use of the small traditional hand-mills, to save themselves the price charged by the mill-owners. But once again social changes were imminent and the feudal lords, the owners of the mills, acquired sufficient power to prevent a competition so harmful to their monopoly. They proscribed and destroyed the hand-mills, obliging everyone to have recourse to their water-mills.

If these facts are disregarded, the spread of the mill may simply appear to be due to the gradual recognition of its technical superiority. In fact nothing less than the decline of the Roman Empire,

Water-mill from the
twelfth-century *Garden of Delights*.

the advent of Christianity and the new organisation along feudal lines were necessary to establish the device. For, with some other developments of the period – such as the introduction of harness and the stirrup, which increased the superior power of the horseman – it became an essential part of the fabric of feudal society, until new developments, both technical and social, opened the way to quite different systems of organisation and to further advances.

We thus see a continual interweaving on the loom of history of the motive forces of technical and social progress. Consequently we shall need to refer to both of these, to help us grasp the underlying factors of the economics of our time.

The theory of this dualism is by no means new. Over 4,000 years ago Chinese philosophy, as it groped towards a view of the meaning of life, initiated a set of related doctrines centred round this concept, in the *I-Ching*, or 'Book of Mutations'. In this remarkable work, which has recently undergone a reappraisal, everything is interpreted as the combination of two principles, the one active and the other receptive; the *yang* and the *yin*, represented by the trigrams ≡ and ≡ ≡. Our warp and woof are somewhat similar. The forces of technical progress would embody action and innovation, like the masculine principle of *yang*, and the social factors would correspond to the feminine principle of *yin*. Each force in its own way is creative: the former initiates drastic changes and the latter humanises technical developments. Moreover, both are mutually influential. Technology annihilates outmoded norms and promotes others in their place; it shatters the vessel of group-acceptance. Society on the other hand makes new techniques possible; it admits them and organises men in relation to them.

Such an association of ideas may seem arbitrary but, as we have just seen, it has been rooted in the human mind for more than a thousand years. In any case, the operative factor is that the action of technical forces on the one hand and social forces on the other is what determines the economies of human groups, just as the woof interwoven with the warp determines the texture of the cloth. Organisation – although etymologically a word which postulates machines – does not have a purely technical connotation. It stands for something more. The so-called techniques of organisation make no sense without a human element, which is at one and the same time their motive force and their *raison d'être*. Yet it is precisely the existence of such techniques – communications, good order and government, the keeping of public records, and so on – which rationalises the organisation of society into something very different from the natural organic growth which is the general concept of society in economies of the traditional pattern.

Types of organisation

The different types of economy that we find will therefore result from the combination of a certain level of technical achievement with clearly defined social attitudes. Such combinations can be classified, and once this is done we shall have a systematic catalogue of the forms of economic organisation in force in the modern world. It is essential to recognise the different economic patterns that exist, so that we can calculate the direction each will take in the future. Quite clearly the Soviet economy will not develop in the same way as that of the United States or Thailand. We must differentiate these several patterns of organisation and classify them so as to be able to surmise their possible development under the pressures of present-day economic forces.

In short, we have to classify the economic systems at present operating in the world, a problem on which all do not agree, and therefore we shall put forward our own classification. Specialists are still debating the basic concept of 'system' and its distinguishing traits. Since so many definitions exist, I will take the liberty of proposing my own, with apologies for its unavoidable length: by *economic system* I understand that aggregate of basic technical and institutional patterns which characterise the whole economic structure of a society, and control its general aims as well as its working methods.

A few brief remarks will, I hope, illustrate this definition. The human behaviour patterns which characterise the system are as much technical as institutional or social, and thus the two forces may be taken into account. Clearly consideration is given only to the most fundamental and characteristic patterns, since a plethora of detail would render the description meaningless. Moreover, these behaviour patterns divide economic activity into two channels: one being the basic resolutions subscribed to by the community and the other the channel along which these resolutions will find an outlet for development.

It is not difficult to see that both these aspects can be related to the technical and social forces that we are here amalgamating. Indeed, the resolutions of a society, whether a singleminded dedication to the production of consumer goods, or a decision to build up armaments, are especially related to the values of

Eighteenth-century silk scroll, depicting two philosophers studying the concept of *yang* and *yin*.

that society, that is, to the beliefs that motivate their attitudes to life. Such resolutions therefore stem chiefly from the social warp. Once any particular course of action is adopted, it can be carried out on different levels: for instance, the consumer goods may consist of stored grain or frozen meat; the armaments may be bows and arrows or jet bombers, according to the state of scientific knowledge and the capital equipment available in that society. To opt for iron and steel production does not of itself determine whether it will be obtained in the smith's forge or in the latest metallurgical plant.

We omit nothing of importance by restricting ourselves solely to a synthesis of the technical and the sociological. Indeed, the paramount concern in any economy is to know the 'what?', 'how?' and 'for whom?' of its production. Now, the 'what?' and the 'for whom?' – which are interdependent – are controlled by the social preferences regarding the most essential commodities and the criteria according to which these are to be distributed to the community; while the standard of technical achievement determines the 'how?' of production. The standard of technical achievement determines the degree of industrial output, while sociological factors determine the preferences within the compass of industrial output, choosing those industries which will give promise of the most effectual development. In conclusion, when economic systems are described exclusively in terms of the two coordinates, technology and sociology, nothing essential is omitted, because the three questions of production, the 'how?', the 'what?' and the 'for whom?' are answered implicitly. The pattern of the finished material is unerringly established by the synthesis of the woof and the warp.

The level of technical achievement

Let us now apply these two criteria to the actual situation prevailing in various countries, to determine the type to which each belongs from the point of view of their future economic development.

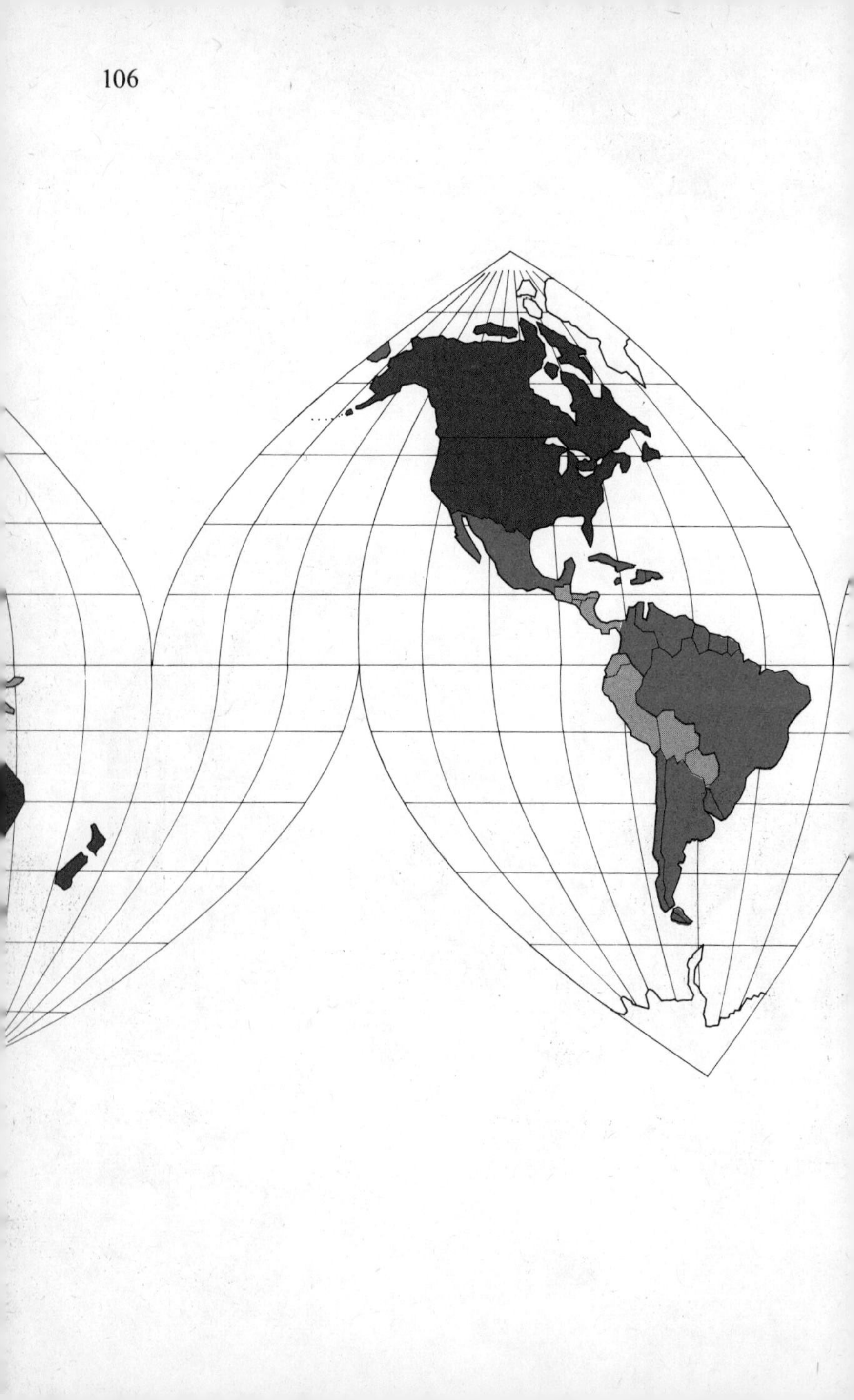

Figure 10. *Technical levels in the world economy*. With the help of various data one can construct fairly acceptable indices of countries' technical levels.

high technical level
intermediate technical level
low technical level

The first obstacle in our path is the lack of a suitable yardstick against which the extent of each nation's technology and sociology can be measured exactly.

In any case, the first is easier to measure. In the absence of any better mean, the power consumption per head of population, already used to demonstrate the present geographical spread of technology, could give us a fairly satisfactory index of the degree of scientific and material progress in each case. Fortunately much accurate work has been done in this field. Outstanding is the elaborate research by Brian J.L. Berry in N. Ginsburg's *Atlas of Economic Development*. Using factorial analysis, Berry combines forty-three variables – such as abundance of transport routes, power consumption, demographic rates, national product, volume of traffic handled by postal and telephone services, printing of newspapers and so on. The result allows us to arrange ninety-five countries and territories on a graduated scale which reflects the level of technical achievement. At the top come Great Britain and the Federal German Republic; at the bottom, Afghanistan.

Figure 10 shows us the results of this analysis. To simplify matters the ninety-five countries which Berry separates out into five levels have been rearranged into three groups only. The most advanced countries are those of Western Europe, together with some countries of Eastern Europe (East Germany, Poland and Czechoslovakia). Australia and New Zealand, together with the USA and Canada, have a comparable standard. The middle group includes the Mediterranean countries (except Italy), the majority of Latin America, the Soviet Union and a few countries in Africa and the Middle East. The remainder of the world is contained in the lowest group, centred round the two giants, India and China.

It is not difficult to appreciate the clear relationship which exists between this geographical distribution and the index of power consumption per person – although Berry's detailed scale is much more satisfactory, taking into account as it does a greater number of variables.

The social warp

Unfortunately, when it comes to plotting a graduated scale of the different kinds of warp or social structures, there is no equivalent scheme of classification available. The work of Woytinsky which I quoted earlier, thorough and painstaking though it is, is based in essence on political régimes, distinguishing between parliamentary democracies (republics and constitutional monarchies) and absolute governments (autocratic monarchies and dictatorships). This involves collating regions as widely divergent in their social system as the republics of Switzerland and Egypt and the kingdoms of Sweden and Ethiopia. It is true that other authors are producing neater classifications, despite the difficulty, but these are based on the inclusion of various other factors which make it virtually impossible to grade such dissimilar prototypes on a single scale.

I am compelled therefore to attempt a differentiation based solely on the criterion of social behaviour, with future expansion as the key concern. It will be taken for granted that perhaps the most decisive factor in economic expansion is the deployment made of available resources, and especially of capital goods: machines, transport, plant, and so on. The optimum use of such capital equipment is fundamental to rapid economic progress. Furthermore, the rising accumulation of capital, or the appreciation of its assets by new tools and equipment, is founded on increased output from human labour and ultimately on the maximum productivity that this labour can achieve without an increase in effort. Hence the decisions affecting the deployment of available capital goods create the environment for expansion, particularly decisions concerning new investments, the creation of new capital by means of national savings. If savings are used to build new factories, motor-ways or schools, the economic progress will be more rapid than if they are wasted on white elephants and in satisfying the demand for luxury goods by the more affluent classes.

For this reason the importance of regulations regarding the

ownership of producer equipment was realised long ago. Socialist platforms claim public ownership of such equipment, since socialism is well aware that the deployment of capital by private ownership is motivated by profit-making considerations or personal preferences. These do not necessarily coincide with the national interest. It is generally better business, for instance, to produce an alcoholic beverage than to found a university. The outcome is the now familiar 'affluent society', in which TV sets and refrigerators abound, while there is a shortage of primary schools and hospitals.

We could, therefore, construct a scale which would range from the maximum private ownership to the maximum public ownership of capital equipment. Nevertheless, we shall see in the next chapter that in non-socialist countries there is much more State control of privately owned capital goods than there was fifty or a hundred years ago. In market economies based on the private ownership of capital, the ownership of a factory is in the hands of numerous shareholders, who, in fact, exercise practically no control. These undertakings are managed by boards, or individuals who, in their turn, as we shall see, find their freedom of action rather more restricted today than formerly.

Thus a distinction must be made between private or public ownership of capital equipment and the power of decisions concerning its use and investment in new production lines. Often, it is true, the one is dependent on the other, but with a view to results the availability of goods is of more consequence than who owns them, especially in view of the restrictions contingent upon ownership in modern countries. This was how Max Weber understood the position when he defined the 'economic orders', or systems providing for the separate 'allocation of the effective power of disposal over economic goods and services'.

In short, acceptance of these criteria will, at one end of the scale, lead to a large number of private decisions regarding the deployment of capital and investment, while at the other end, these decisions will be to a large extent under public and centralised control. In the first instance, the connection will be rather with market economics, based on the private ownership of capital, while in the second, it will be with socialist economies.

These criteria are easy to apply in theory but extremely difficult to apply in practice, since it is impossible to measure in any particular case to what extent these basic economic decisions can be attributed either to public or to private influence. Attempts at quantity estimation based – like Akerman's for instance – on the amount of national production absorbed by and handled through the national budget do not give satisfactory results, because the data cannot be compared from nation to nation, and what is formally considered 'public' for budgetary purposes is not always so in practice. Yet, as we have already seen, this same discrepancy between the official and the actual also invalidates classifications based on extraneous data, such as political constitutions or declarations of policy, and so recourse to such criteria would not resolve the difficulty either. On the other hand, present political forces, especially in the emergent countries of the Third World, modify certain situations even before they have materialised into data which can be assembled for analysis. The independence recently achieved by so many African nations, for instance, has so far failed in some cases to produce an organised system of society which is stable enough to be identified. The same thing is happening even in some South American countries, although they have given rise to comparative studies as interesting as R. H. Fitzgibbon's *How Democratic is Latin America?* or R. Vekemans and J. L. Segundo's *Essay on the Social and Economic Typology of the Latin-American Countries*, published by UNESCO.

For all these reasons I refrain from constructing a world scale like that employed to convey the geographical distribution of the three levels of technical achievement, to illustrate the respective private or public nature of the basic economic decisions in each country. A geographical representation would have only the appearance of exactness and would, of necessity, raise some very debatable points. Nevertheless, even if the criteria are not applicable in practice to all countries (owing to a lack of concrete information and the impossibility of an objective survey) they retain, I think, a certain relevance, because they are applicable to some of the most prominent countries and therefore allow us to examine the probable evolution of these countries. In the Soviet Union, for instance, it is unquestionably the state that decides the deployment of almost the entire economic output, while in the USA such decisions proceed pre-eminently from the private sector. Accordingly, once the possible evolution of each country has been studied, we have sufficient evidence to enable us to make similar predictions for those other nations which are organised along corresponding lines to the USSR and the USA, whichever they may be.

Present-day economic systems

Consequently, the two criteria, technical and social, will be systematically combined in one diagram, in which the various types of economy will be marked out inside a rectangle, whose vertical and base lines represent the previously explained coordinates fixed for the technical and social scale respectively. As we have said, the lack of sufficient information prevents the accurate classification of every country in the world, but we shall classify a few examples, making use of sufficient supporting data to enable us to judge the future. In succeeding chapters we shall study the foreseeable future of the different systems, and this will enable us to predict where the present economic forces are taking each country according to its allotted subdivision or system.

Figure 11 represents the present world economic scene by a rectangle. We now have to fill in this rectangle with a series of subdivisions, each of which will classify a different system. To give them dimension, we shall assume the vertical of the rectangle to correspond to the level of technical achievement, marking it off at three points corresponding to the three technical levels, which intersect the rectangle horizontally. The most advanced countries will be found at the top of the rectangle, the intermediate ones in the centre and the rest at the bottom.

The base of the figure, on the other hand, corresponds to the sociological scale. The further left a country is, the more centralised or public will be the control of decisions relating to investment and capital equipment; while instances where private decision is supreme, indicating capitalist societies or market economies, will be located further to the right. A vertical line divides the area into two, according to whether the system proclaims itself as based on the private or the public ownership of capital – socialist countries on the left and capitalist on the right. We have, of course, just contended that certain official statements or equivalent political reports in some governmental systems do not always tally with the facts; but the principle of public or private ownership is the most satisfactory guide available to the control of decisions, at least from an objective point of view. Moreover, each of these halves is shown divided down the centre, according to whether the emphasis is laid to a greater or lesser degree on the principle of public or private ownership. Thus we have constructed four columns which, reading from left to right, represent: fully centralised systems; centralised systems modified by certain concessions to the market and private control; private decision-control systems, but with considerable state direction of the economy; and finally the most typical market or capitalist system.

It is unnecessary to add that the two extremes are never absolute; even in countries where there is most centralised control there is always some private scope and vice versa. In any case, the subdivisions are not foolproof. The system in France is not actually much unlike that of the USA or Great Britain, which, as we shall see, also clearly manage their economies by various measures of state intervention: budgets, legislation affecting the economy or industrial relations, public works, and so on. Nevertheless, in France these measures seem to emanate from a central control in successive economic plans which, moreover, seek to influence

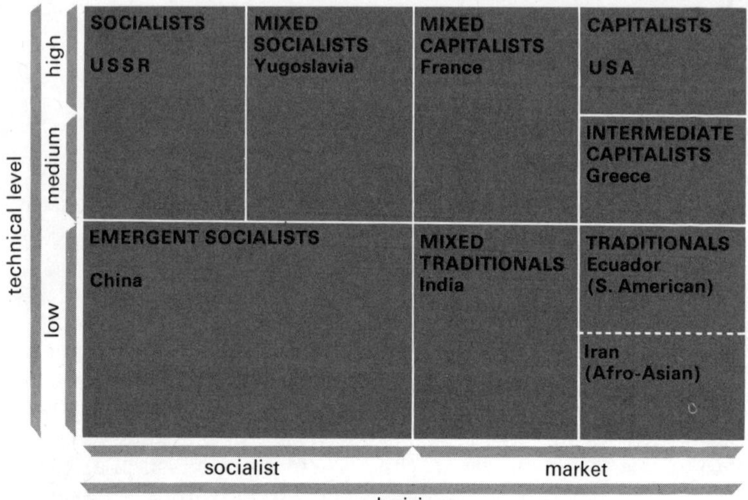

private decisions in a much more positive way than in other capitalist countries. In the same way, it can be debated whether the greater latitude allowed the private sphere in some socialist countries of Eastern Europe, represented in the other half of the diagram, is a relic of their former capitalist organisations, still relatively recent, or whether it is a deliberate modification of their basic socialist principles.

In subsequent chapters we shall analyse these problems and the table presented here will be fully substantiated. Meanwhile I make one final observation. It will have been noted that there are not twelve compartments in the diagram, as would be expected from the combination of three horizontal sections (for the three technical levels) with four vertical sections (the different types of social warp previously defined). This discrepancy is dictated by practical considerations that will now be explained.

In effect, there are fewer non-capitalist countries than countries with a market economy, and it is not worth sorting them into the three technical levels, since some subdivisions would remain unfilled. Therefore the left half of the rectangle is divided horizontally into two parts only: the bottom section, for nations with least technical achievement, which we propose to call *emergent socialists* for want of a better term, and the remaining sections for countries with high and medium levels of technical achievement, which we subdivide into socialist and mixed socialist countries, according to their social organisation. The latter subdivision is not extended to the lowest technical level, because the admissible countries are few and a profound economic dualism, common to all underdeveloped countries, exists in them. Traditional forms of life, collective but not centralised, of a family or tribal nature, are maintained by this dualism, and they coexist with the central scheme of the economy for the general welfare. Hence these countries always have mixed industries, not through any deliberate central decision (as occurs in some European socialist states), but simply through the survival of traditional modes of life.

The same reluctance to create needless subdivisions in our table would lead us to dispense with any distinction between the upper and intermediate technical levels for countries classed as *mixed capitalists*. This distinction is retained, however, in order to differentiate between countries which are *capitalists* and those which are *intermediate capitalists*. Finally, countries which are less technically advanced are classified as either *mixed traditionals*, having a pronounced leaning towards central planning, or *traditionals*, which are rather more swayed by private decisions. In the latter group, the admissible countries are so numerous that it proves an advantage to subdivide the lower right section, with one level for the *Latin American* countries which are more technically advanced so that some are already in the upper section, and another for the *Afro–Asians*.

For greater clarity one specific country is inserted as an example in each of the subdivisions. The diagram is considerably simplified but it will, later on, prove an acceptable basis for detailed analysis. I want however to dispel any possible misunderstanding brought about by such an over-simplification. It is clear, for instance, that a low technical level does not necessarily indicate an inferior culture, but simply that the availability of machines and equipment is insufficient for an accelerated rate of economic development. I am the first to admire the astonishing artistic achievements of certain Eastern cultures in lands to which material efficiency and productivity are alien. We must always bear in mind that the lines intersecting this field are only very approximate. Their purpose is to serve as a foundation for the evolutionary theory which will be developed in the coming chapters.

The theory demands one further proviso, for it is as well to recognise the direction we are taking if we are to make predictions. We must guard against the common error of systematic extrapolation: in other words, against believing that where a bend on a mountain trail hides the track from our view the path will continue to maintain its present direction. Nevertheless we can assume that the forces at work will go on behaving in the same way at least for relatively short periods of time, providing that we leave the door open for the unforeseen. Under the next heading, therefore, we will take a brief look at how the economic systems at present discernible in the world came into existence.

The emergence of present-day economic systems

Some of the social systems we have discussed, such as the traditional types, have their roots in remote antiquity. Others, like capitalism, are relatively modern. In this analysis we shall consider only the period after 1900: earlier systems do not interest us here if they do not survive today. We shall also discount modern systems that have enjoyed only a brief existence, such as fascism, which is only a form of capitalism aggressively on the defensive and camouflaged by an irrational mythology, which is nevertheless able to capture temporarily the enthusiasm of the masses. The urge to fascism still persists in places. But its present-day forms resemble typical capitalism more closely than did its Italian or German models. Besides, modern fascists lack the technical resources necessary for a serious aggressive drive. Nor is there any point in referring to cooperative systems, even though they are somethimes included in standard works comparing economic systems. No specific examples exist of a basically cooperative organisation, and there has been scant justification for the beguiling notion that a co-operative society is the automatic cure for the shortcomings of private ownership. The outstanding instances of extensive cooperative organisation of the economy can only be examined within systems which, like those in Scandinavia, least require such a cure, thanks to other factors. Cooperative combination is really only an occasional appendage to existing structures.

To go back to our diagram, it is evident as figure 12 shows, that at the beginning of this century the whole world field was divided into the three types of economy set out in the vertical column on the extreme right of figure 11: capitalist, capitalist with medium technical level, and traditional. Before the modern era, all the social components were of a traditional or pre-technical nature, many of them unaware of the existence of others; and they formed a complex world pattern. The course of history, the progressive unification of human capacity in the last few centuries, and the influence and spread of European capitalism, which we have discussed, have simplified this pattern, so that no fewer than fourteen of the twenty-one civilisations so far extant, as identified by Toynbee, have already disappeared, although two have generated successors. As we saw in a previous chapter, several technical levels emerged within this pattern of traditional societies, and consequently the three capitalist systems referred to could be distinguished by 1900.

The Soviet revolution of 1917 introduced a phenomenon little short of momentous: the first modern country founded on the state ownership of capital goods. The Union of Soviet Socialist Republics (as it was established in 1923) sprang from sources which were wholly of European origin, and which persisted intact despite the considerable contributions of Lenin, who set about putting Marxist ideals into practice in his enormous country. Yet the European nature of this genesis which makes socialism the true heir of capitalism, does not lessen the acute contrast between the two, or the far-reaching importance on the world scene of the

Figure 12. The emergence of present-day economic systems.

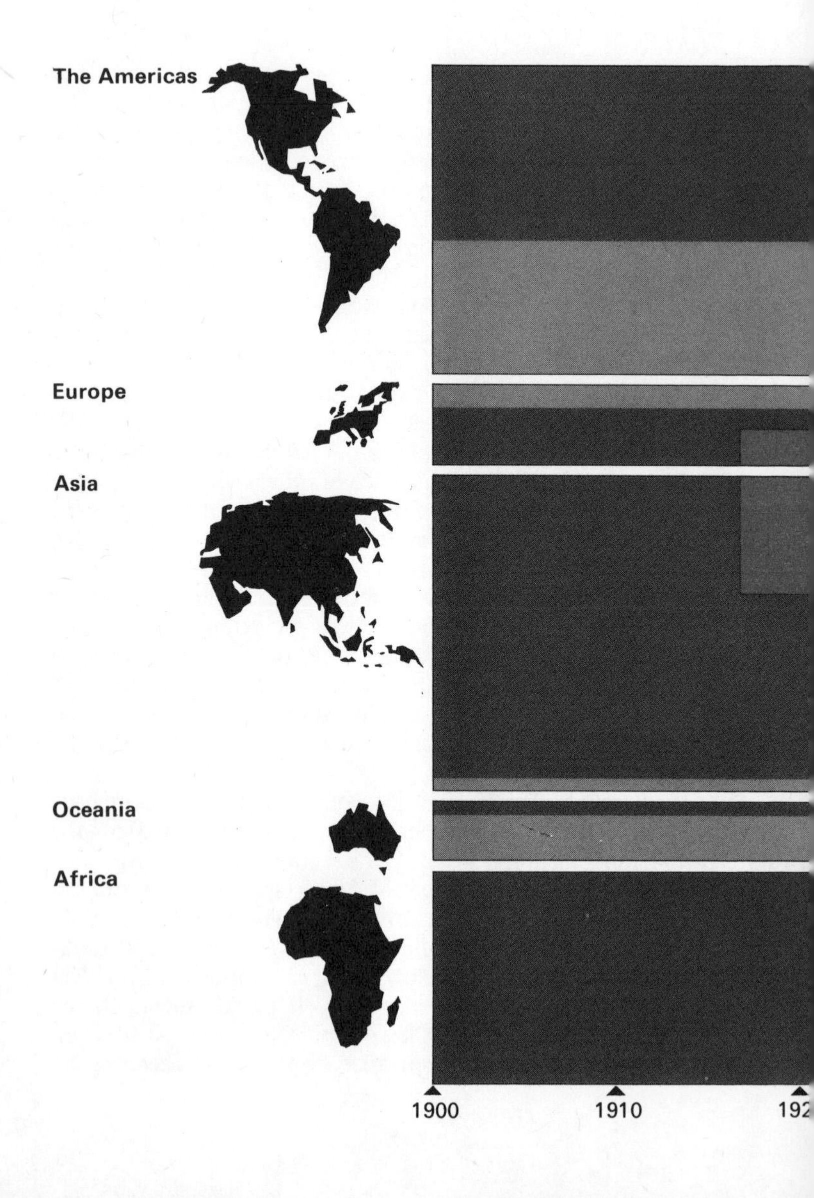

developed capitalist countries

intermediate and traditional countries

socialist countries

The width of the horizontal bands is proportional to the surface area of continents and countries

first socialist country. Its novelty immediately caught the attention of the underdeveloped countries, for until then they could imitate only the single model available: the capitalist system. At first, Western Europe and the United States preserved unimpaired their influence over the politicians of other countries, owing to their high standard of economic efficiency. This was particularly the case during the first period of Soviet control, when the tremendous problems that arose as a result of the change-over made many capitalists believe that 'that' would end up in ruins. Even so, those longing for rapid development were now beginning to turn their attention to the possibility of socialism.

Until the Second World War, the Soviet Union continued to be an isolated, albeit highly significant, phenomenon. But with the birth of the People's Democracies in Eastern Europe after 1945, the USSR like the USA became transformed into the nucleus of a system and the bi-partite world structure arose which was described in chapter 4. We have to remember that in the heart of this group, there now appeared in their turn the first examples of 'mixed socialism'; at the same time the unquestionable efficiency

African students alongside Russians in a language laboratory at the Patrice Lumumba Friendship University, Moscow. Till quite recently capitalism was the only economic system open to developing countries once independence was achieved, but now socialism provides another model. In addition to technical and economic aid programs, more and more African and Asian students go to universities in socialist countries.

of centralised planning for development aroused in capitalist countries like France an interest in this centralised planning, which gave rise to 'mixed capitalism'.

At the same time socialism, accelerated by the Second World War, was spreading to China, and in 1949 Mao Tse-tung proclaimed the People's Republic. Here was the first example of 'emergent socialism', while the crumbling of the European colonial empires in Asia, together with the urgent necessity for development and the desire for efficiency in planning, promoted the birth of the 'mixed traditional' system in some of these Asian nations, notably India.

At this juncture instances of all the systems listed in our typology were in existence. But the spread of socialism did not stop there. The Egyptian *coup d'état* of 1952 brought the first of the specialised forms of 'African socialism', not always easy to define, which have spread throughout the continent of Africa. Meanwhile, events in Korea and SW Asia brought fresh contributions to emergent socialism. Finally, in 1959, socialism appeared in the American continent as a result of Fidel Castro's revolution in Cuba; its regional compass may have been extremely restricted but it has had a noticeable influence throughout the entire Western hemisphere. The whole process is statistically reflected as follows: in 1917 socialism extended over only 8½ million square miles, which were the confines of the USSR before the last war and represented about 15 per cent of the inhabited globe. Half a century later it has doubled its extent, which now (though because of the uncertainty of some of the African positions this is only an approximate estimate) exceeds 17 million square miles, almost one third of the earth's surface.

The field of forces

This outline completes the present-day picture. We now have some definite 'bodies' – the systems classified – and two forces: technical and social. Our present description of the field can be compared with a simple diagram of bodies in physical space. It does not illustrate clearly for us the perspectives of the immediate future. Like all morphology, it gives a static description. We must now make that description dynamic and study these diverse systems in actual operation. Some idea has already been conveyed by the historical development described in the last paragraph, but we need greater accuracy and we cannot be limited to mere prognostication from the past. We must be stricter in systematising our dynamic concept, and give a better interpretation of the forces acting upon the present economy.

To do this we shall imitate the physicists by applying the 'field' concept, so abundantly employed during the last century. The mechanistic interpretation of the universe, still deeply impressed upon the mind of Helmholtz a hundred years ago, barred the way to progress until the concept of a field containing all the lines of force in a single space was advanced. When what the physicists call 'an experimental body' is introduced into such a field, it will be displaced along the lines of force which compose the field and will reveal their existence and characteristics.

We can represent the world economic scene as a field of this type, in which we have identified the existence of certain forces, technical and social. At once the systems classified in this chapter become so many other 'bodies' which are displaced in accordance with the corresponding lines of force. As soon as we are able to trace these lines with certainty on the rectangle in figure 11, which we have used to represent the whole world economic scene, we shall have transformed it into a field and we shall have a scientific idea about the direction towards which each system will be displaced as time goes on. Prognosis is allowable, for I have observed from the start that it is not my intention to prophesy, but to delineate the immediate future before the lines of force in operation at present suffer appreciable variations.

Our next task will consist of tracing these lines of force on the economic field presented in this chapter. The following chapters will deal with this problem.

6 Towards a planning system

A system based on money and goods

This book is being published just after the ninth centenary of the Norman Conquest of Britain in 1066. I refer to this date, because the Bayeux tapestry, which has preserved for us a life-like portrayal of the event, furnishes two illustrations, one of William the Conqueror's ships and one of a horse doing farm-work, which serve as an appropriate introduction to this chapter.

According to Lefebvre des Noëttes, this is the oldest drawing extant of a horse with the revolutionary equipment of stirrups, metal shoes and harness, which were introduced into Europe between the ninth and tenth centuries, probably by way of the nomadic peoples of the East. Perhaps such advances seem trivial to us today, but the beneficial effect they had upon agriculture and land transport has been compared by historians to the impact made by the steam-engine in the eighteenth century. Without going into detail, we should note that it has been proved that the load haulage of an animal so equipped is three or four times that of the same beast accoutred as it would have been in ancient Rome.

The Bayeux tapestry does not portray any new technique in the ships: on the contrary, it shows vessels that were about to become obsolete since they still use a lateral oar as a rudder. A century later the modern rudder made its appearance, hinged at the stern and operated by a horizontal balance-beam. Today we pay little attention to this invention either, but it proved decisive in navigation. A German chronicler has recorded that, as a Crusader sailing along the Spanish coast towards the Holy Land in 1189, he suddenly heard the pilot shout some orders and could not believe his eyes: the vessel was actually moving against the wind under sail and without the use of oars. It was one of the greatest marvels of the journey for this warrior and he felt obliged to put it down in writing. Max Weber has stated that this is the first account on record of a manoeuvre at sea against the wind relying only on the new tiller.

The reader will probably be wondering what the horse and ships

The invention of the rudder was the most revolutionary advance in medieval navigation. *Right* The Bayeux tapestry: at the time of the Norman Conquest ships were still being steered by an oar. *Below* Black marble font at Winchester Cathedral: by the twelfth century fixed rudders were in use, enabling a ship to sail against the wind.

of the Bayeux tapestry have got to do with capitalism: simply that they are symbols of a technical acceleration which was able to widen the scope of transportation and commerce. Naturally this was not the only stimulus to trade; other influential factors played their part, such as the underrated first agricultural revolution in Northern Europe. There were other, non-technical factors, such as the influence of Islam, as Jacques Pirenne's well known study seeks to prove, and the peaceful settlement of the Hungarian and Norman invasions. But the basis of capitalism was undoubtedly the development of commerce, allied to progress in transportation. In the opening words of *Das Kapital*, Marx puts it in this way:

The wealth of societies in which the capitalist system of production has control, in our view takes the form of a 'mighty storehouse of goods' with trade as its basic practice.

Indeed, the system lays emphasis much more on goods than on men, who are treated as a form of merchandise because of their labour: hence the importance of technical development and attitudes that favour the unhampered growth of trade. The fusion of the rational attitude with the medieval advances in administration, whose effect was stressed in an earlier chapter, could have made no real impact if a speedier exchange of goods had not been made possible by improved methods of transportation.

Trade was all important to the expansion of the merchant cities of Italy and the Hanseatic League, and, with other factors recorded by economic historians, led to the birth of capitalism. It must be pointed out that modern research reveals the final years of the Middle Ages and the period of the Renaissance, from the fourteenth century to the end of the fifteenth, to have been an age of prolonged economic depression. Some authorities link the economic hardships to the loss of population in Europe from 1340 onwards, due to the Great Plague. Others take the view that the expansion of trade at a time of economic difficulties was a crisis of development, and a sign of alteration in the structure of society: it was a direct result of the appearance of capitalism, whose growth was being stifled in the rigidly hierarchical world of the Middle

NTO:PLENIS VE
NTE RR A:
ONIS
TIS

Ages and whose vast schemes were being frustrated by lack of financial backing. The capitalist system, as we shall see, was to survive similar crucial phases in its growth.

Release from the stranglehold of medievalism came from an unexpected quarter: the geographical discoveries of the Portuguese in the East and of the Spaniards in the West. These navigators and colonisers opened up the way to new worlds and awakened a flood of inventive genius at a time when the precious metals from the Americas were beginning to supply the wealth essential to capitalism and economic expansion. Until then numerous currencies had been used as a means of exchange, instead of a standard coinage in the modern, token sense. The gold of the Indies, coined by the new monarchies, gave capitalism the opportunity of rationalising an economic tool vital to the smooth functioning of its market system. The axle was now provided with the two wheels essential for its successful progress; improved transport methods and imported gold had truly launched capitalism.

To glimpse its final destination, under the pressure of present-day forces, we have had to emphasise the primary dependence of capitalism on commercial and financial markets. However, the smooth operation of these markets was hindered by guild rules and mercantile regulations, so that the mere distribution of money and goods was not enough. Hence arose the connection between capitalism and liberalism, which I shall deal with later. For the moment I shall simply stress that the system strove to keep restrictions to a minimum by aiming at more and more freedom of movement for economic enterprises.

This resulted in the continued growth of rational attitudes from the stagnant waters of tradition, encouraging a technical acceleration which, in turn, converted the first mercantile capitalism into a better known and more typical form: industrial capitalism. Within barely two generations a decisive change took place in England. Until 1760 home industries in which the craftsmen did the work in their own houses had predominated. By 1820 these same workmen were already going to the factory to do their work.

The first passenger locomotive, 1808. The nineteenth century was to be the century of steam.

The centralisation of industry was being hastened by the technical necessity of siting machines close to the steam-engine, from which power could be transmitted only for the short distance permitted by axles, belts and pulleys. Centralisation grew with the added stimulus of the wider markets afforded by the new revolution in transportation, by rail and sea, which made use of the unprecedented power of the same steam-engine. It is even possible that the steam-engine almost became airborne, to judge from a scaled-down model of a steam aeroplane built by Stringfellow in 1848.

Many hold that the railway revolution marks the most representative feature of typical capitalism: mechanised industry. The novelists and poets of the period waxed eloquent over the symbolic meaning of the railway, the man-made Pegasus of the technical age. A quaint advertisement for the first passenger locomotive flaunts two arrogant publicity slogans: 'Mechanical power subduing animal speed' and above it the challenge, 'Catch me who can'. Five years after Stephenson had won the locomotive prize with his famous *Rocket*, the Newcastle to Carlisle company bought an engine from him, and one of the three coaches forming the train on the inaugural run (March 1835) was named *Social*, as if to express the nineteenth century's progress along its metalled way.

The USA, whose future achievements had already been forecast by Tocqueville, was to cross the continent with the 'iron horse' and railways were to reach the Pacific. In the meantime the tracks in Europe went on multiplying to form an intricate network. Before this was achieved, however, the system would have to overcome another difficulty due to investing in more enterprises than it could conveniently handle at any one time and to oversubscribing to the building of railroads which made serious demands on capital. Consider for instance the crowded events of the decade ending in 1848: the building of the first French railway from Paris to Saint-Germain in 1837; the foundation of the Manchester School, the embodiment of free trade and *laissez faire* in 1838; the establishment of the metric system in France in 1840 – though the highly capitalist society of Great Britain did not opt for this elementary rationalisation; the appearance of superphosphates and the first artificial fertilisers in 1842; the reorganisation of the Bank of England by Peel's famous and far-reaching law of 1844; the inauguration in 1844 of Morse telegraph, which put an end to the Chappe visual system of signalling towers; the triumph of free trade with the Repeal of the English Corn Laws in 1846; the discovery in 1847 of nitro-glycerine, which would pave the way for public works like the Panama Canal, after Nobel had shown how to control it by converting it into dynamite; and finally the Great Famine of 1847 in Ireland.

Both technical and social phenomena were now interwoven, inspiring a cumulative effort: new railways, increasing competition, colonial expansion, finance for domestic projects; all these placed the system under very severe strain which took effect in the economic crises of 1825, 1837 and 1847, successive hammer blows which aggravated the social misery described by Dickens and Balzac. The tension mounted and in 1838 Proudhon published his book *What is Property?*, whose title reads like the opening of an indictment. Entrepreneurs lacked financial backing, workers had more than enough reason to be resentful. A crisis, brought on by development, had to break out somewhere.

Two outlets provided simultaneous relief, for 1848 was the year both of the *Communist Manifesto* and of Sutter's discovery of the Californian goldfields. The *Communist Manifesto* made its appearance when monarchies were tottering as a result of the revolution of 1848, and even collapsing altogether as did the rule of Louis-Philippe in France. After recovering from the revolution, however, the system was in a stronger position, for it crushed the forces of labour and removed any possibility of action for some time. Moreover, since America was again sending her gold to Europe (this was shortly to be followed by a contribution from the Australian gold-mines), the financial worries of capitalism were over. A new period of expansion followed. During the next ten years the world's output of gold increased tenfold, bursting the limits by which current banking policy exercised control over the extension of credit.

The crisis brought financial considerations to the fore and from then on industrial capitalism developed a financial system which was to be protected by the end of the century. Finance became centralised like the factory system. The banking houses of the Rothschilds and the Pereyres in France and the merchant bankers in England were to provide backing for railways in Spain and other countries and for various other enterprises. The three great French banks (*Comptoir National d'Escompte*, *Crédit Lyonnais* and *Société Générale*), between them increased from 64 branches in 1870 to 1229 forty years later. Rigidity of legal standards was also instituted as at the outset of capitalism, and further facilities were extended to the huge modern commercial undertakings. Between 1855 and 1862 the principle of limited liability became law in Great Britain, and from 1867 in France the previous legislation requiring a special law for each stock company set up was abandoned. So *high finance* was born, as earlier high nobility had been

~~Sunday~~ Monday 24th this day some kind of mettle was

177

~~discover~~ found in the tail race ~~that~~ ~~that~~ looks like goald ~~first discovered by James Martial, the Boss of the Mill.~~

~~Sunday 30 clean & has been~~ all the last week our metal has been tride and proves to be Goald it is thought to be rich we have pict up more than a hundred dollars woth last week

---

February. 1848

Sun 6th the wether has been clear

Manifest

der

Kommunistischen Partei.

Veröffentlicht im Februar 1848.

London.

Gedruckt in der Office der „Bildungs-Gesellschaft für Arbeiter"

von J. E. Burghard.

46, Liverpool Street, Bishopsgate.

Титульный лист первого издания
«Манифеста Коммунистической партии»

Left Diary entry recording the discovery of gold at Sutter's Mill, California, in 1848. *Right* Title page of Karl Marx's *Communist Manifesto*, which appeared in the same year. If 1848 proved a year of opportunity for free enterprise, it also marked the opening of a new era for socialism.

born. Shortly afterwards, in 1879, a Rockefeller lawyer named Samuel C. T. Dodd invented *trusts*, and with them a method of coordinating a mass of undertakings into an efficient system of handling assets. The new stage in the development of capitalism is characterised by increasing coordination and organised expansion.

The increasing organisation of capital, however, entailed a decrease in the importance of the individual, who was seen as one more cog in an all-powerful machine. Capitalism has thus moved further and further away from its primary form in which the private entrepreneur was the pivot of all initiative and the maker of decisions. The merchant of the Renaissance needed only a small staff of assistants and agents. The industrialist in the nineteenth century was helpless without numerous technicians and a large labour force though he continued to be their visible and effective chief. In the modern organisation, as we shall see, the capitalist is no more than a part of the whole. Three factors have contributed to this: the internal structure of the enterprises themselves, their nation-wide scale and the effect of foreign influence.

As regards the internal structure of companies, the expansion fostered by the advantages of large-scale production has made individual direction impossible. It has been replaced by an administrative bureaucracy in which personalities, even those of the chairman, are completely discounted. As regards the national scope of these giant concerns, their increasing power has promoted the establishment of other powerful bodies to act as a social counterbalance, with the aid of increasing State intervention. Finally, as regards the external sphere, the loss of colonial markets coupled with the demands of two great world wars has necessitated collective readjustments which themselves have led to more direct control of the economy by the State.

All this means that under the pressure of economic expansion society has developed away from the world of political liberalism and a social organisation based on the individual. This is the direct result of the technical and social forces in operation and clearly indicates the direction which capitalism is now taking. This direction would be immediately obvious were it not that after several generations of thinking in terms of liberalism and associating it with the idea of maximum progress, it becomes difficult to accept the unremitting lesson of the past – *autres temps, autres moeurs*. The irrefutable teaching of history shows that no system is everlasting; liberal capitalism, which for many is capitalism under another name, cannot be the system of the future and it is not even the system of the present. If we do not fully grasp this we shall be unable to envisage the ultimate goal of present-day economic forces. We must, therefore, rid ourselves at once of the idea that capitalism is the 'natural order of things' in society and its only possible channel for future progress.

Capitalism as a phase

We must therefore regard capitalism as a phase in history, and indeed as a much shorter phase than some others. The capitalist economy is a product of modern Europe. It has undoubtedly been far-reaching; it contains within itself good points as well as bad; it is powered by an unprecedented dynamism and has spread to the rest of the world; it has everything to be said for it except that it cannot be the final world system.

When official slogans reiterate that man attains freedom only in the capitalist system, it is important to underline that the system's political doctrine used to be liberalism with the slogan *laissez faire*. But much has happened since the first merchant capitalists, constricted by the numerous fetters of a traditional society, put rationalism and the spirit of financial gain into practical effect. Modern economies are no longer interested in liberalism or *laissez faire*, but in a disciplined organisation which favours their growth under the conditions of modern technology, just as freedom favoured their growth in the past. In this they remain faithful to their rationalism, which does not conflict with the spontaneous behaviour of *laissez faire*, as might seem to be the case at first sight. On the contrary, both courses are perfectly compatible if economic liberalism is conceived as the result of previous planning: that is, as having been deliberately designed by the capitalists, after they had weighed up all the advantages to be gained from non-intervention at the highest levels, since their economic potential dominated the world of supply and demand. The establishment of the free market was thus the result of a rational calculation; the lack of a plan in *laissez faire* was a plan in itself. It is not surprising that in the Age of Enlightenment the subtlest logic could coexist with Rousseau's idea of the noble savage.

Thus the capitalists, in their fight for liberty, based their socio-economic decisions on the results of competition in the open market since it was there that they were strongest: in short, it was *their* liberty that they were defending. It is perhaps more difficult to explain how the other social groups came to leave their entrenched economic positions so readily – feudalism, the organisation of guilds, mercantilism – and accepted the challenge in that field of open competition where the new entrepreneurs were most powerful. It seems most probable that they could not avoid doing so. However, they swallowed the bitter pill more easily by developing the palliative doctrine that such a competition was the 'natural order' of society, thus reconciling logic with faith and intellectual enlightenment with spectacular hopes for the future. The capitalists' liberty became *the Liberty* through the ideology which passed down from Grotius and Pufendorf, through Mandeville and the physiocrats and was finally popularised in Adam Smith's formula of the *invisible hand.*

According to this formula, one has only to leave each individual completely free to satisfy his most selfish desires for collective well-being to be achieved, of its own accord and without the need for any planned direction from above.

The good administrator should therefore confine himself to making it easy for each man to satisfy his own egoism. Once this idea had become generally accepted capitalism had defeated the attitudes that hindered its early advance. This implies the theoretical negation of the social structure in a radical way since the doctrine of capitalism conceived the economy as a cluster of human molecules, related to each other on a purely economic basis. Schumpeter could therefore say that Ricardo had no ideas on sociology and John Stuart Mill could assert that the science of economics was more like mechanics than chemistry, by which he meant that it was not concerned with stable formulae among elements but with balances among forces connecting molecules. Even in 1909, an economist as distinguished as Pareto could write that 'Society, as distinct from individuals, is an abstraction which does not correspond to anything real'. Capitalism had achieved as far as possible an economic theory without sociology. In the conception of *their* liberty as *the* liberty, the capitalists marked out a sort of combat area, in which no rules prevailed and where the capitalist could challenge his opponents but at the same time say, like the self-confident bull-fighter: 'Leave us alone. Let no one interfere. If you interfere it is a crime against the natural order of things.'

I do not mean, of course, that Quesnay or Adam Smith should have deliberately devoted themselves to an ideological interpretation of capitalist expedients. Yet their social theory ran parallel to economic practice. Both were facets of the same social situation in which rational attitudes could clearly be seen in conflict with the traditional society from which they had emerged: attitudes which were embodied in the over-simplified psychology which was attributed to that molecular being, *homo economicus*, responsive only to the stimulus of financial gain. 'Nature', wrote Bentham in a much quoted passage, 'has placed Humanity beneath the rule of two sovereign masters: pleasure and pain'. This formula would still be rich in content although, if every human aspect is to be included, all positive stimuli must be termed 'pleasure' and all negative ones 'pain', and the statement becomes a platitude. The economists simplified it still more: not for nothing did they represent a system founded on material things, money and merchandise. They reduced human motives to the Newtonian centrifugal and centripetal pull of two impulses: profit and loss. Thus double entry book-keeping is made the foundation of man's being. Such a psychology is natural to capitalism. Because it is abstract and over-simplified this schematisation is unacceptable to us today, but the view then current of the general pattern of mental behaviour was nevertheless based on it and on the role of the *invisible hand* in making everything for the best.

Europe has been accustomed to this idea for so long, that many people still regard it as 'natural'. As a result they consider all the other economic systems that history and ethnography have evolved as foreign to man's nature. They still hold that by nature man is an individual, like an autonomous molecule in free motion within the social orbit. Yet the opposite is true. It was proved some time ago first by historians and then by anthropologists, that the prevailing tendency in the world has been for men to live together in social groups and even submerge their personalities within the 'extended family', an integration typical of all traditional societies. If a wide enough view of history and geography be taken, the idea of the individual as created by capitalism is an exception. To judge by frequency of examples, the subordination of the individual to the group is much more in the natural order than his elevation to the status of author of his own decisions. Economic individualism is a mere phase in history, an experiment related to the needs of a certain period and essential to its deliberate aim to create a modern society from the stagnation of tradition. Its artificial

character is evident in the fact that, in spite of its doctrines, the free competition in which its economic theory was founded could never have been fully realised.

The truth was already known to Aristotle, who made man a 'political animal' and who considered that only gods and wild beasts could live outside a society. Toynbee mentions that the Greeks could not conceive of any beings living alone except the monstrous Cyclops, described in the *Odyssey* as 'creatures who do not take care of one another'. He makes the comment:

It is significant that this isolated manner of life is not ascribed to ordinary human beings; and, in fact, no human being has ever lived in the Cyclopean way, since man is essentially a social animal inasmuch as social life is a prerequisite of the evolution of human from sub-human.

Let us disabuse our minds, therefore, of the prejudice that capitalist liberalism is the only natural order of things. Let us deprive this system of the undeserved epithet 'natural' to which it has no more claim than any other form of society. Capitalism is neither more nor less than one more phase in history, even if it is the one that affects us most, because our lives are involved with

Rags to riches. An early Du Pont powder mill and its mile-long successor today.

it. Only when we are no longer thus biassed in our judgment shall we succeed in tracing the future of this phase.

From entrepreneur to organisation

Once free of prejudice we can see more clearly the different influences which have for so long been undermining the individual entrepreneur's power of decision. In the first place technical progress has steadily raised the optimum size of firms to fantastic proportions. In 1954 Berle summarised some statistics of Adelmans, according to which 45 per cent of the industrial production of America, then estimated as a quarter of the entire world output, was in the hands of 135 companies. Moreover, their actual influence was greater than the figures show, because it extended to firms nominally independent but in reality subject to the decisions of the more powerful caucus. The same author cited as an example of this the various agents of General Motors, whose garages and installations were valued at three thousand million dollars and whose turnover and output were controlled by the policy of the

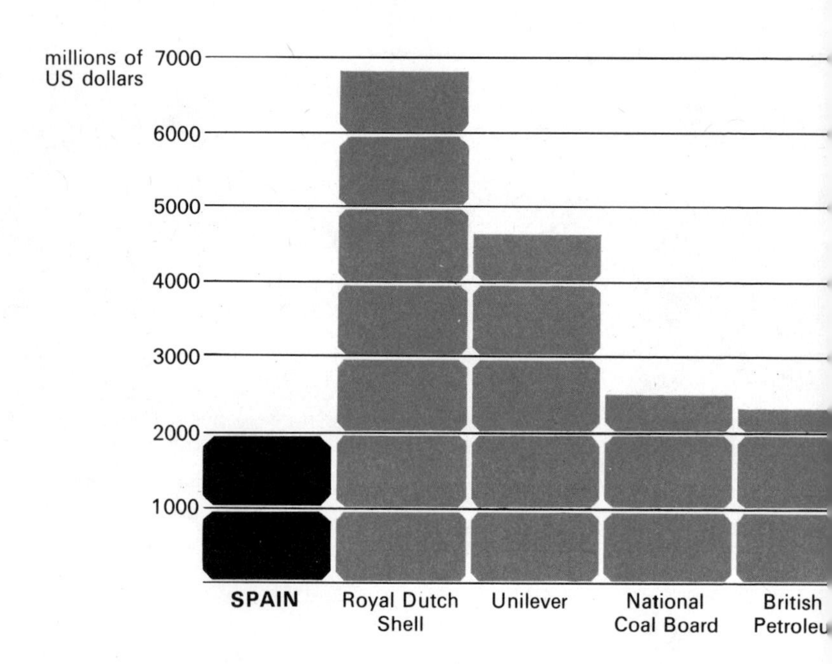

giant company they represented. In Germany, the annual statistics given in the *Frankfürter Allgemeine Zeitung* later showed that the hundred biggest companies in the country together made up a third of the industrial capital; while the three largest banks could raise 59 per cent of the total financial capital unaided. Further examples of huge undertakings are needless, for they abound in the textbooks and in commercial propaganda itself (figure 13).

In this vast scale the figure of the entrepreneur has naturally undergone a profound change. He is now no longer the autonomous individual described by both conservative and socialist economists in the past. The successful middle-class business-man

Figure 13. *Giant concerns.* Even if we ignore the vast concerns of the United States, we can still obtain some idea of the size of modern units of production by comparing the 1964 turnover of the ten largest European firms and the total budget expenditure of a semi-developed European country such as Spain, with a population of thirty-one millions. Spain's national expenditure is the basic unit of comparison in the chart.

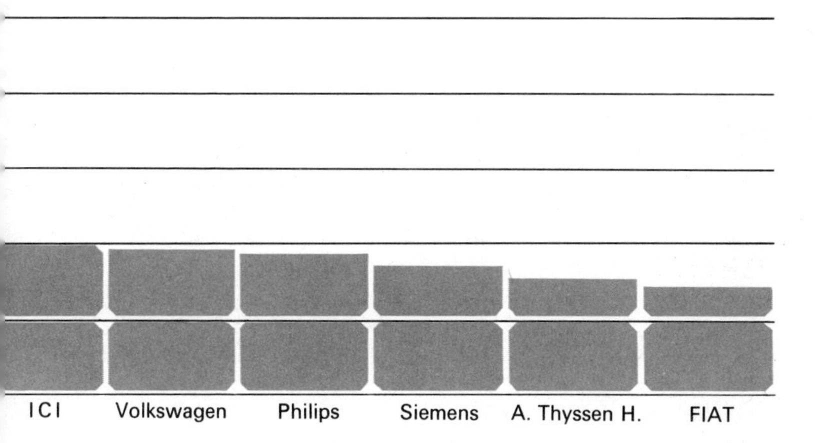

portrayed by Balzac in 1848 had already been changed into Theodore Dreiser's *The Financier* by 1900, and fifty years later into the managing directors of companies described in Cameron Hawley's *Executive Suite*.

The transformation of the entrepreneur, the key figure of capitalism, is the best guide to the evolution of the system. Even fifty years ago the world of the entrepreneur centred round well known personalities. F. L. Allen had no difficulty in naming the eight persons (which included two of the Rockefeller family) who had the greatest influence within the economy of the USA. They were men who imposed their will on the cut and thrust of the market; men like John Pierpont Morgan who stopped panic on the New York Stock Exchange almost singlehanded in 1907 and on one occasion interrupted one of his lawyers, as he was putting forward the legal objections to a scheme of his, with the remark: 'I do not keep a lawyer to tell me what I can or cannot do but to explain to me how I can do what I want'. In short, these were men who personally directed their companies using them as the tools and levers of their own wills.

Such are the men who are in danger of extinction now that huge organisations are taking their place. Even forty years ago a Thyssen was still the embodiment in Germany of those industrialists, now almost figures of the past, whose names were household words and whose caricatures appeared in newspaper cartoons. The firm which Thyssen founded still survives under the name of *August Thyssen Hütte, A G* and is the key member of the sixteen development units into which the Allies broke up the Thyssen Trust in 1945. But one must hunt through the archives to discover who are the main physical heirs of the old founder. We learn that the principal stockholders at present are the widow of the last Thyssen and their daughter Countess Anita de Zichy. If we remember how often those old financiers previously featured in the Press we are struck forcibly by the fact that though she is wealthy, a countess and the owner of a famous name, the heiress to the Thyssen fortune is of less interest to reporters than her ancestor was and infinitely less newsworthy than any starlet at the Cannes or Venice Film Festivals.

This is hardly surprising. The principal owner of a vast company no longer exercises any decisive role. As Berle has written, the new times have brought the disappearance of the capitalist, although capital and capitalism continue to exist. Can one indeed still speak of capitalism? Not by nineteenth century standards. In 1951, the American journalist William I. Nichols wrote an article entitled *Wanted – a new name for capitalism*, which received widespread publicity and was reproduced in the *Reader's Digest*. Nichols discussed the tremendous changes which I have been treating here and in his conclusion requested his readers to submit some possible new term. He received fifteen thousand replies and the astounded author exclaimed: 'In all my journalistic career, I have never touched on such a sensitive spot in public opinion.'

A new name is certainly needed since the cornerstone of the system has shifted: the individual entrepreneur has been caught up in the web of administration. This is primarily due to the inevitable accent on larger units of organisation. As I have suggested before, when the yearly turnover of many huge corporations is several times larger than the national budget of a country like Spain, it is impossible for their control to be in the hands of a single individual. A team of managers, who are becoming more and more professional, is essential and they very often take over the duties of the owner. In his study of the entrepreneur in America, Bendix remarks that of those born about 1790 only 5 per cent were non-owning managers. The percentage for those born about 1845 rose to 21 and today the figure has reached 48 per cent. Moreover, another 34 per cent of owners today have been trained as professional managers and are thus furthering company bureaucracy.

The form of organisation which is replacing the individual is no longer the administrative board of the past, made up of the family and a few friends with vested interests. Today the organisation is a tree with many branches, sometimes intertwined, a system with inter-dependent channels (figure 14): the numerous departments and directors, whose decisions, before they can take effect, are to an increasing extent vetted by a host of experts. Formerly a clever lawyer or an inventive engineer could be consulted, but today the experts form a body of economists, market research specialists, publicity experts, psychologists, sociologists and public relations agents. Formerly the business man at the top decided for himself and was guided above all by his own experience and insight, although he obviously listened to his colleagues. Today he has to think twice before he disagrees with the technical experts, especially since his immediate subordinates, as well as the boards of experts and his

Figure 14. *The modern organisation of a capitalist enterprise.* In a modern business organisation, decisions have become institutionalised and are based on complex evaluation. The executive departments reflect this decision-making organisation on a smaller scale.

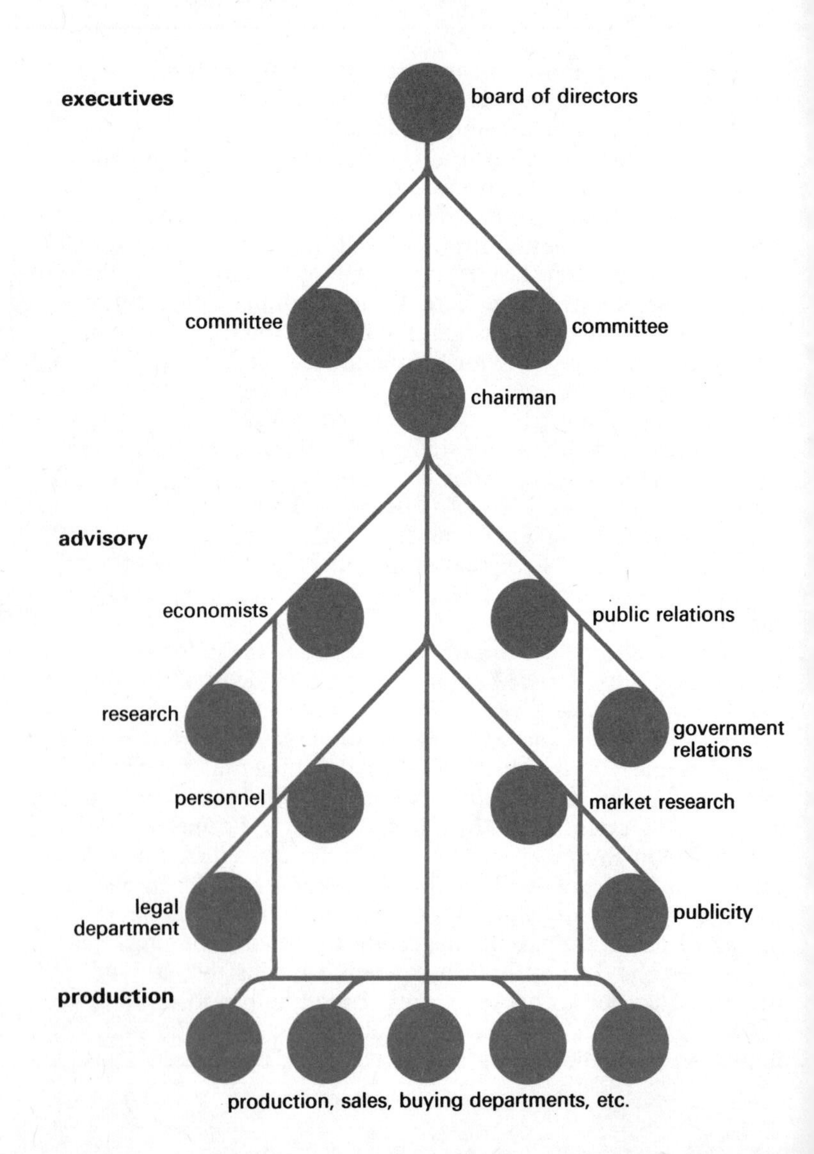

rival concerns, are keenly alert for any sign that 'the Old Man is slipping'. It is not surprising that American doctors have coined a special term, *executive stress*, to define the physiological tension peculiar to the business man who takes final responsibility for a decision whose actual source cannot be named since it proceeds from the organisation as a whole.

Nobody denies that the 'professionalisation' of the entrepreneur is a modern phenomenon. James Burnham gave it a considerable political slant in his book *The Managerial Revolution*, sub-titled *What is happening in the World.* Another popular work, *The Organisation Man* by W.H.Whyte, makes a study of the newcomer to the organisation who has usurped the role of the old entrepreneur. Many other authors have analysed the transformation of the company along more or less academic lines. The change is already so obvious that I need hardly do more than quote the following example from Vance Packard's *The Status Seekers*:

In a typical corporation, the head of the hierarchy assigned to a floor gets the corner office with the nicest view, and the offices of his subordinates branch out from his corner in descending order of rank. Physical closeness to the center of power is considered evidence of status; and nobody wants to be put out 'in left field'.

Desks, too, typically are categorised by rank. Mahogany, of course, outranks walnut; and walnut outranks oak. The man who is entitled to wall-to-wall carpeting is likely to have a water carafe, which has replaced the brass spittoon as a symbol of flag rank, and also probably has a red-leather couch.

In the film *The Apartment*, the rise of the poor employee to the dizzy executive heights, was symbolised by the right to that absolute final token of status: a personal key to the executives' private washroom, and in some the basin has even been known to have had gold-plated taps. Elsewhere there are even more subtle distinctions at the top. For, and again I quote Vance Packard:

At a Mid-Western oil firm, however, a fine line is drawn. The vice-presidents, like the president, have a private washroom; but it is literally that. Their washroom has no toilet, as the president's has.

Not without reason has Allen proposed the term 'managerial system' rather than 'capitalist system'.

State control

We have now seen how the company gradually passed out of personal control because internal pressures continually demanded the maximum development, which was impossible without a complex organisation. However, other factors have also helped to restrict the entrepreneur's power of self-determination, and his insistence on free trade under the old form of capitalism. These factors are social and point to something more than the loss of personal control – increasing state control of the economy (figure 15). This is the result of historical changes which, as we have seen, took place under two combined influences: one endogenous and the other exogenous.

As far as internal influences are concerned it must be remembered that the entrepreneur never had absolute freedom of action. His will was bounded by legal and political principles, as is the playing surface of a football pitch by touchlines. Within that area, however, true liberal doctrine condemned state interference in free competition, because only free competition would realise the maximum profit which, under Adam Smith's *invisible hand*, was to yield society the greatest benefit. Despite this theory, which was in full force by the mid-nineteenth century, state intervention soon became imperative to counter indefensible abuses which did not lie too heavily on the consciences of those who adhered to a system based upon money, goods and free trade. The reduction of man to a mere equation of work in terms of goods, for instance, led to obvious exploitation. The condition of children in industry brought numerous outcries from moralists and literary men, which resulted in the first capitalist restrictions of free trade: the Apprentices Act of 1802 in England and the 1819 Act regulating the employment of children in the cotton industry. France followed suit in 1841 with her first law dealing with child employment. In 1844 another

Lloyd George comforting the sick with the promise of social insurance. Difficult as it may be to take a poster of this nature seriously, it is significant that State aid was considered a necessary vote-winning measure at the time. The National Insurance Act was passed in 1911.

Mr. LLOYD GEORGE'S National Health Insurance Bill provides for the insurance of the Worker in case of Sickness.

Support the Liberal Government

in their policy of

SOCIAL REFORM.

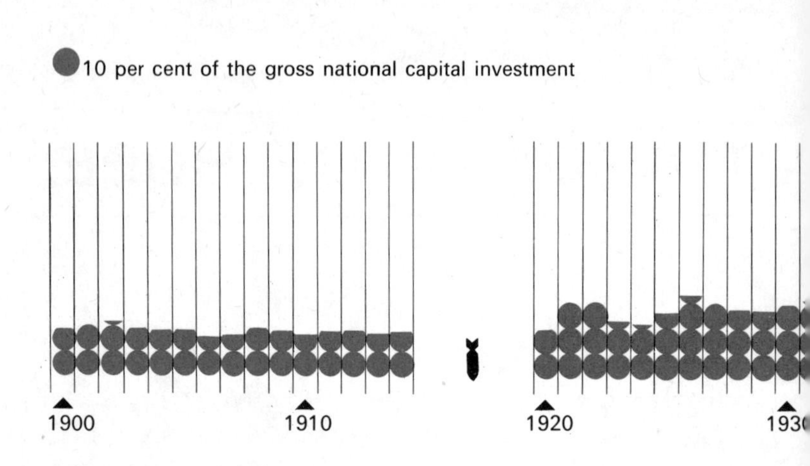

law was passed in Britain dealing with the similar condition of women in industry.

Social pressures were gradually building up against a liberty of action which was enjoyed primarily by the capitalist. The first International Working Men's Association was founded in London in 1864 and from 1871 workers' organisations, already in existence, were recognised by law in Great Britain. Under increasing pressure from public opinion, governments also had to take measures to protect consumers, and began to come to grips with the trusts, as the Sherman Law, passed in America in 1890, witnesses. The twentieth century ushered in the first British laws on social insurance, with which the names of Lloyd George and Winston Churchill are associated, a fitting culmination of attitudes which had advanced considerably from the sale of sweated labour in the markets of the first capitalists. Bismarck had begun to travel the same road, influenced by the socialist intellectuals. Minimum wage scales appeared in Australia and New Zealand in 1894; in Great Britain in 1900; in France in 1914. Even the conservative Roman Catholic Church acknowledged the existence of the new tenancies in the encyclical *Rerum Novarum* in 1891.

It is not surprising that state intervention should start with those labour conditions in which the human problem was most glaring. I do not intend to give the whole process in detail but it is

Figure 15. *Public investment in Great Britain.* The discs represent the percentage of the gross national capital investment carried out by the public sector in the corresponding year. The increasing role of the State in the economy is reflected in the greater proportion of capital investment in the total national investment. Up to 1914 it was less than 20 per cent, since 1948 it has exceeded 40 per cent.

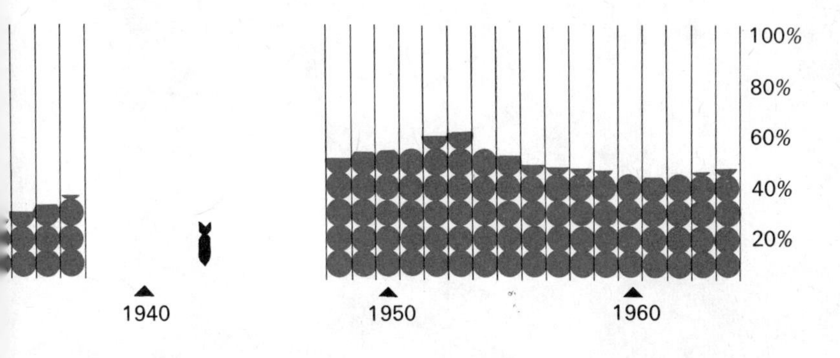

today impossible, even for neo-liberals (who for that very reason advocate a genuine reparation for past wrongs) to believe in the automatic action of the *invisible hand.* The liberal capitalism of the nineteenth century is dead and buried. Its concept of liberty undoubtedly produced an astonishing technical acceleration and a consequent rise in productivity. Yet that very concept created a technical giant beyond the power of any single individual to control, with a resulting breakdown of human values within the system. A factory can be neither set up nor run by the entrepreneur working on his own. Each individual is not a self-contained unit whose social relations are tantamount to a kind of 'external trading' with the other units. We are all completely bound to each other. Society, and not the individual, has produced the productive equipment, and the assumption of privilege by any one person is far less justified now than in the days when craftsmen were almost self sufficient. These and similar ideas lead the state to play an increasing role in industrial relations and gradually to take over the responsibility for incomes policies.

At the same time pressures arose from international events which favoured increasing control by the state. The First World War was responsible for directives and plans which, though relaxed at the end of the struggle, according to the policy then current, left indelible traces. The decision to return to the normal

conditions of the capitalist 'natural order of things' seemed to be justified by the prosperity of the 'twenties. There was even a relaxation of some of the restrictions hitherto in force: the Webb–Pomerene law amended the Sherman anti-trusts legislation in America and in Germany a special tribunal set up in 1923 to discriminate between 'good' and 'bad' cartels relaxed restrictions.

However the world slump which began in 1929 revealed more sharply than ever before the inherent contradictions within the system. In 1931 the pound sterling abandoned the gold standard. This disaster to the golden symbol of a century of financial power was equivalent to striking the colours. The democrats triumphed at the polls in 1932 and the Roosevelt Administration took office. The new president's interference in the economy outraged the traditionalists and two years later a Supreme Court ruling was obtained which declared unconstitutional the *National Industrial*

The Great Depression caused widespread unemployment in the United States.
Left Mrs Roosevelt serves unemployed women in a New York soup kitchen. *Below* Dole queue.

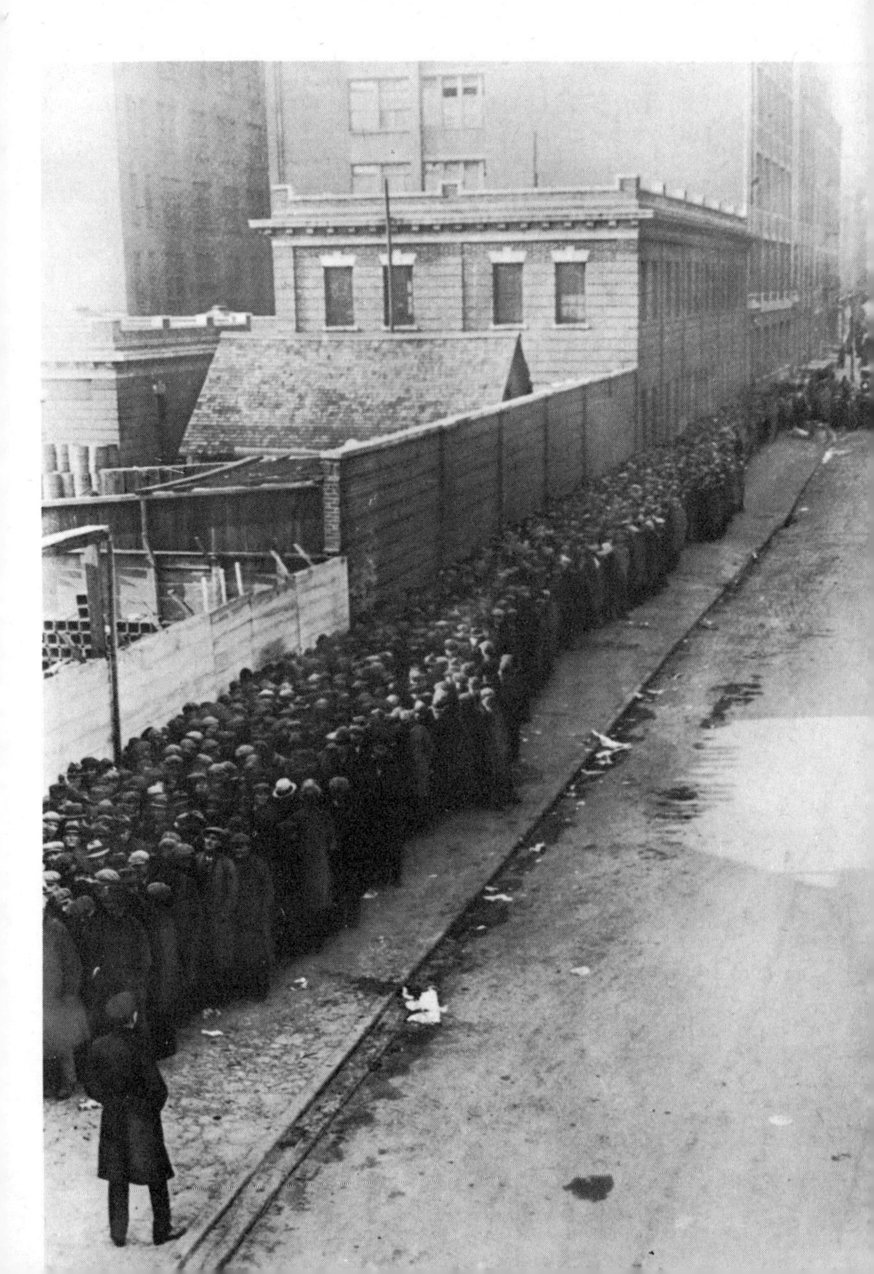

Recovery Act of 1933. However, it could not delete the effect of other measures like the *Muscle Shoals–Tennessee Valley Act* of May 1933 which inaugurated the transformation of the Tennessee Valley, and is regarded today as a milestone in modern regional policy.

The policies of other countries followed much the same direction, as any modern history of economics will show. Great Britain accepted the Beveridge Plan for social security (whose basic assumption was that the state had a duty to the worker 'from the cradle to the grave') and embarked upon a regional policy with the 1934 Act on Special Areas, dealing with the commercial aspect of farming in the Act of 1931 and by the setting up of *Agricultural Marketing Boards* in 1933. In France, as in other European countries, it became fashionable to use the term 'directed economy' for the current form of intervention – perhaps to avoid the term 'plan', which was still taboo in the capitalist world, chiefly because the Russians had sanctioned it in 1928. Be that as it may France set up her Wheat Bureau in 1936, and instituted measures for the nationalisation of the Bank of France. Meanwhile Germany and Italy had adopted a yet more overt policy of state control to cope with preparations for war, and to overcome difficulties, such as those caused by the economic sanctions imposed on Italy by the League of Nations following the Abyssinian war. The repercussions of the Depression compelled some kind of state intervention in foreign trade. In France, as elsewhere, it took the form of quantitative share restrictions or quotas. The same thing happened in the United States, where the control of the economy gradually passed from Wall Street to the ministerial departments in Washington, although Wall Street still exerted considerable influence.

Just as the birth of capitalism produced its own ideology so its development has also produced changes in the climate of opinion. In the nineteenth century the theorists of capitalism viewed the world as a great sea of free enterprise occasionally broken by the reef of some monopoly. In the age of the Rockefellers and Morgans Professor Sumner of Yale inveighed against the idea of assigning

Figure 16. *Nationalisation of sectors of the economy.* During the last few decades some European countries have increased their direct participation in basic sectors of the economy by pursuing a policy of nationalisation.

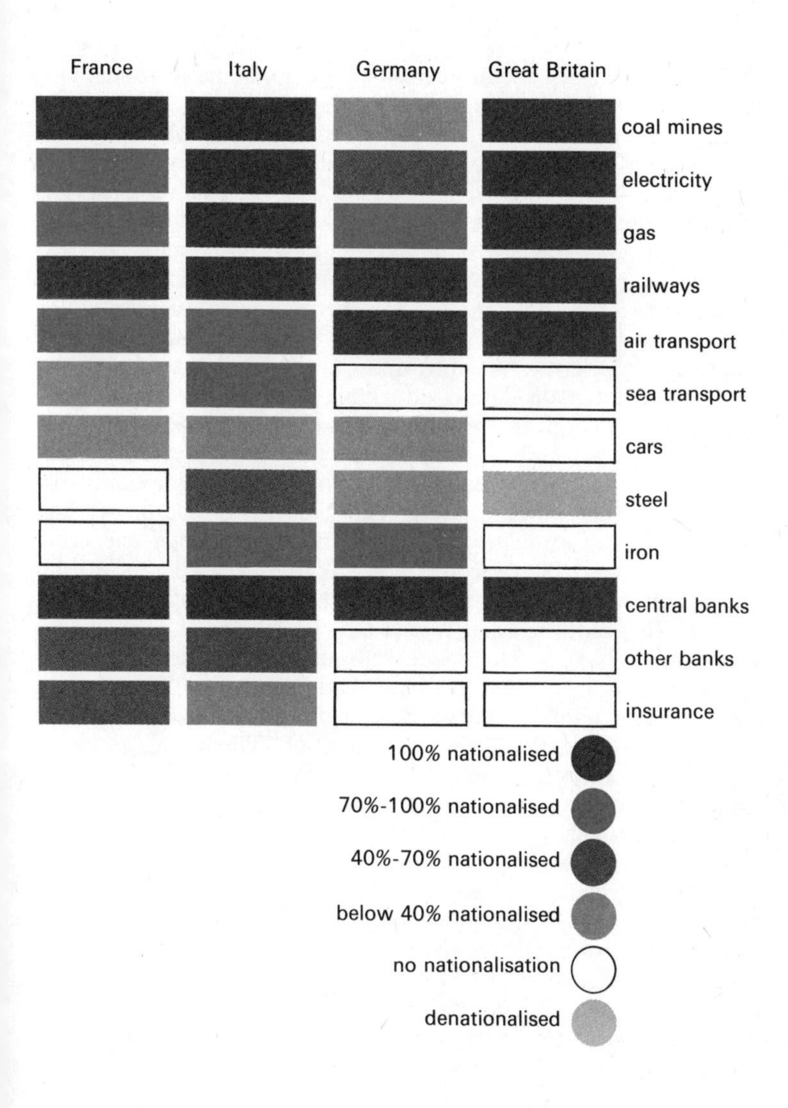

the government the role of guardian angel to the nation when God had set up the principles of political economy for that very purpose. Yet by 1930 such theorists of imperfect competition as Chamberlain or Joan Robinson saw the world as something very different from a sea of free enterprise; it was in reality made up of several powerful monopolies, each conflicting with the other, in which the egalitarian safeguard of market supply and demand was not allowed to operate. The micro-economy of marginal profits was turning into a macro-economy – in other words, it was becoming a theory based on society and not on the individual. When the Depression came and the unemployed crowded the streets, the economic theorists in their comfortable arm-chairs were forced to consider their plight. In 1936, in his *The General Theory of Employment, Interest and Money*, Lord Keynes incorporated the problems of unemployment into standard economic theory, stressing the essential function of the State as guardian. Economic theory had once more become *political economy* and thus a *social* science.

The exigences of the Second World War demanded almost total centralisation in every country, besides coordination of the respective allied economies. It is true that afterwards, as in the First War, there was a return to decentralisation, but in no sense at all had the situation reverted to what it had been before 1939. Indeed the very term 'state intervention', typical of the 'thirties, is entirely inadequate for defining the present position. Today the dominant trait is state control of the entire economy in every basic facet of living and its influence is on the increase. In many instances, it is exercised through the nationalisation of services or industries which were previously in private ownership (figure 16). By 1960 the railways were nationalised in all the main European countries; the central banks and atomic power stations are owned by the nation almost everywhere; the coal mines in Great Britain, Italy and France are state-owned; electricity and gas are under complete state control in Britain and Italy and partial state control in France; in the majority of countries all, or nearly all, the air-lines are state-owned. Direct state intervention through nationalisation is supplemented by indirect state regulation of the entire political economy by such means as taxes, excise duty, investment levies, subsidies or grants to adjust personal inequalities, measures to improve depressed areas and state legislation to counteract unemployment or offset deficiencies in supply and demand, so as to maintain a high level of employment and general economic activity.

In conclusion, the world of the present cannot be aptly symbolised by the steam-engine. Coordinators and planners, schemes and laws, card-indices and registers – the symbols of bureaucracy – are more representative of the age than machines. It is true that these forms and files are a continued effect of the rationalisation fostered by technology. But the law itself is no longer the application of reason to the practice of high principles and a lofty standard of values, so much as a code of norms respected purely and simply for its power to achieve the objectives, usually material, of the state. The present-day structure of capitalism is therefore more aptly symbolised by the firm's record cards than by the machine worked by man. This wave of rationalisation created capitalism and the technical approach. It has led to an economic organisation which will soon entail the state conducting the national economic orchestra.

Nobody today disapproves of this central control of the economy, much less demands, as did the old liberalism – neo-liberalism has completely waived the point – the economic neutrality of the state. The concept of government as a kind of passive arbitrator, ruling on exceptional matters such as national defence, public order or general health, has given way to the idea of the state as a conductor setting the tone and the beat for the individual instrumentalists who are the units of economic decision. The Second World War afforded the proof that such a system is much more productive; and productivity is the ultimate criterion of a world preoccupied by economic efficiency as the basis of expansion and development. Even conservative ideology has rejected the old liberal doctrines which charged the Soviet system with being wasteful and took for granted the matchless efficiency of an economy based on the market. This can be shown in the work of a distinguished Yale professor and ex-economic adviser to President Eisenhower, Henry C. Wallich, published a short while ago under the significant title *The Cost of Freedom*. He concludes with these words:

> The essence of the principles that we have examined in this book can be expressed very briefly. In the way in which we conduct our affairs, it seems an undeniable fact that we value a free economy principally for the service it renders to freedom, both political and economic. The virtues of its productivity, however impressive they may be, come second. If our major concern were maximum production at all costs, a directed economy of the kind used in the last two wars would probably recommend itself most to us, as it does to the communist world.

To be still more brief, the theme of the book is the admission that a planned economy directed towards production is more efficient than a market economy, even though the latter, in Wallich's view, concedes a greater measure of freedom.

Towards planning

To judge by world events, it seems that people are not very interested in paying for liberty at the cost of reduced efficiency. This is not difficult to understand. In the first place, maximum production at all costs is the chief concern of many backward countries, which cannot defer their development any longer. The millions of people who do not get enough to eat from one day to the next are not greatly interested in enjoying freedom to die of hunger in the streets. In the second place, when the present-day heirs of liberalism try to retain as much as possible of their old position by pointing out the advantages of liberty (after admitting they were wrong in ascribing greater efficiency to a market economy), they are skating on very thin ice, and immediately provoke their opponents to ask what is the nature of this liberty and, above all, for whom is it designed. It is possible that the United

States as a whole can permit itself the luxury of maintaining liberty at the cost of a slower economic expansion than in other countries. Yet it is doubtful whether there would be agreement from the thirty or forty million Americans living on the verge of that new poverty, so vividly described by Michael Harrington in his book *The Other Country*. The problem can be put another way: circumstances being what they are, one has a right to wonder whether the price of liberty for those who can afford to do without it is not being paid by those whose abject standard of living makes the question of liberty irrelevant for them.

I believe that the facts justify such a statement of the situation, though the reader will perhaps question it. It cannot however be denied that the economic warp of capitalist society is all the time tending towards increased planning. Economic forces are today heading towards the outcome which we foresaw when considering technical progress and its consequences in the field of company regrouping and state control of the economy. Other forces, such as the 'countervailing power' (to use Galbraith's phrase) achieved by labour organisations and by a growing social sense in the public, are being fused into the same design based on planning. Other people, too, have a special part to play in this design: the experts in the new tools of economic analysis, national accounting, and the input-output tables evolved by Leontiev, all giving advice to public administrations on how to perfect their national economic plans.

I repeat that the idea of a neutral state is completely obsolete and that increasing central control of the economy is a *fait accompli*. France took the lead in the West when she set up a General Commissariat of Planning on 3 January 1946. The fourth Plan, approved by law on 2 August 1962 and now fulfilled, had the following objectives: general expansion of the economy, distribution of production between internal consumption and provision for new equipment for future growth, the formulation of a social policy on incomes, adjustments by subsidies and other controls, measures to redress inequalities in the different geographical areas of the country and even – to the indignation of the surviving liberals – decisions on the amount of goods to be consumed.

The general trend needs no further discussion since it can be easily gathered from current events. I shall therefore conclude this chapter by summing up the future direction of present economic forces. This is towards an increasingly planned way of life and central control of the economy. Only those who are unwilling to see this can doubt it. At the beginning of the century the Spanish Nobel prizewinner, José Echegaray, who was an engineer and Minister of Finance, as well as a dramatist, had already grasped the situation, as these words from an article of his published in 1909 will demonstrate:

Throughout the nineteenth century, or at least until its last few years, the trend of the individual prevailed. Of late there has been a complete change of scene. Pure individualism is being replaced by socialism in a more or less radical form.

With these conclusions, we can begin to tackle the problem set out at the end of the previous chapter, and resolve the lines of force bearing on the sections in the theoretical field there presented. According to our previous reasoning, those lines on the right of the diagram which correspond to the capitalist systems examined in this chapter, will be directed to the centre of the field. Consequently, in forecasting the most likely evolution of the market economy systems, on the analogy of the lines of force in a magnetic field, we must expect a tendency in the systems in the right half of the field to be displaced towards the left. This means a trend away from societies based on individual economic decisions towards an organisation whose decisions are increasingly centralised.

This tendency must be related to another trend before we can define the effective lines of force. We must take into account the role of the technical woof in social development, bearing in mind that scientific progress will tend to displace the systems in the right half of the field from lower to higher levels. This means that the lowest technical levels, which correspond to the traditional economies, will move towards others of a more rationalised character.

In short, the evolution of the systems – the movement of the 'experimental bodies' – will be the result of interplay between these two dynamic forces: the trend from right to left, or from market systems towards increased planning, and from bottom to top, towards an improving technical level. The resulting lines of force will therefore appear as arrows pointing diagonally upwards from the bottom right-hand corner, or, in geographical terms, from south-east to north-west, as shown in figure 17. This means that the trend in capitalist countries will be a long-term development towards a more socialised warp and a still more technicised woof. This is the outline of the future for those of us who dwell in the capitalist world. It is clear that the paths converging on the horizon will be different in every case – some countries will undergo a swifter technical transformation than a social, and vice-versa – but the goal to which all are bound seems clearly established. I have been guided not only by the previous argument but also by the consideration of another dynamic force, which will be discussed later because it operates in both halves of the field.

Another consideration prompted by these conclusions will be discussed later: does this tendency towards a planned state mean that the capitalist countries have already started to veer towards socialism. This is the belief of many conservatives, alarmed by state intervention and by the other symptoms described earlier. On the other hand, socialist writers express the opinion that although capitalism differs today from what it was a century ago, the principal traits of the system have not changed in essentials. In the capitalist world founded on money and goods, the proletariat continue to sell their labour in order to live, while the middle class, which continues to be the dominant class, employs them and pockets the unearned increment. Therefore systematised planning is merely the new capitalist method of preserving class privilege for, since it controls the apparatus of government, it can use this to impose its class decisions, representing them as proceeding from popular demand. It is simply state capitalism.

The two views on this subject can be re-expressed in different

Figure 17. *The lines of force in the capitalist countries.* In the capitalist half of the field (see figure 11) the resulting lines of force impel countries towards a planned way of life, at the same time improving their technical level.

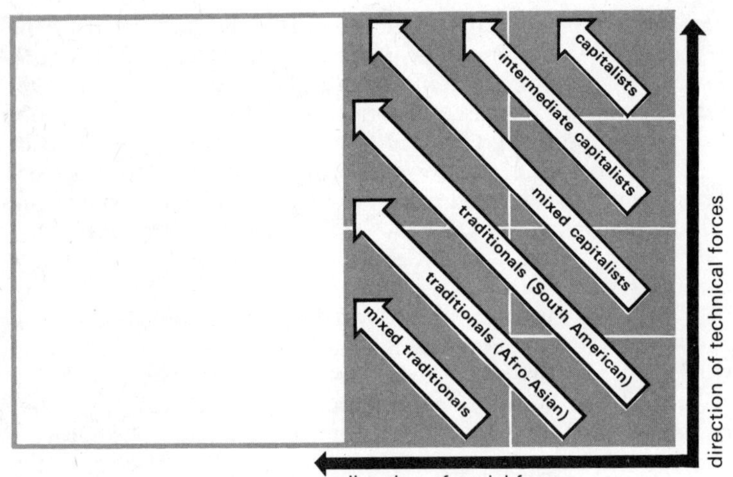

ways. In my opinion, the socialist writers are undoubtedly correct. But at the same time it cannot be denied that the individual entrepreneur who originated capitalism has lost ground, even if his disappearance has served to consolidate the interests of his class as a whole. It is certainly true that a system of planning is not in itself socialism, because it has hardly any effect on the private ownership of capital equipment, apart from the nationalised industries already mentioned. But it is also true that the central control of decisions has demanded greater sacrifices by capitalists than appears at first sight in their attitude. Their faith in the *invisible hand* has suddenly collapsed, as Keynes declared in his famous speech in 1926. The idea of the market as an arena for 'free' competition and the guiding-light of economic decisions has steadily lost ground before the influence of state intervention and its principles. The State conducts the orchestra and if certain groups still control the arm which wields the baton, they have to avoid creating discords; the result is a policy of levelling-out differences of wealth with a greater sense of social justice. Whether it is the result of sincere altruism or of a far-seeing self-interest, some points in the socialist programme have already been put into practice in capitalist countries. In the groups responsible for making decisions there is a mental attitude at work which is steadily rejecting out-moded dogmas and closing the gap between the two extreme points of view.

When the moment for drawing conclusions arrives, I shall defend the thesis that there is no point in discussing whether present-day capitalism is drifting towards the socialism that we know today, because the gradual transformation of the system would lead it in any case to the socialism of the future. The socialism of the future *must* differ from that of today, unless we are to accept the unchanging nature of the social warp, which is something that history has proved false. What then will the socialism of tomorrow be like?

To give a rational answer to this question we shall examine the probable trend of the lines of force in the left half of our field.

7 Towards the new socialism

'Eppur si muove'

In answer to our question about the future of socialism, we have the official statement of the senior socialist state. The present programme of the Communist Party of the Soviet Union, which replaced the one of 1919 and was approved unanimously by the 4,813 delegates to the Twenty-Second Congress, on the afternoon of 31 October 1961, ends with these words:

The present generation in the Soviet Union will live in Communism.

This foresees Communism as the society of the immediate future although, with Moses when in sight of the Promised Land, Khruschev, who proclaimed the programme, is no longer leading the people. Yet the communism foreshadowed in this announcement is not that which Marx and Engels foresaw: it is not the state-less and money-less society. The State and the Party will endure for an indefinite period; nor is there any suggestion that money should be abolished. In short, the ultimate evolution of human society envisaged by Marx is not being proclaimed, but a form of socialism whose technical and economic development is stressed much more forcibly than the structure of the future social warp.

There is however good reason to believe that the date and the contents of the programme were influenced more by tradition and by current pressures than by a rational vision of the future. It seems certain that the clash of personalities between Khruschev and the new generation of leaders, the Sino–Soviet tension, the Yugoslav programme of 1958 and other factors, made it expedient to launch a solemn declaration of policy to reinforce the official line. It is difficult therefore to accept this official statement about the future and we must do our own thinking about the evolution of socialism if we want to determine the direction of the lines of force in the left half of our field.

To do this it is imperative to take history into account once again. Though the history of socialism covers a much shorter period it is no less dramatic than the history of capitalism. We have no need to go back to ancient and medieval times as we did before, when we sought the early foundations of capitalism. Socialism, though the object of ardent passions, arose rationally within the heart of rational capitalism. It does not in this respect run counter to capitalism but claims to be its superior, because capitalism rationalises only economic decisions which do not materially affect the interests of certain groups, whose privileged position is criticised by socialists, under the charge of unfair discrimination. These vested interests gave rise to the conflict between the two attitudes: while the capitalists attempted to vindicate them by invoking certain social beliefs, the socialists took their stand with those whom the system oppressed, revealing a firm opposition to those beliefs and having recourse to rational analysis. The conflict between the Middle Ages and the modern capitalist world was incapable of an harmonious solution because each spoke a different language and one of them had to disappear. The clash between present-day capitalism and socialism is equally stubborn, not because the two do not speak the same language but because 'there is none so deaf as he who will not hear'. What gives capitalism most cause for concern in its undeniable, though repudiated, descendant socialism, is that it replies to criticism with the same rational arguments that capitalism itself had used against the previous system.

In 1848 capitalism was able to suppress the first manifestation of socialism. From then on Marx began to hope for a progressive evolution, by which capitalism would mature into a socialised system. He hoped for an impetus similar to that by which the modern world had crystallised from the stagnation of medievalism. Yet this maturing process, as we have seen, has led not to socialist ownership of capital equipment but to State capitalism. Nor did socialism have its first victory in the most mature country but, on the contrary, in Czarist Russia. This must not lead us to imagine that it was a chance occurrence. Socialism – whether Marxist or the Russian version of Chernichevski and Herzen – had in fact been sowing its seed for some time. Moreover, the absolute power of the Czarist régime was extremely vulnerable if only because it was incredibly anachronistic. No one who studies John Reed's fascinating eye-witness account of those ten days which shook the world in 1917, can fail to be moved by the mixture of reason and passion, of logic and violence, which the outbreak of the October Revolution aroused in a people capable of endless political wrangling yet endowed with an exceptional genius for corporate action. 'Before a train from Petrograd reached Moscow', Reed wrote, 'nearly every carriage had its supplies committee organised and each committee had already broken up into small political groups which were arguing about basic principles'.

As if eager to reproduce the ideological evolution of the West in a few decades, Russian socialism at its outset had its catacombs and its martyrs, followed by its Middle Ages of illusion and near mysticism, which though inspired by no religious zeal, had the same results. It later had its Stalinist absolute monarchy and now, apparently, has its version of the presidential Republic; and this too is passing, though its knell has not yet sounded. The process of evolution has bequeathed this system too its dogmas and its myths, since man is not brain alone and since, when Russia stood condemned in the eyes of the world, it was essential to present a solid front, proof against the tiniest shafts of criticism. The monolithic nature of the Soviet Union, so often censured by others, is the natural outcome of its early childhood. The strictures of the world have raised her attempts at self-justification to the status of dogma, without toleration of the faintest heresy. Tolerance can only come from a position of strength and doubtless this conviction of strength is the motive force of the USSR.

The present position must be known before we can plot the system's future. The facts are obvious but one must be reminded of them because a large number of Westerners refuse to accept them owing to a strange mental block whenever the 'taboo' word socialism is mentioned. Just as the theologians denied Columbus' assertion that there were lands in the West and Galileo's theory that the earth rotates on its own axis, so capitalist intellectuals denied that socialism was feasible. Even in 1920, an economist as talented as Von Mises could state that a socialist economy would not work, because it was not possible to carry out the necessary calculations. At the same time, however, he was fully aware that both Pareto, and Barone, in 1908, had constructed model schemes illustrating socialist theory. Von Mises' book was translated into English in 1935 without the author's deeming it necessary to revise his position, even though there had already been fifteen years of Soviet rule; and by 1928 the American Fred M. Taylor had completed Barone's ideas in his study *On the Direction of Production in a Socialist State*. In 1934–5 two noted economists, Robbins and Hayek, declared Barone's solution correct in theory, but believed it inadequate for producing practical results. Despite the immediate reply of the Pole Oskar Lange, this negative idea remained uppermost in the Western world, although Galileo's remark about the Earth could have been repeated: *Eppur si muove* ('But it does move').

It must nevertheless be admitted that the adherents of socialism can produce few theorists to match the massive academic strength of their opponents. The one man who had the scientific genius to forge theories of equal weight, Karl Marx, was much more concerned with the pressing problem of criticising capitalism than with concocting 'cookery book recipes for the stews of the future', as he said in a much-quoted remark. When Von Mises was writing, Lenin, driven by necessity, had in fact worked out various principles to guide the great nation emerging from the ruins of the Czarist collapse. The literary intellectuals, however, had little relish for his theorising and only trifling support could be expected from them. It is certainly true that when Robbins and Hayek were expressing doubts, even though with less vehemence than Von Mises, socialist supporters could point to the undeniable survival of the Soviet Union, which by then had started its Second Five-year Plan. The attitude of the economists, however, was that 'that' was different and had scarcely any bearing on 'true' economic science, as unfolded to the human race by Adam Smith.

'That' was indeed different, and it was not easy to discover its exact nature. It was an historical upheaval, a far more significant eruption of social discontent than the French Revolution, as Bertrand Russell declared on his return from a visit made soon after the explosion, his impressions of which he published in 1920. It was tackling every obstacle that lay in its path, and those it could not surmount it was skirting round, to return to the attack later. Following this policy, after he had carried out the first stage of socialisation in depth Lenin adopted the *New Economic Policy* in 1921 as a strategic withdrawal. This made allowances for certain economic activities, chiefly in the rural sector, that were liable to be stigmatised as 'capitalist', and in April 1925 the *Kulaks* or wealthy farmers were granted the right to rent land and employ paid labour. Such concessions relieved the tension and avoided a break in the social warp, strained to breaking-point by the struggle for freedom.

Far left In 1917 violence ushered in the new regime in Russia and, *left*, austerity followed it in order to achieve the 'union of Soviets plus electrification', Lenin's definition of Communism. In 1956, however, events outside Russia caused changes in Soviet policy. *Below* A patriot lies dead in Budapest, the victim of his people's struggle against Stalinist oppression.

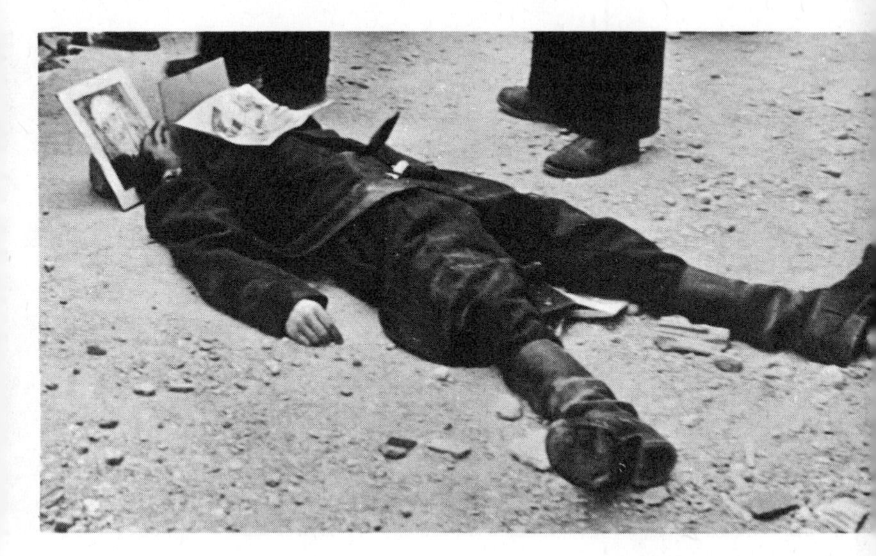

In reminding the reader of this change of direction in policy, I am not trying to sum up in a few lines the economic history of the USSR, which would be impossible. I merely wish to emphasise that just as the word 'capitalism' has varied in significance with the passage of time, so, too, has the word 'socialism' in its much briefer history. The stage reached with the NEP (New Economic Policy) now offered a breathing-space for reflection on the future course of the economy, which was hesitating between industrialisation and agricultural reform, despite the famous slogan launched by Lenin in 1919, which defined Communism as the 'union of soviets plus electrification'. Lenin's objective of industrialisation won the day and the first five-year plan meant the end of the concessions granted by the NEP and the introduction of a new stage.

This new phase stepped up the centralisation of various production units, each controlled by departments under a People's Commissar, which became Ministries in 1946. This system of

Soviet policy was also influenced from within. *Below* Recitation by the poet Yevtushenko. *Right* Window of the Moscow Central Department Store. Less than a third of Russians today can remember the Revolution or have any personal knowledge of the tremendous sacrifices of the past. Yevtushenko praises Mother Russia while dispensing with social realism; so too do people aspire to a more comfortable life, in which consumer demands are more exacting than in the past.

centralisation was the result not so much of a prepared theory as of the practical application of a rational spirit, free from the numbing dogmas of capitalism. The dread of unconsciously slipping into such mental shackles explains the old socialist attitudes of Engels and Plekhanov carried to extremes by Bukarin in 1920. They looked upon the classic science of economics as an offspring of the chaos which reigned in the market economy and therefore to be shunned at all cost in a socialist society. As late as 1931, as Alec Nove observes, the Central Office of Statistics changed its name to the Central Office of National Economy, because the word 'statistics' connoted chance events and was therefore an unsuitable term for rationally planned activities.

It is not strange therefore that very valuable contributions to the theory of the socialist system should have originated outside the Soviet Union. In 1938 there was a reprint of Taylor's book, quoted above, along with another by Lange; soon afterwards other

authors such as Dickinson and Lerner added the weight of their authority, and there gradually emerged the theory of 'market socialism'. But within the official circles of capitalist intellectuals socialism continued to be taboo. Even in 1942 Schumpeter headed Part Three of his *Capitalism, Socialism and Democracy* with the question 'Can socialism work?' With all the weight of his scientific authority, he roundly answered, 'Of course it can'. Meanwhile the sudden reversals of the Second World War began to convince many people of the Soviet economy's ability to support a vast military effort. Nevertheless the belief persisted that its pragmatic methods would in the long run prove less efficient than the market economy. As we indicated earlier, doubt as to this supposed inferiority was beginning to seep into the capitalist world. It was now admitted not only that socialism, in spite of everything, was making progress, but that its economic results compared favourably with those of capitalism. This point deserves special attention, as much for its testimony to an intrinsic change of attitude as for its undeniable psychological impact on the underdeveloped countries which are seeking examples to copy among the most technically advanced countries.

Efficiency of the systems compared

The factor which was chiefly responsible for awakening serious thoughts about the productive potential of the USSR in the minds of the general public was perhaps the successful launching of the first artificial satellite in October 1957. Vain attempts were made to denigrate the success of *Sputnik* by imputing it to the concentration of all efforts on this one objective to the exclusion of other needs such as domestic consumption. Even if this were true, the satellite could never have gone into orbit without a level of scientific and technical attainment until then associated in the public mind only with the United States and the most advanced capitalist nations. Clearly, socialism was capable of achievement. More or less capable than capitalism? That is the question that many were now asking.

The reply can be only relative. No definitive comparison between the two systems can give scientific satisfaction because their respective statistics are the subject of endless controversy and, besides, two structures with such different objectives have no common ground for comparison. The reader will find an excellent treatise on the difficulties in the *Theory of International Comparisons of Economic Output*, compiled by Peter Wiles for a volume of essays on the subject of planning. The Soviet point of view is presented in H.G. Shaffer's work *The Soviet Economy*, which does not, however, probe the question deeply, but merely offers some data on the history of events which have wrought the change of attitude in the West towards Soviet progress. As can be seen, I have preferred to use Western sources for information discrediting capitalist aims and Soviet sources for figures and statistics which are less favourable to the USSR. I hope by this means to avoid the propaganda or prejudice of both camps.

The chief point of comparison, presented in figure 18, which is taken from Robert W. Campbell's *Soviet Economic Power*, is most striking and immediate. The illustration shows primarily the expansion index of Soviet industrial production with 1928 as the base year, and, granting a link between industrialisation and technological advance, reflects technical acceleration. According to official data issued by the Central Office of Statistics in Moscow, industrial production in 1958 was probably thirty times higher than in 1928, to rise to almost fifty times in 1965 according to the objectives of the Seven-year Plan then in force. Of course, such data are completely refuted by Western experts, so Campbell has taken several American estimates from which we have selected for figure 18 those of Shimkin and those of the *National Bureau*, which show a fair measure of agreement. The result is far below the Soviet statistics, since the level reached in 1955 is only seven times higher than in 1928. Even so this is a very satisfactory industrial increase if comparison is made with the United States where the same source puts the annual increase in the period 1929–57 at 3·2 per cent, scarcely two and a half times higher than in 1928. The difference is large enough to prove that technical acceleration in the Soviet Union is more rapid than in the capitalist world.

I must reiterate that there is only a relative value in such comparisons, since besides qualitative differences in output there are other factors which, as we shall see, are a matter of present concern to the Soviet government. Moreover, industry is the field in which comparison most favours the Soviet Union. If we were to consider agriculture we should find that the official Soviet indices themselves show a level of production in 1958 only double that of 1913, while the same source shows a level thirty-five times greater for industry over the same period. Again, the production of some of the more important consumer goods in the Soviet Union is still far below that in America, as is recognised by A. Aganbegian in a paper published in the Soviet Union and included in the volume

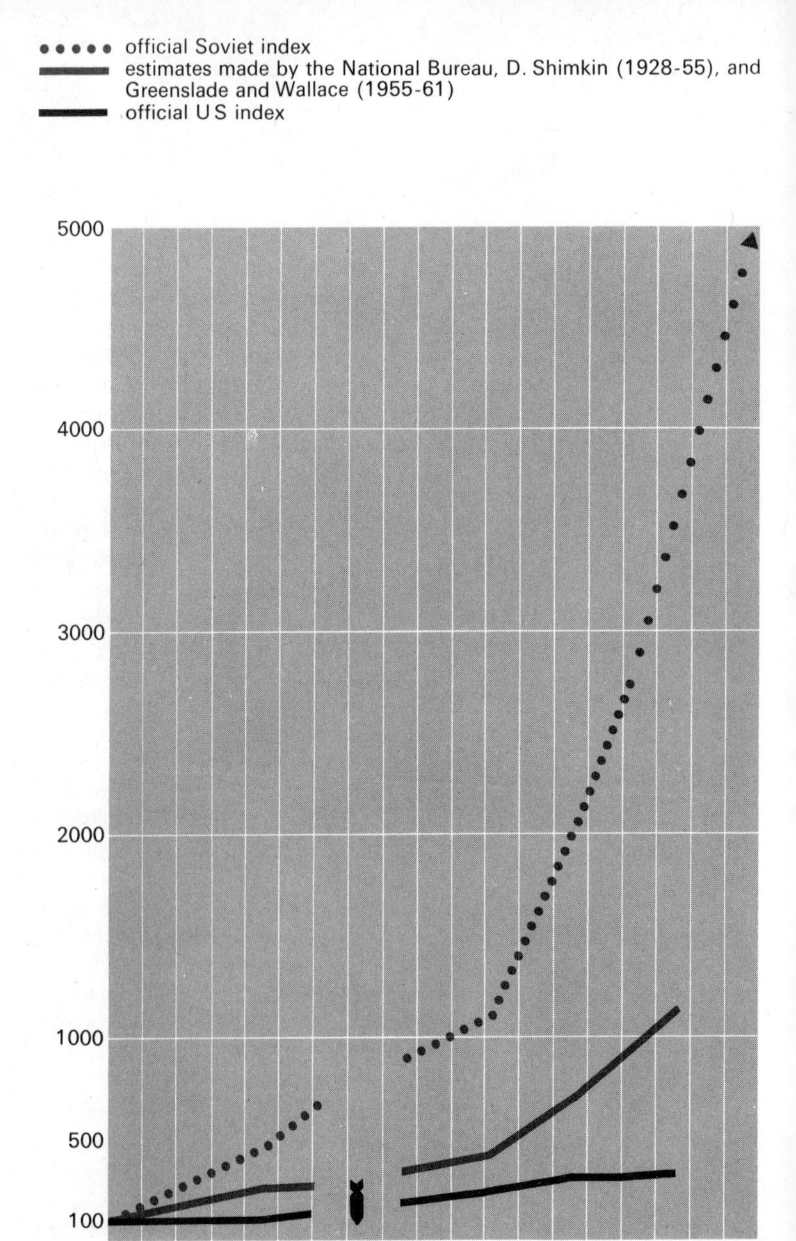
official Soviet index
estimates made by the National Bureau, D. Shimkin (1928-55), and Greenslade and Wallace (1955-61)
official U S index
5000
4000
3000
2000
1000
500
100
1928 '32 '34 '36 '38 '40 '42 '44 '46 '48 '50 '52 '54 '56 '58 '60 '62 '64 '66

Figure 18. *Industrial growth in the USSR and the USA*. Although the official Soviet index is not accepted, western economists estimate that Russian industrial production in 1961 was eleven times greater than in 1928, while American production was a little over three times higher.

The Soviet Economy. This book, which makes use of data from Kosygin and other Russian economists, states that in 1959 the consumption per head of milk products was only 89 per cent of the American level; meat consumption, only 48 per cent; eggs 35 per cent; sugar 72 per cent; with various percentages for the several items shown in figure 19. Nevertheless, as in the comparison of industrial expansion, whose outcome was unfavourable to the USA, these observations must be qualified. It should particularly be noted that much more attention is paid in the USSR than in Western countries to social or collective consumption – items such as education and health – but with the important exception of housing. Here again, drawing a parallel between worlds whose standard of values differs so widely gives an unreal picture and the resulting figures should not be accepted as an accurate guide to quantity but as a rough guide to emphasis and degree. Even so the capacity for and rapid rate of economic development of the USSR cannot be questioned by the impartial observer.

The only comparison which might give a satisfactory result is empirical: a contrast of the achievements of the socialist economy in Russia with what might have been if the old Czarist régime had been allowed to evolve without radical changes. Such an experiment is impossible, which reinforces the beliefs of some Western economists that by 1917 the most difficult part had already been accomplished. Thus Rostow declared that the Russian economy had laid the foundations for its industrial expansion in the twenty or twenty-five years before 1914. And since this expansion was based, in Rostow's words, on the fact that 'the old blocks and resistances to steady growth are finally overcome', and 'the forces making for economic progress expand and come to dominate the society', it might lead us to believe that the Czarist régime would have been as successful as the Soviets.

This thesis is untenable. One has only to point to the brake exercised on many underdeveloped countries by the old social structures whose property distribution resembles that under the

Czars. Agriculture is kept at a primitive technical level, and there is no diversion towards industry of that concentrated effort which the socialist state has built up since its early days. As I have maintained throughout this book, technical progress is not the explanation for everything and alterations in the social warp are an essential feature of progress. If we are to continue our study of the likely future of the Russian upheaval of 1917, we must give closer attention to recent events which may have a bearing on the evolution of the Soviet system. For it is not only capitalism that is changing: all life is evolving.

The recent setting

The word 'thaw', the title of a novel by Ehrenburg, has become the generic term for these changes. It found concrete expression in Gregory Chukrai's film, *The Blue Sky*, where, in a famous sequence, the announcement of Stalin's death was followed by a series of shots showing the first Spring streams reappearing on the ice-bound plains, a symbol that the hero's troubles with officialdom were over. There is no doubt that since 1953 the changes have been radical and sweeping. In poetry, they have been manifested in the new voices of young poets like Yevtushenko and Voznesenski and in the long suppressed voices of older ones like Anna Akhmatova, whose *Requiem* circulated in manuscript form for several years and has only just been published; in the novel, with Ehrenburg's *Thaw* cited above, Dudintsev's *Not By Bread Alone* and Solzhenitsyn's *A Day in the Life of Ivan Denisovich*; in the theatre, with such successful plays as Simonov's *The Four*, staged at the Contemporary Theatre; in music, with Shostakovich's *Fourth Symphony* which, though already being rehearsed in 1936, was not allowed to have its première until 1962 since it did not conform to the Stalinist dogma on art; in science, with the factual acceptance of Heisenberg's uncertainty principle and the reinstatement of Einstein in an official article in *Pravda* in 1955. Nobody can deny these and many other changes of outlook, although interpretation

Figure 19. *Consumption per head of population in the USSR and the USA*. Consumption per head of various articles in the USSR is expressed by the black segments as a percentage of the US level.

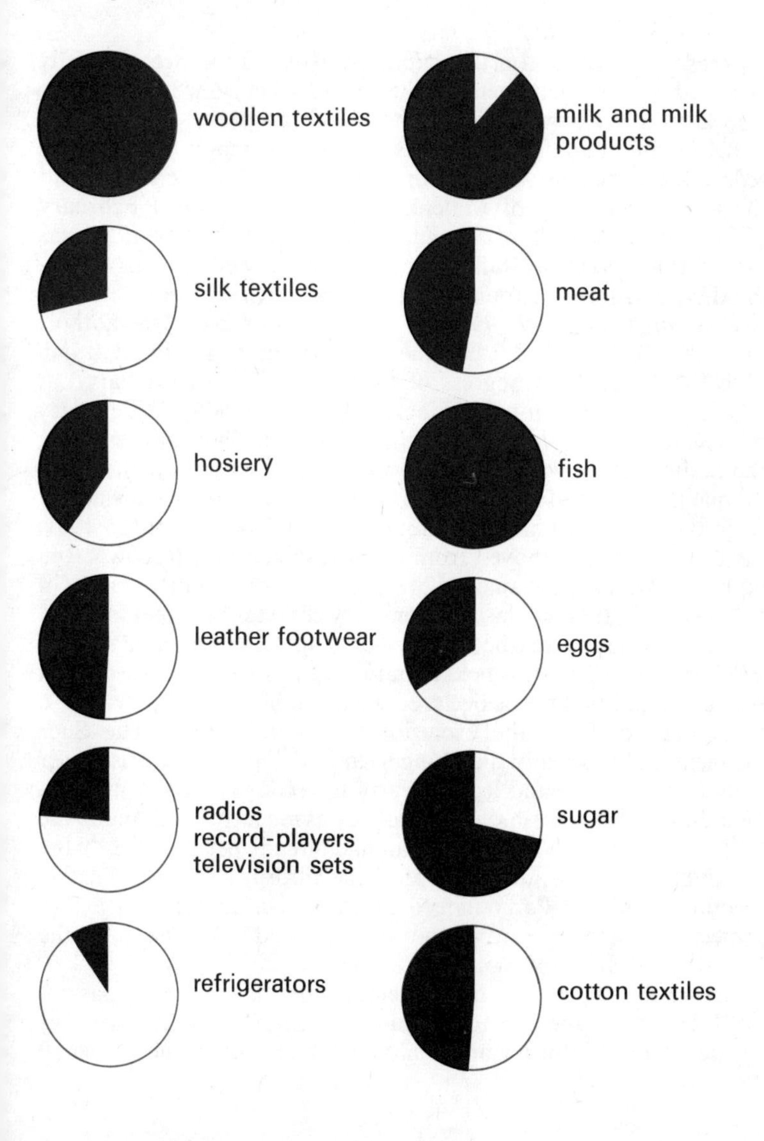

of these may vary. In the capitalist world they are generally accepted as an amendment, while in the socialist world they are viewed as a reaffirmation of purpose and progress.

Before offering our judgment let us trace the major events which reflect these changes. The death of Stalin on 5 March 1953 and the brief ascendancy of Malenkov, which ended on 8 February 1955, were followed by the Khruschev era. The year 1956 was momentous, and an Italian Communist, a well-known correspondent in Moscow, found in it inspiration for a work entitled *The Great Turning-off: From Stalin to Khruschev*. The author, Giuseppe Boffa, called 1956 'the impassioned year', for it began with the Twentieth Congress of the Soviet Communist Party, at whose famous session behind locked doors on Friday 24 February Khruschev violently denounced the Stalin cult. That same evening, the Stalin factory was referred to in the press as simply 'the automobile factory of Moscow'. The name of Stalin began to disappear from the fronts of buildings, monuments and maps, until in 1961, his body too was removed from the mausoleum in Moscow's Red Square – where now once more the body of Lenin remains in isolation – to the small historic cemetery close to the Kremlin walls.

Official censure reached a further stage. In the same year a technical conference was held about the law of value in the socialist economy, and Stalin was declared mistaken in confining the law to consumer goods to the exclusion of capital goods. The Suez problem and especially the Hungarian uprising and the crisis over Communism in Poland led the Party to reconsider many matters, including economic organisation. Consequently, although the outlines of the Sixth Five-year Plan had already been passed by the Twentieth Congress, at the close of the Fifth in 1955, the Central Committee of the Party agreed in December to set out further projects for a new programme which would take shape as the Seventh Plan for 1959–65.

Before this, however, the Supreme Soviet of the USSR passed, on 10 May 1957, the Law for the improvement of the administrative organisation of industry and building, whose importance we shall consider later on. In October of the same year the USSR astounded the world with the launching of *Sputnik* and, to conclude this rapid survey, in January–February 1959 came the Twenty-First Congress, which approved the Seventh and latest Plan, with the Declaration of Moscow in December 1960, signed by the delegates of eighty-one Communist Parties throughout the world. Naturally the 'thaw' has not always maintained the same even flow and even in March 1963 Khruschev condemned Ehrenburg's deviationism before a body of writers and artists. Nevertheless, the general pattern of its evolution continued to follow a single course. The new generation of economists have followed the lead of their literary colleagues by replacing the men of the old guard. The substitution in May 1960 of the old Bolshevik Voroshilov by the metallurgical engineer Leonidas I. Brezhnev as President of the Supreme Soviet was symptomatic of this attitude. From the Spring of 1961 onwards, official censorship of articles by foreign correspondents in Moscow became less strict. In October of the same year the Twenty-Second Congress took place and the new Party Programme already mentioned was ratified. Finally on 14 October 1964 the Khruschev era came to an end and Khruschev was succeeded by Brezhnev and Aleksei N. Kosygin.

Since it is not possible to examine in detail the many issues relating to the changes recorded since 1954, and particularly since 1956, we will focus on three points which vitally affect economic evolution: the tendencies towards decentralisation in a system based on planning, the new trends in the behaviour of managements and the increasing regard for consumers.

Economic decentralisation

It must be realised at the outset that a country of over eight and a half million square miles cannot organise its economy without a chain of regional subdivisions, each responsible for its own administration. In the time of Lenin the first State Commission for Electrification (GOELRO) marked out eight economic areas and the Committee of State Planning itself (GOSPLAN) appointed a sub-committee in May 1921 which proposed the division of the country into twenty-one economic regions. These were abolished in 1930, but the administrative subdivisions were retained, and although during the Third Five-year Plan (1938–42) a further economic grouping took place, it remained true that an overall control predominated and that regional decisions were made in Moscow by various specialised economic departments. By mid-1950 industry alone had twenty-seven ministries, each responsible for a different activity (Aviation, Motor Vehicles, Armaments, etc.), which it controlled over the entire land area of the Soviet Union. In addition there were fourteen other ministries of economics (mainly for agriculture and commerce), one for each Soviet republic, under a central authority which coordinated the economic activities of each area throughout the whole of the USSR. It was a truly centralised organisation.

The drawbacks of the system help to explain the vicissitudes that befall the hero of Dudintsev's novel, mentioned earlier in this chapter. The Fifth Five-year Plan (1951–55) tried to strengthen regional control by the introduction of some new measures, though the system as outlined was not greatly modified; in fact it was further complicated by bureaucratic organisation within the different republics. With reference to the reform of 1957, the Soviet author Evenko quotes such instances as the Soviet Republic of Russia with its 84 federal and republican ministries and departments and the republic of Uzbekskaya with 52. He goes on:

> Such a system of industrial administration was putting artificial obstacles in the way of a solution to several urgent problems, notably rational specialisation and the cooperation of the state enterprises situated in each zone. . . . The subordination of state enterprise to a central department of the same line of business was causing a weakening of the normal regional bonds that link different branches of industry at work in the same economic zone. In some cases, regions were actually being hampered in their attempts to settle economic problems by deploying to best advantage all available raw materials, money and labour and particularly their production output.

Thus the 1957 law on administrative organisation states:

As there are currently more than 200,000 industrial state enterprises and 100,000 public works in progress in the USSR it is impossible to direct production with firm efficiency from the ministries and departments bearing branch responsibility. There is a pressing need to give wider powers and authority in the economic field to the individual republics by shifting the accent of daily economic control from the centre outwards, to the areas of economic administration.

In other words, the development and increasing complexity of the Soviet economy was impairing the efficiency of an over-centralised system, for obvious reasons. The process has its counterpart in the capitalist world, where as we saw, the ever-growing corporations of big business proved less and less capable of control by a single individual. The real factor behind this recent decentralisation is the insistent demand for technical progress, for which an adequate organisation is imperative. Nevertheless an attempt has been made to justify these Soviet reforms by the purely Leninist precept of 'democratic centralism'. Whatever its motive, the law of 1957 considerably adjusted the degree of centralism imposed during the Stalin régime. Whereas a high percentage of economic decisions had until then continued to come from Moscow, the new system largely delegated the onus of decision to the regional centres. Thus the step had been taken from the former 'ministerial' system to the new Sovnarkhozi or 'Economic Regional Councils'. In July 1957, a hundred and five of these Sovnarkhozi were set up for mutual coordination in economic areas and these, in their turn, were grouped into eighteen 'large areas' (figure 20). The new law thus effects regionalisation by delegating decision to different levels, limited by the directives and measures approved by the Seven-year Plan, to which the whole economy is subject, and which guarantees its unity of direction. In a few cases, because of the special nature of certain enterprises – such as railways, for example – a large central ministry is retained as under the old system and the regions have fewer delegated powers.

With this new organisation, the Seven-year Plan could go into operation in 1959 on the assumption that the Sovnarkhozi would shoulder the burden of the direct control of state enterprises and works by handling as much as three-quarters of the Soviet industrial output, including all the cast-iron and iron ore, nearly all the steel, sheet-metal, non-ferrous metals, coal, oil, cement, all chemicals and heavy industry (turbines, locomotives, vehicles, combine-harvesters and so on), the sugar industry, almost all the textiles and animal fats and numerous articles for home consumption.

In view of the high degree of these delegated powers as well as their qualitative importance, many Western economists have regarded the reform as no less than a readjustment in socialism. Although it is unquestionably a vital change, it is equally possible to interpret it as an improvement in socialist planning, which is the construction put upon it by Soviet authors. The fact that the plan not only provides for decentralisation to a certain degree, but puts it into effect, does not necessarily detract from the unity of decision; much less does it alter in any way that fundamental principle of socialist doctrine, the public ownership of capital goods. Just as in the West the growth of state control has not basically altered the capitalist system, which has merely adopted another method of handling productive capacity through private groups working according to their respective interests, so in the USSR the greater flexibility in execution that they are striving to attain through decentralisation is, in principle, perfectly compatible with the organisation of the system on socialist lines.

Hence the move towards decentralisation was clearly incorporated in the new programme of the Communist Party, part 2, section 1, paragraph 3 of which states:

> Local organs must play an even greater part and increase their personal role in the management of the economy. Henceforth certain management functions must be transferred from Union organs to organs of the republics, from organs of the republics to regional organs and from regional organs to district organs. The work done by the Economic Centres must be perfected, since they have proved to be the most practical means of controlling industry and construction, given the present level of production.

Notwithstanding this blessing from the Party programme, recent events reveal a new change in Soviet economic trends. In October 1965, the plenum of the Supreme Soviet decided at its policy meeting to abolish Sovnarkhozi. Other recently created organs are disappearing as well (in particular the USSR Council of National Economy and the Supreme Council of National Economy, which was created to coordinate the work of the former body with that of Gosplan – the State Planning Commission) and overall control of industry is being entrusted once again to central ministeries each of which is in charge of a particular branch of production, as was the case before the reforms of 1957.

Clearly these measures are intended to correct the policy of regional decentralisation already discussed. Their official justification was that in practice Sovnarkhozi had gone to extremes in reversing earlier policies, i.e. they had displayed an exaggerated concern for regional matters and had neglected the general interests of the country. This explanation leads one to believe that, although for the moment the regional emphasis in the organisation of the economy has formally been abandoned, this is because there had been excesses in carrying out the 'regionally orientated' policy rather than because the reasons in favour of some degree of decentralisation, or the facts which warranted it, were no longer valid. As we explained above, these reasons are the actual growth of the Soviet economy and its increasing qualitative complexity, both of which make it difficult to achieve good results if control is excessively concentrated and if the situation is similar to that of the classical textbook entrepreneur who is unable to cope with the task of controlling the huge enterprises of modern capitalism. Accordingly Sovnarkhozi were set up and have now been abolished for exceeding their terms of reference and perhaps also for other relevant political reasons. But this error in the practical application of the regional criterion cannot hide the fact that Soviet production is becoming increasingly complex. Nor does it destroy the case for a more flexible and efficient organisation of the economy than that provided by unlimited centralisation.

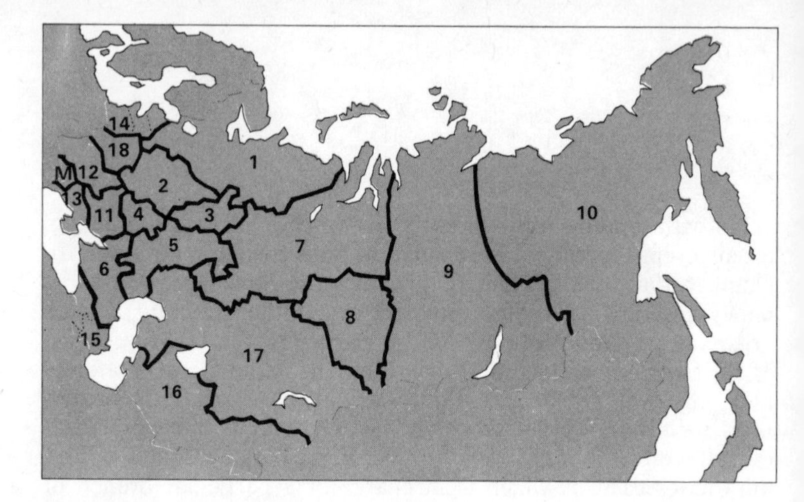

This is the view of such distinguished experts as Professor Nove, who in a commentary on the latest Soviet developments in the British journal *New Society* (7 October 1965) underlined the continuity of Soviet growth, notwithstanding the new measures, and went on to say:

> The essence of the problem is that the old centralised system of economic management is in process of breaking down. This is reflected statistically by a reduced growth rate, and the Soviet press is full of articles and speeches, both by economists and politicians, which express dissatisfaction in the sharpest terms. None of the defects from which the economy suffers are new, in the sense that they all existed under Stalin's rule too. However, the crude priorities of Stalin's centralised planning are manifestly unable to cope with present needs. This is due partly to the fact that the economy is much bigger, more complex, more sophisticated than it was, as a consequence of rapid growth in the past, and partly to the greater complexity of the needs which must be satisfied. The simple priorities of Stalinism had to be diluted.

The most conclusive proof that this is an accurate assessment of the situation, and that facts are imposing a certain decentralisation of decisions, is that the measures taken in October 1965 bear out our thesis in other respects. If, on the one hand, Sovnarkhozi have been abolished during this period, on the other hand the functions and degree of initiative of the factory managers have been increased, as we shall see.

Figure 20. *Important economic regions of the USSR.* Until May 1957 the direction of the Soviet-economy was centralised in Moscow. Now there is a certain degree of decentralisation, which functions without prejudice to the central economic plan. **1** North-west. **2** Centre. **3** Volga/Viatka. **4** Central Black Earth Region. **5** Volga. **6** North Caucasus. **7** Urals. **8** Western Siberia. **9** Eastern Siberia. **10** Far East. **11** Donets/Dnieper. **12** South-west. **13** South. **14** Baltic. **15** Transcaucasia. **16** Central Asia. **17** Kazakhstan. **18** Byelorussia. **M** Republic of Moldavia.

Management of industrial enterprises

Effectively the law of 1957 involved more than a merely regional trend, but in fact it was immediately interpreted in its full rigour by Soviet factory managers (not only by Western economists) as a kind of economic 'thaw', which would make it possible for them to steer a less obstructed course in the future. Hence there was an encouragement of the feeling that decentralisation should not be restricted to regional organs and indeed should be extended to the factories and plants themselves, whose managers had formerly been reduced to the passive role of reaching, or exceeding, as best they could, the targets assigned to each by the Plan or by the appropriate branch Minister.

So a favourable atmosphere was building up for the theories that startled the general public in the West in September 1962, under the arresting title of 'the Liberman Affair', when Evsei Liberman, a professor of economics at the Institute of Technology and Engineering at Kharkov University, published his article. The germ of these ideas had in fact appeared some time before, when in 1956, as we saw, the problem of the socialist theory of values was restated publicly. Apparently Liberman himself had begun his serious work on the subject in 1955. In collaboration with other writers, he had already published in 1959 a book on 'The economic stimuli for putting the plan into practice in Soviet industry'. But his famous article which appeared in August 1962 was his first in a technical journal and when it was reprinted in *Pravda* on 9 September, it became an immediate subject of controversy.

It is difficult to sum up Liberman's suggestions in a few words. In essence he proposed to relax direct state intervention in the management of the state enterprises so that all that was binding on the manager was to maintain the production quota, the type of produce and the price. If the Western reader finds this still too restricting, he should note the implied freedom of decision in such important matters as the labour strength, investment and the use of different methods or new techniques. The most staggering suggestion, however, was that the old method of gauging the success of each state enterprise, based on various quantitative coefficients and the simple arithmetic of debit and credit, should be abandoned and replaced by a 'profit rate', a new scale of assessment, worked out as a ratio of profit gained to capital used and regulated by a mean of the various normal profit levels in the different branches of economic activity. If the rate exceeded the figure laid down as the norm, the bonus and incentive payments of the manager and his workers would be increased accordingly. In this way management would be stimulated not only to exceed the figure of planned production and the balance of income over expenditure but to improve the ratio between this balance and the capital invested. Thus there would be an incentive to try out new ideas and to boost output, since it would be to the manager's own advantage to obtain the highest results with the minimum of equipment or outlay.

Soviet factory managers welcomed Liberman's scheme wholeheartedly, though the planning officials were rather more reserved. However, the distinguished econometrician and academician Nemchikov supported Liberman, and in November of the same year, a Commission examined the proposals and at least accepted the ratio of profit to capital as a criterion of production, though not as an exclusive criterion. Even Khruschev recognised the virtue of the scheme in its direct bearing on output efficiency; and yet the matter was let slide. 1963 brought new tensions, indicated by Khruschev's speech before the representatives of literature and the arts. Then on 17 August 1964 no less a person than Vadim Trapeznikov added his support to Liberman in an article in *Pravda*. This personage was the 1951 Stalin Prize Winner and Director of the Institute of Automation and Telemechanics of the Academy of the Sciences of the USSR; as we shall see, his special standing gave weight to Liberman's proposals when he suggested their application to Soviet scientific progress, which is beyond all question linked with the evolution of the economic system.

In September when Leontiev, a corresponding member of the

Academy of the Sciences, joined in the dispute, Liberman seized his opportunity and published another article in *Pravda* (20 September). The affair had again become the topic of the moment and this time the new ideas were put into practice in two textile factories, one in Moscow and the other in Gorky. Until then the retail stores nominated by the planners had had to take the goods of both factories, even though lack of purchasers forced them to stockpile, in spite of the relative scarcity of cloth. From the second half of 1964 both factories were authorised to decide which type of cloth should be produced on the basis of public demand, to assess which a show was held in the factory itself before it went into production. The first sales, though at slightly higher prices, were a success, although the factories could not interpret them in terms of profits since they lacked the power to readjust their own prices and costs, which were not geared to the new type of demand. The experiment therefore produced arguments in favour of granting managers a variable price system. If Liberman had not quite ventured to suggest this, Trapeznikov most certainly did so in his support of him.

The new Party programme covers this aspect too. Under the same section heading quoted above it states:

> Extension of operative independence and of the initiative of enterprises on the basis of the state-plan targets is essential in order to mobilise untapped resources and make more effective use of capital investments, production facilities and finances. It is necessary for enterprise to play a substantially greater part in introducing the latest machinery . . . In the process of Communist construction economic management will make use of material and moral incentives for high production figures . . . Initiative and successes in finding and using new ways of improving the quantitative and qualitative indexes of production should be specially encouraged . . . It is necessary in Communist construction to make full use of commodity-money relations in keeping with their new substance in the Socialist period. In this, such instruments of economic development as cost accounting, money, price, production cost, profit, trade, credit and finance play a big part.

Both Khruschev's successors made similar statements in the

early days of their rule. In a solemn speech to commemorate the forty-seventh anniversary of the October Revolution, delivered on 6 November 1964 in the vast hall in the Kremlin where the great Congresses take place, Brezhnev used a quotation from Lenin to stress the superiority of man over the bureaucratic machine. He declared that the development of heavy industry must be subordinated to the needs of the entire economy and even to a more rapid rate of progress in agriculture and the light industries. He went on:

> Today, as never before, there is an obvious need to apply economic incentives for the development of production. Economic stimuli must encourage enterprises to make better use of their production funds, use raw materials and semi-manufactures economically, get new machinery running more quickly, improve the goods produced and raise the productivity of labour at every factory.

One month later, in his address to the Supreme Soviet on the State Plan for Economic Development in 1965, Kosygin, the President of the Council of Ministers of the USSR, declared:

> If we are to improve the management of our economy and our system of planning we should grant more economic independence to our enterprises and increase their responsibility for the making of more efficient decisions with the aim of achieving the objectives of the Plan, at the same time strengthening the authority of managers, inspectors and foremen. The removal of all kinds of bureaucratic obstacles and of artificial forms of control over production will provide tremendous opportunities for the labour force to develop its initiative in order to achieve new economic advances, both in the factories and on the collective farms. The introduction of cost accounting, the fixing of true economic prices, the revival of the role of profit and of systematic and compulsory material incentives to productive effort are vital conditions for the speedier advance of our economy. At the moment the application of profit and loss accounting is confined to each separate enterprise and indeed, on this basis, it does not seem to be applied at all. We must institute more systematic profit and loss accounting and extend it fully to all the vital sectors of our national economy.

If the programme of economic reorganisation adopted in October 1965 implies a correction of the policy of regional decentralisation, at the same time it confirms the trends we have been discussing, insofar as it envisages relatively greater autonomy in the management of enterprise and a re-evaluation of profit as an index of efficiency. Thus in a major speech, Mr Kosygin announced, in addition to the abolition of Sovnarkhozi already mentioned, that from then on every enterprise would be largely free from the mass of detailed working instructions formerly provided by the central and regional organisations.

Top-level planning decisions would be expressed in general terms only, and it would be left to the managers to decide the details; the earlier criterion of efficiency – achievement of the planned quantity of production – would now be replaced by a new one – achievement of the planned turnover – and this would require managers to pay attention to the market, a hitherto unnecessary procedure. However, if so far enterprises themselves had had very little freedom to encourage their labour force, now there were new prospects of significant wage increases, not only in connection with changes in the level of production but also with improvements in quality and increases in profits of the enterprise. In short, although some Soviet economists may perhaps have desired an even greater swing in this direction, it is undeniable that in October 1965 a new move was made towards greater decentralisation (within the limits imposed centrally by the Plan, of course) and towards a revival of profit as a basic index of efficiency in the management of enterprises.

To repeat, all this must not be interpreted as an abandonment of socialist principles. A recent article by Professor Liberman (already the outstanding spokesman for these new ideas) published in the West with the significant title 'Russia harnesses the profit motive', points out that socialist profit is generated by economies of production and not by exploitation in the purchase of raw materials or in the sale of finished products, and goes on to justify its compatibility with the Socialist system using arguments which we cannot reproduce here, but which can be read in their original translation in the *Sunday Times* of 10 October 1965.

We would merely stress that this official information confirms the continuation of trends towards decentralisation in the USSR based on greater autonomy for management. Moreover, this article is evidence of the continued existence of other aspects of these trends, which we have already referred to and now propose to discuss.

Consumer markets

We must now deal with the new important role of consumer demand, as a result of which turnover rather than production is now the measure of an enterprise's efficiency. The greater freedom of action now enjoyed by managers, especially in the consumer goods industries, has thus become the vital link which adapts and unites the general aims of the Plan with the concrete demands of the public. As Liberman says in his article:

> Total consumer demand is a quite planable quantity here. But just what to satisfy it with – for instance, what colour of blouse or what style of suit to produce or how better to organise their production – is not the prerogative of centralised planning. This is sooner a question on which the stores should come to an understanding with the factories.

This kind of understanding already takes place in the USSR – above all in the light consumer goods industries – thus extending the first experiments made in the Mayak and Bolshevishka factories in Gorky and Moscow respectively.

Fundamentally, the same kind of factors, deriving from the growth and growing complexity of the Soviet Economy, which necessarily involve the setting up of similar systems of organisation everywhere, wield their influence here. As a result the structure of modern management in Soviet industry is similar in form to that of a large Western corporation, as can be seen by comparing figure 21 with figure 14. The only difference is that, with the public ownership of capital, the whole of Soviet industry interlocks in a single huge corporation. To return to the delegation of decision, it is even more illuminating to contrast with the Stalin era the third

Figure 21. *The organisation of modern Soviet industry.* A high level of technology requires modern forms everywhere. A comparison of this diagram with figure 14 reveals considerable similarities.

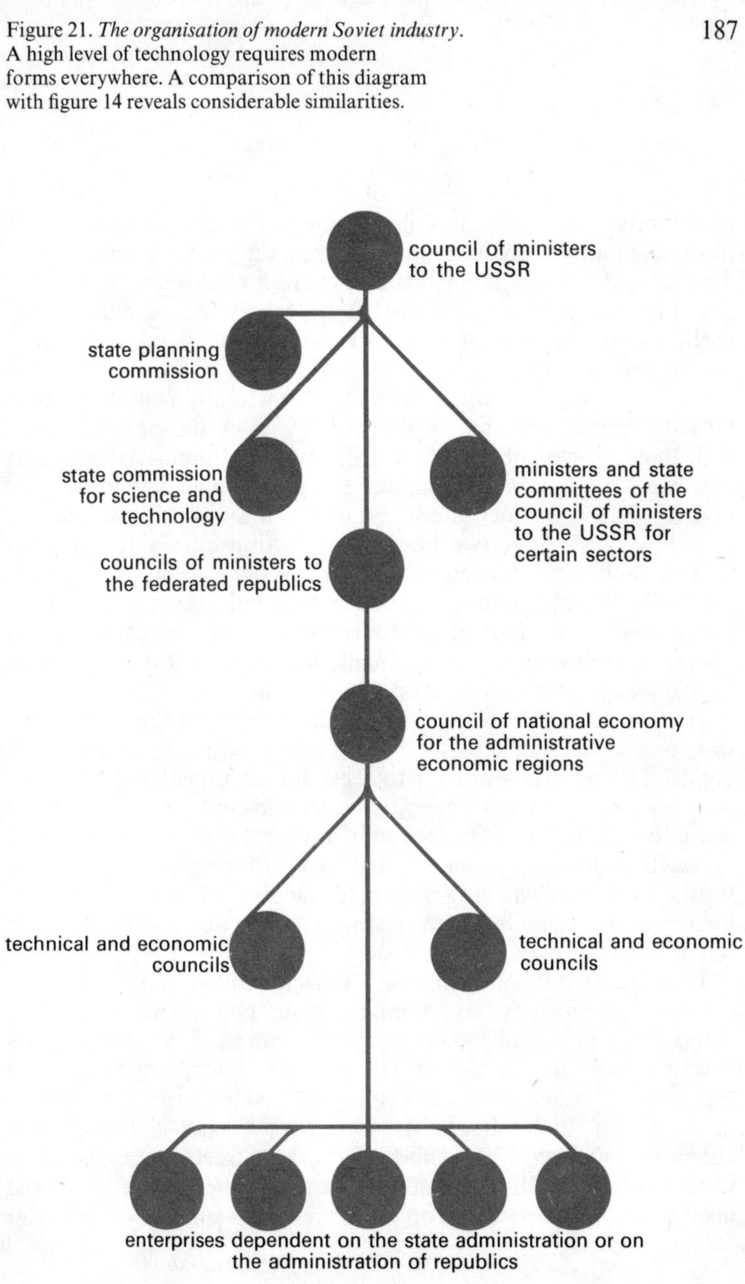

of the points referred to earlier, namely, the increasing attention of the Plan and of Soviet economic direction to consumer demand. This does not really involve the delegation of decision but rather the influence of the decisions of others on the planning body itself. The increasing concern with consumer demand is therefore one of the most interesting aspects of the new phase.

Obviously the consumer has never been totally neglected but it must be understood that in the early years of the Soviet régime, with their avowed object of electrification and industrialisation at any cost, machinery and capital equipment had a much higher priority than consumer goods. Figure 22 draws on Soviet sources to indicate how these two lines of production have varied in relation to each other through the several economic plans. Whereas the 1928–32 programme planned an annual increase of capital goods three times that of consumer articles, the seventh, now in operation, allows for a very small difference in ratio, although capital goods, on which development depends, are still dominant.

The same diagram shows that in the fourth plan, just after the war, preference was actually given to the production of consumer goods. The reason is not far to seek, for an urgent restocking of consumer markets was imperative after the continual drain of the war effort. But this was not the only motive, for post-war consumer production has not been confined to restoring stocks to their former levels but has in fact marked the start of an era characterised by a much greater concern for consumer demand than any in the previous history of the USSR.

The figures do not completely reflect another point: that the economic authorities have even begun to give their attention to specific demands, which were formerly ignored. Travellers, paying a return visit to the Soviet Union after a long absence, have expressed their delight at the displays of fashions and fancy goods in the shops. In his book, *A New Russia?*, H. E. Salisbury describes the strikingly gay effect of Gorky Street where the shop windows had an 'indefinable Parisian air' about them with the display of ladies' dresses on dummies and lengths of material

Figure 22. *The production of investment goods and consumer goods in the USSR.* In the early Five Year Plans almost all Soviet productive effort was concentrated on industrialisation, and consumer needs took second place. Since 1945 the difference between the growth of production of investment goods and that of consumer goods has become less marked.

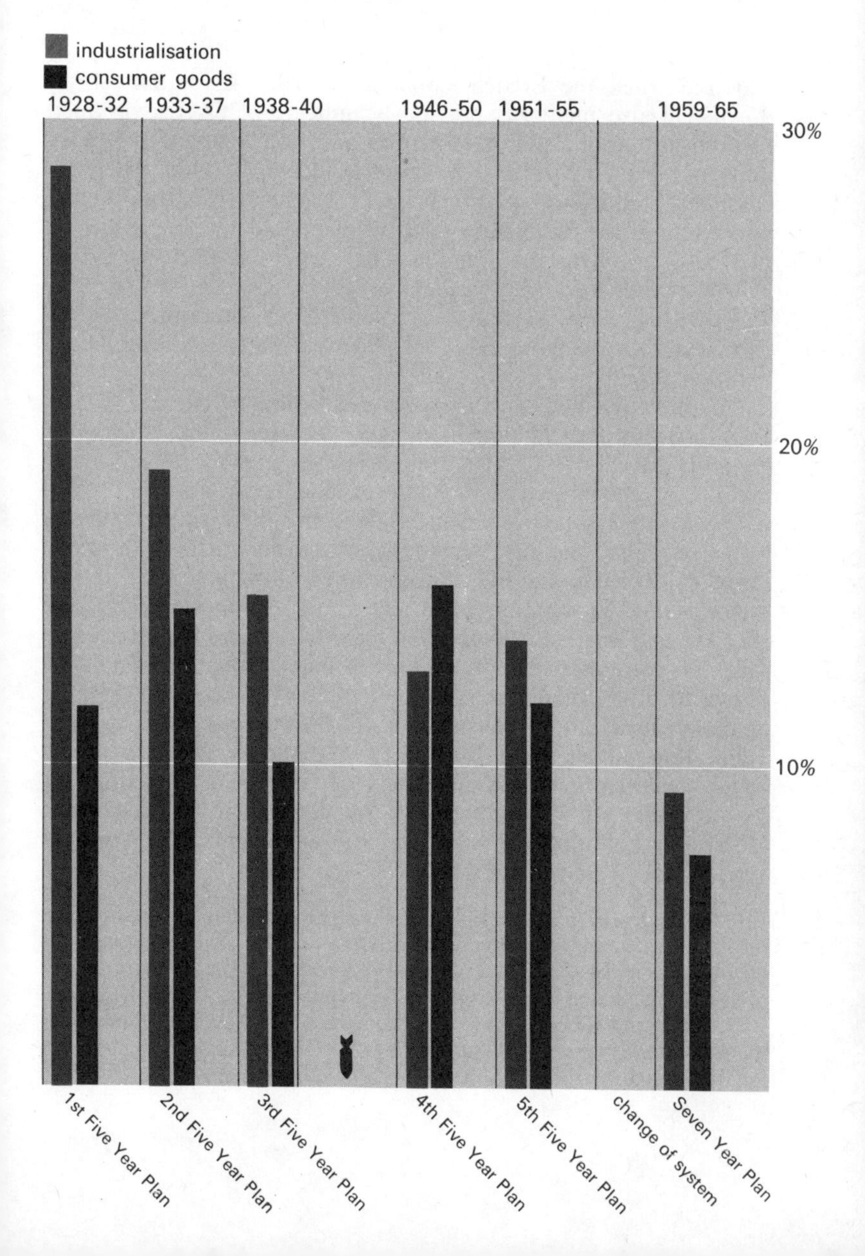

acquired when the French stand at the 1961 Exhibition closed down. He also mentions previously unheard-of foreign products as 'non-utilitarian' as Indian bronze vases, gleaming Czech glass, nude porcelain figurines – 'a rarity in decorous Moscow' is his comment – and good quality Western jewellery. It is true that he also refers to the established practice of queuing in shops, but the fact of the innovations remains. The supply necessary to satisfy a new qualitative and quantitative demand cannot of course be achieved overnight. Moreover, a complete imitation of the capitalist countries cannot be expected when so many basic needs are still unsatisfied.

Undoubtedly, consumers have a wider field of choice, even in such frivolous matters as fashion, as Soviet publications themselves certainly reveal. And economic decisions are more and more taking consumers' requirements into account – an assertion which rests on more solid information than the mere impressions of travellers' tales. We have already observed, for instance, how the ideas of Liberman and his colleagues were initially applied in two factories, and brought about an experiment to decide production according to demand. Besides the many references to the need to raise the consumer level made by the Party, attention should be drawn to other official pronouncements on the need for stepping up the present rate of consumer production.

Limiting ourselves to the official statements already quoted, which demonstrated that autonomy of enterprises and attention to the market are also supported by the present leaders of the USSR, we note that Mr Kosygin in his statement of 9 December 1964, already referred to, said:

> In the process of fulfilment of the plan enterprises should take into account the growing demands to the produce they put out, from the viewpoint of its quality, and make use of the technical opportunities for the improvement of goods manufactured. To enable the enterprises to feel better the market fluctuations and the changes in the demands of the buyers it is necessary to make extensive practice of establishing direct contacts between enterprises (or trusts) and the shops selling goods to the population.

And later on he reiterates:

> Plans for the production of consumer goods must be based on orders from consumers, taking into account the establishment of direct contacts between industrial enterprises and trading organisations. The use of such methods of planning will undoubtedly be progressive, for planning based on orders is more concrete; it better meets the requirements of the economy and the population.

In the speech alluded to on the occasion of the forty-seventh anniversary of the Revolution, Brezhnev takes the same line and stresses:

> The growth in the income of the Soviet people leads to a growing demand for more varied and better quality consumer goods. We shall bear this demand in mind and make use of all opportunities and all the achievements of technical and scientific progress in order to develop large scale production of these consumer goods and to reduce their price. . . . It is also necessary to change our attitude towards services and public entertainments and towards those employed in these activities.

This further quotation from Liberman's article shows that these trends are continuing today. As Kosygin stated in the plenum of October 1965, closer links must be established between production and consumption and the orientation and efficiency of enterprises must be improved accordingly. After this book had gone to press, confirmation of the trends described in this chapter came from the report issued after the Twenty-Third Congress of the CPSU which took place in Moscow from 29 March to 8 April 1966.

Cybernetics, sociology and lines of force

The new trends therefore are established facts and they clearly presuppose a change of attitude which will involve a correction of previous criteria. This is confirmed by such an authoritative text as the comprehensive volume entitled *Principles of Marxist Leninism*, which has now taken the place of the Stalinist work as the official handbook of the system. In it can be found passages as significant as the following:

Perhaps a wide application of the principles of financial autonomy in enterprises (we refer to their commercial and monetary relations) is not inconsistent with the tasks of constructing a communist society in which the very concepts of goods and money eventually disappear. As we know Stalin in his *Economic Problems of Socialism in the USSR* stated that if circulation of goods were increased 'progress towards communism would be inevitably halted' and 'the circulation of goods is incompatible with the prospect of transition from Socialism to communism' . . . but a conclusion of this kind could only have occurred to him because he failed to understand the role of commercial and monetary transactions in the preparation of conditions for the step to communism. For skilful use during production of the lever of income stimulates above all the continued growth of the productivity of labour and consequently ensures that abundance of goods without which the passage to communism is impossible.

In this sentence lies the key to the present third programme of the Soviet communist party, which is essentially one of economic development and increased productivity. The leadership of the country is slowly passing from the old dogmatic revolutionaries into the hands of new men with a highly technical approach. It is significant that Brezhnev and Kosygin are a generation removed from Mikoyan, Suslov and Khruschev himself. And the new members of the Praesidium, Podgorny, Poliansky, Voronov and some members of the Secretariat like Demichev or Shelepin, are a generation later still: a generation with a more rational approach, and which is now replacing the old revolutionaries who still cling to the almost mythical relics of Bolshevism or to Stalinist doctrines. If the establishment of the Soviet state demanded a strictly doctrinaire approach, a certain degree of rational criticism cannot today be denied the younger generation, who did not experience the times of trial, and who do not therefore have the same feelings about the civil war, the revolution or the foreign bloc.

These changes need not necessarily be interpreted therefore as a change of direction in the course of socialism. The evolution of the system is motivated by the twin forces of technical acceleration and social transformation, which underlie the changing scene of capitalism. They are likewise conditioning the evolution of socialism in a direction which we shall understand more fully if we analyse their basic trends still further.

Technical acceleration, particularly its qualitative diversification, is of prime importance in the recent evolution of the Soviet Union. The growing complexity of industry and economic activity in general has steadily outmoded the elementary planning of the early years, when the principal concern was electrification with a few other basic necessities. The over-centralisation of economic decision made it markedly less efficient, especially in the Asiatic areas of the country where progress had received a boost during the last war, and also with regard to the management of a vast far-flung industry. The attempts of the older generation to resolve this problem by appealing to the almost axiomatic virtue of certain Leninist and Stalinist catch phrases had been increasingly overtaken by the tide of events. The trend was away from the ingrained distrust of statistics and economic theories – displayed when Kantorovich's first notions of a programme along modern lines were ignored – towards the present unquestioned acceptance of these very methods.

In other words a process of rationalisation had suddenly established itself, much more rapidly than in the history of capitalism. This process owed much to the organisation of scientific pursuits, which has also undergone a recent change with the far-reaching reform of April 1961, by which the State Committee for the Coordination of Research, composed of scientists and government representatives, was established. As it is not possible to analyse all these changes in detail, I will concentrate on one of the most significant: the first developments in cybernetics, which were still almost 'clandestine' up to 1953–4, because of a deep distrust in the official mind of all the adjuncts of bourgeois ideology. Nevertheless, those years saw the appearance of the first Soviet electronic computers of the 'Strela' and 'BESM' types. Since then the lapse of the dogmatic veto against such highly specialised modern equipment has furthered development in this field, which is today the responsibility of the Department of Mechanical and Technical

Control under the Academy of the Sciences. In *The Facts Rebel*, Paloczi–Horvath has analysed the technical and social importance of these innovations, whose recognition in the setting up of the Ministry of Automation coincides almost exactly with the famous denunciation of Stalin at the Twentieth Congress about the beginning of 1956. It will be remembered that the head of the Institute for Research into Cybernetics was the same Trapeznikov who supported Liberman. This in itself is further proof of the connection between the development of new techniques, and the ideological trends favouring the replacement of a doctrinaire direction of the economy by the scientific objectivity of theory and calculation.

We cannot trace the evolution of cybernetics in full. The chief stages were the famous Conference on the Philosophical Problems in Natural Science, the translation in Moscow of the works of Norbert Wiener (the founder of cybernetics), the assertion in the Soviet Encyclopaedia that cybernetics was to be considered a super-science, and the setting up of an automatic piston factory in the Soviet Union. The reader can trace the progress of cybernetics in Paloczi–Horvath's work, where one instance in particular reveals the acuteness of the struggle between scientific rationalisation and party dogma. The author tells us that in 1962 specialist Soviet publications produced the information that electronic computers had been used in experiments on price systems in relation to three different aspects of Marxist theory: value, cost of production and mean value. It turned out that none of the three concepts was of the slightest use in supplying information to guide the decisions of the planners!

It is not surprising therefore that technical specialists are replacing the politicians. Side by side with the effects of this technical influence we have general sociological factors stemming from the inevitable emergence of the new generation to replace the old. Although they are part of the heroic past, memories of the revolution carry little weight with the younger generation. The young are much more concerned with existing conditions, and they find that their standard of living compares unfavourably with that of the West, even if it is an improvement on the past. They are proud of their country's successes in outer space, but these also awaken a yearning for the material advantages proper to a great nation. The attention currently being paid to consumers is in large measure due to this natural yearning. As the *Principles of Marxist Leninism* admits, 'the higher the standard of living, the greater the abundance and variety of goods and services considered essential by the people'.

There is no need to labour the point. The new generation with the special problems it poses is not only directing increased attention to the market and accelerating technical decentralisation but is also responsible for the re-establishment in the USSR of another discipline traditionally denounced as 'bourgeois': sociology. The stereotyped concepts of the party have proved inadequate and too rigid to adapt to the winds of change that are blowing through the community. These shortcomings are a serious drawback to *rapprochement* with other nations, at a time when the Soviet Union is desperately anxious to influence the alien societies emerging within the Third World. It is not surprising, then, that in 1956 – again the year of decision – the Soviet Union sent a delegation for the first time to the Antwerp convention of the International Association of Sociology and followed this up by sending increasingly active delegates to later conventions at Stressa and Washington. In 1958 another meeting took place, this time in Moscow, sponsored by UNESCO and attended by sociologists from the Western world. In this field too there is a noticeable tendency for the old schematic theories of the early days to be superseded by a more detailed analysis of social realities.

We can now make some observations on the lines of force in the left half of our diagram in chapter 5. As in the right half, technical progress creates an upward trend from bottom to top, whereas the factors that we have been studying in this chapter produce a horizontal trend to the right, reflecting a trend towards the improvement of socialist prospects by increased attention to consumer

Figure 23. *The lines of force in the socialist countries.* In the socialist half of the field (see figure 11), the resulting lines of force are directing countries to a greater degree of decentralisation, at the same time raising the technical level.

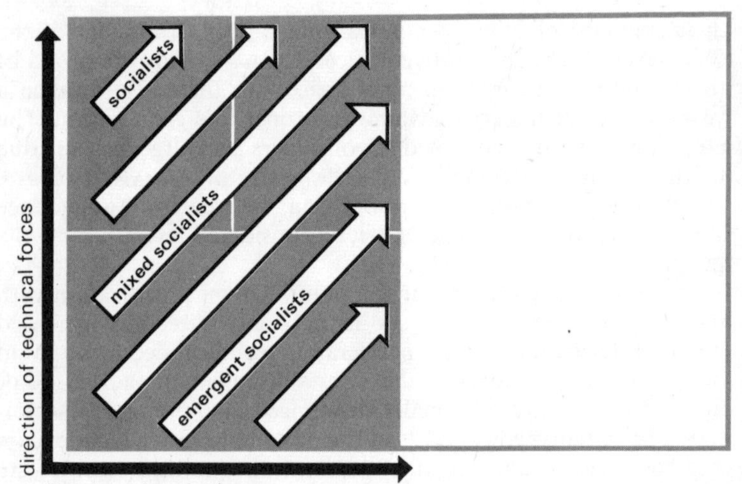

demand and especially by the increased efficiency of economic plans resulting from the decentralisation of decisions, without loss of the principle of public ownership of capital. These two trends fuse as lines of force which move diagonally from the bottom left to the top right. Expressed geographically, the direction of these forces is from south-west to north-east, as shown in figure 23.

The evolution of socialist countries is thus towards a higher technical standard, with the retention of their public ownership of capital goods and their overall economic plan. However, they have a social warp in which there is a much greater regard for consumer demand than in the past, with increased initiative for managers and in the echelons of each sector of production.

I must, however, as in the previous chapter, end with a proviso. The increased regard for consumer demand and the attention paid to management are not signs of a meeting of the ways, much less of a return to capitalism. The evolution which I foresee requires time, which in its turn implies social change. If a convergence were possible, what could be the form of the capitalism of the future united with the socialism of the future? However, when the paths are so different and the starting-points are so divergent, it is inappropriate to talk of convergence on, or a nearer approach to, a still distant prospect. The modifications that have already taken place in both capitalism and socialism provide evidence enough to state that the future will not reproduce exactly either of the two systems as they are at present. There is also the effect of two further factors to be considered: the unpredictable nature of technical progress, which we shall not go into here but whose effects will unquestionably entail social upheavals, and the increasing role of the emergent countries in the world economy. We have already referred to this and since we must examine it in considerable detail, it deserves a chapter of its own.

8 The emergent countries

Tradition caught in a cross fire

In the last two chapters we have traced the direction of the lines of force in the two halves of the field, capitalist and socialist. We must not forget, however, that we have reached our conclusions by taking into account only those societies with high technical levels. In fact, we have practically confined ourselves to trends in the USA and the USSR, both strongly representative of their respective groups. This must not prevent us from examining what is happening in the rest of the world, especially in the emergent countries to which the majority of the human race belongs. Although these countries are only beginning to have a direct say in world affairs at present, the time is coming when their influence will without doubt be considerable.

I will refer briefly here to the European People's Democracies, for even though their structure is based on the Soviet model, the trends towards decentralisation noted in the previous chapter, often appear more strongly there. It should be noted, however, that among the Russian Marxists symptoms of specific decentralisation in say Poland or Yugoslavia, are regarded not as signs of a progressive evolution but as remnants of the recent capitalist past, which must be gradually discarded in the march towards socialism.

Whether a regression or a sign of progress, decentralisation is a definite trend and has been given the backing of such an eminent authority as the late Oskar Lange, who returned to his native Poland after the War as vice-president of the State Council and director of the central body responsible for planning. It is no surprise that even the journal of the Soviet *Gosplan* had already published in 1961 an article by the Polish economist W. Brus about 'the experiment in the use of material incentives in Poland', setting forth ideas in full agreement with those of Liberman.

For Eastern Europe, 1956 was also of decisive importance with the Hungarian uprising and other government crises, particularly in Poland, where a scheme on the lines of the Soviet NEP of the 'twenties, though of course against a different background, was inaugurated. There followed changes some of which, like the setting up of the Workers' Councils in the State enterprises, seemed very promising at the outset but eventually came to nothing. There were however other innovations in the economic structure which were more lasting, such as the wider powers granted to the state enterprises and the beginning of regionalisation on the lines of the decentralisation recently established in the USSR.

More lasting were the reforms in Yugoslavia, which in 1956 led the Soviet leaders to charge Tito with being 'revisionist'. But Yugoslavia held her ground, even refusing to sign the Declaration of Moscow in 1960, to which the Communist Parties of eighty-one countries pledged their support. This attitude gave wide publicity to the Yugoslav experiment, not only because of its intrinsic merit, but also because of the realistic manner in which it tried to combine a mild form of market economy with socialist ownership and central planning.

Yugoslavia began to take this course at the end of 1949, as a result of the difficulties encountered in trying to put through the First Five-year Plan of 1947–51, drawn up in imitation of the classic Soviet model. In 1950 basic legislation was brought in giving workers' collectives the task of running the economic enterprises of the State, with control vested in all the workers when plants were small or a Workers' Council when they were on a large scale. The actual management devolved upon a committee headed by a director chosen by popular vote and endowed with very wide powers regarding the employment of labour, industrial relations and internal discipline within the structure established by the central planning authority. The relative autonomy of such managers after 1957 was mentioned by the Organisation for Economic Cooperation and Development in Paris (in its official report published with the full approval of Yugoslavia), with the comment that 'the process of the country's economic expansion has been accompanied and expedited by a real and progressive decentralisation of the power of decision'. That shrewd observer Galbraith,

Yugoslav workers carrying an industrial chart to a meeting of the Workers' Council. Yugoslavia's 'market socialism' is designed to give the workers real control over output and industrial policy.

after paying a visit to Poland and Yugoslavia in 1958, declared his 'clear impression that the market socialism of Yugoslavia is a system on the march'. It may be concluded that the Yugoslav system, while answering all the requirements of a socialist society, is beginning to bridge the gap between socialism and an advanced capitalism, represented by the 'indicative planning' of the French. The French system is the most pronounced at centralisation within a market economy; while Yugoslavia is trying to create market opportunities in a socialist economy.

The variations introduced into the basic Soviet model by the European socialist systems are too subtle for specific analysis in a work whose principal aim is to present a view of the whole world picture. The emergent countries have chief claim to our attention since they are the new actors on the world economic stage, and although the Latin American countries have enjoyed political independence for a hundred and fifty years or so, they have now reached a crisis of development. The tide of political sovereignty has been recently let in to the Afro–Asian world, and its effect during the first decade of the post-war period has been to liberate the whole Southern half of Asia, from Indonesia to Israel; the following decade saw the same result in Africa (figure 24). No fewer than sixteen new African countries attained full independence as recently as 1960.

Throughout the vast world of Afro–Asia, the melting-pot of the age, forces exist whose potential is still untapped or is only beginning to be explored. These human forces in ferment will prove the decisive factor of the future and they are already assuming their role. In his reply to the Communist Party of the Soviet Union on 14 June 1963, Mao Tse-tung, the leader of the most important of these emergent peoples put it like this:

> The vast territories of Asia, Africa and Latin America are the areas where all the contradictions in the contemporary world come together; they are the most vulnerable of the regions which are under imperialist domination and constitute the storm centres of world revolution.

I make no claim for absolute accuracy in predicting the lines of

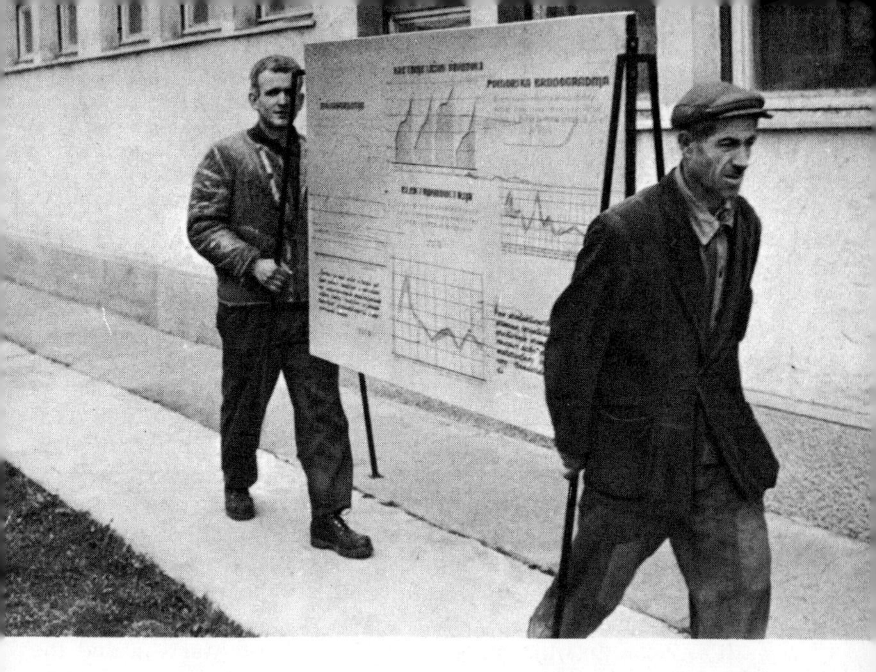

force in this field, where the presence of so many old and new tensions makes it inadvisable to advance more than very general observations. At the risk of mistaken emphasis, I shall take the full impact of these new nations into account, for their influence on the future course of mankind under pressure from population, technical and social forces cannot be ignored.

We have already noted that it is in these emergent nations that the population problem is most acute. Further analysis of the problem is unnecessary if we assume that the population explosion will be checked by the spread of rational methods after the breakdown of religious taboos; nor is further discussion needed to gauge the future direction in which the technical pressure will drive these new countries. Their obvious aim is to reach a higher technical level than they have at present, following the technical trend established in our lines of force, and their progressive development will produce an upward trend in our diagram.

The future characteristics of the social warp are by contrast much more uncertain. The emergent nations are not simply replicas of Europe which lack only technical knowledge to be converted into advanced nations as we know them. They resemble

Figure 24. *African independence.* During the decade 1955–65 two thirds of the African continent gained independence – twenty million square kilometres of territory and two hundred million people in all.

in some ways the traditional societies which existed in Europe a thousand years ago, but their backgrounds are very different and a straightforward repetition of European progress cannot be expected. To begin with, the present historical acceleration is against this, since the emergent countries are being compelled to by-pass certain stages in the historical evolution of Europe. As it would have been nonsensical to expect the United States, when they gained independence in the eighteenth century, to have adopted a temporary feudal system before passing from a primordial native existence to the social structure of contemporary Europe, so it is senseless today to imagine that the new African nations should adopt, for example, the parliamentary system of Victorian England.

It is clear that the more orthodox form of Marxism and the present capitalist ideology make equal claims as the only systems to emerge from social evolution, but circumstances do not favour the adoption of either and further variations can be expected. The immediate and most overwhelming factor in the present acceleration is the existence of the United States and the Soviet Union, each presenting a possible model for the emergent nations. Today's upheaval in the Third World is not the product of slow germination within its own structure, but the inevitable result of colonisation. Then there is the influence of ideas gained by minorities educated abroad, and put into effect at home. These minorities have offered their fellow-countrymen a social warp in which the old traditional threads still endure but are worked into the new capitalist or socialist pattern demanded by modern technology.

It is not easy to reconcile traditional and modern social attitudes; the fusion of the two does not necessarily produce a facsimile of the original. Successful adaptation to technical and social progress requires a new mental approach, which it is much harder to instil on a vast scale than it is to drain marshes, build dams or tunnel through mountains. An eminent authority on American political institutions, Clinton Rossiter, has drawn up a list of prerequisites for the smooth running of the capitalist system along democratic

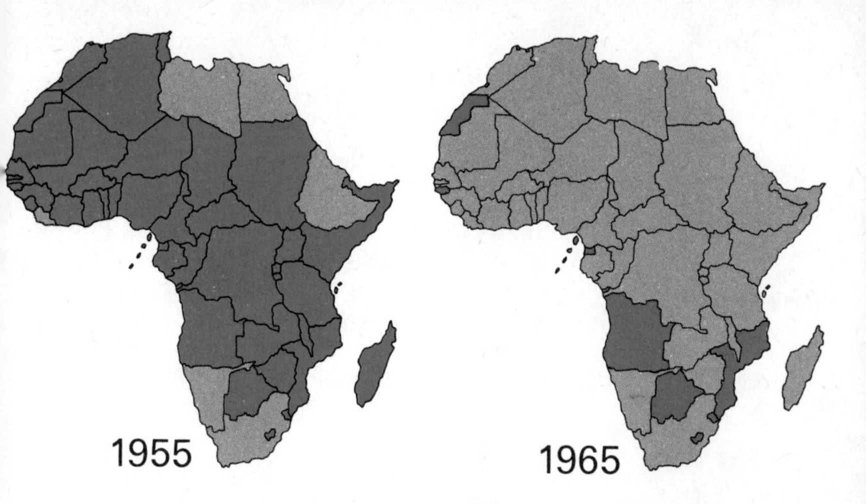

lines: a progressive society, a literary culture, universal education, a system of incentives appropriate to individual initiative and so on. On a journey to India, he confirmed that scarcely any of these prerequisites exist there, and yet the system works tolerably well. A similar discovery awaited the Soviet scientists Avakov and Mirskiy, when they tried to apply Marxist tenets dogmatically to the social structure. They discovered that the classic dichotomy of bourgeoisie and proletariat was invalidated by new factors when expressed in terms of the peasants of the Third World. They observed, too, that the proletarian groups were so small and had been formed in a manner so different from the proletariat of nineteenth-century Europe, that the revolutionary method would have to be modified. Those on the other hand who conduct objective researches into the nature of the social warp, will not be unduly surprised by their findings. Mao Tse-tung's analysis of the social categories in China thus works much more satisfactorily than the traditional Marxist scheme.

We can begin by considering the concept of the social tensions of the emergent peoples as a three-cornered conflict, involving the traditional warp, the capitalist organisation and the influence of socialism. They experience in the first place a conflict between the traditional and the modern, described as 'dualism' in an earlier chapter. This is especially acute because tradition is still very much alive in these countries, and the new is being violently thrust upon them. On top of this, they have become an arena for capitalism and socialism, in which the victor may well be neither system. For the present there may be a compromise between the two and a further compromise with tradition. This is the three-cornered conflict which will serve as our frame of reference when we consider some concrete examples of traditionalist societies in the Third World evolving through the cross-fire of socialism and capitalism.

The wind from the East

I have already quoted Mao Tse-tung for his realistic view of the social classes and for his shrewd vision of the emergent countries as the melting-pot from which the pattern of the future will be cast. I shall therefore take China first, for today she rivals the USSR as the authentic socialist model for the nations of the Third World. In taking up this position Mao's China is the true heir of the old China, which from her earliest days regarded herself as the centre of the world, 'The Middle Empire'. In his remarks about the present disagreement with the Soviet Union, C.P. Fitzgerald refers to this ancient conception of China as the sole trustee of the highest standard of civilisation amid foreign barbarism and adds:

> There can be no doubt that this view, in a modern form, is prevalent in China and is positively stated in the many polemical articles which have appeared since the dispute with the Soviet Union has come into the open. The Chinese now claim to be the upholders of pure Marxism, and denounce Russia as faint-hearted, 'revisionist', and too ready, for fear of nuclear war, to betray world revolution.

China has always looked upon herself as the hub of the universe. She did so in her trade with ancient Rome, when her chroniclers called the Emperor Antoninus An-Tun. She did so in 1542 when the Portuguese merchant Fernando Mendes Pinto reached the East, where he wrote his book *Pilgrimage*, in which he expressed an admiration for Oriental civilisation so unbounded that he wished the laws of China could have been imitated in Portugal. In his eyes the Chinese were justified in their claim, that, compared with them, all foreigners were mere barbarians!

The putting of Western theory into practice in this age-old tradition has achieved staggering results in modern China, which are capable of deluding the emergent countries. Technical acceleration within this vast and teeming country cannot be denied (figure 25) even if the exact extent of the advance is open to question (since official figures are not yet available even for 1960 or 1961). Western or Soviet competitors may deride the failure of the Communes, or to give them their proper name, the 'Public Associations of the People', and the 'Great Leap Forward' started in 1958; yet though this policy certainly had to be modified, without any corresponding signs of recovery until after the crucial year of 1961, Chinese industrial production has advanced at an impressive rate, although the extent claimed is rather optimistic.

It is as impossible to deal with this expansion in a few lines as it is to discuss in brief the involved rivalry with Moscow. One thing is indisputable: results such as these are not achieved by merely transplanting technical knowledge. An indispensable aid has been a social warp highly effective in mobilising and moulding human behaviour on a vast scale. The adjustment of the whole of a mighty population to the new tasks confronting them is a greater achievement still, when one remembers the alphabet difficulty and the comparative dearth of means of communication in such a vast land area, a fact which surprises even the experts. A. Doak Barnett, although scarcely fond of Maoism, writes as follows:

> Some years ago, a foreigner who had just toured Communist China came out to Hong Kong and remarked, with awe in his voice: 'I never thought that human beings and society could be reconstructed so easily'. If he meant that the changes of recent years had been relatively painless, he was very wrong. The plastic surgery that the Communists had been performing on Chinese society for over a decade had been painful indeed for millions of Chinese . . . But if, in using the word 'easily', the visitor actually meant 'rapidly', it is easy to share some of his awe. The Chinese Communists have dramatically demonstrated that an effective totalitarian régime can achieve extensive social change at a breakneck pace.

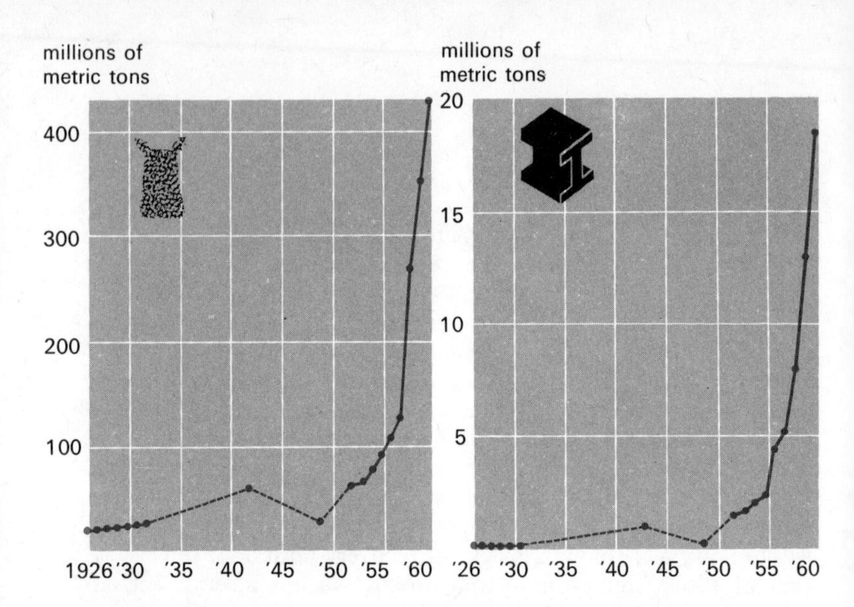

It is not easy to give an objective assessment of such transformations, for it is usual either to exaggerate them for propagandist reasons or to minimise them by adverse criticism. The West has, for instance, been scathing about the break-up of family life in China, completely disregarding the disturbing effect of modern capitalism on the close-knit family of the past.

The explanation for the upheavals of modern China is rooted in its people, a nation of infinite patience and adaptability which does not call itself the masses, but *lao pai hsing*, the Hundred Old Names. To us this is a more rhetorical label, but to the Chinese similes rather than syllogisms or systems are the essential formulae: witness slogans like 'Great leap' or 'walking on two feet' (agriculture and industry), which in themselves embody a whole programme. There are others not so well known like 'converting the whole country into a chess-board' (strengthening the structural inter-dependence of society). Let us remind those who can only think in terms of socialist dogma – Soviet dogma – that this nation has spent several thousand years calmly absorbing all her invaders until they have been assimilated into the very fibre of China. It is only reasonable therefore to wonder if socialism will not also be absorbed and refashioned in this 'Middle Empire', where attitudes

Figure 25. *Industrialisation by the people.* Although the exact figures are open to question, nobody can deny the tremendous progress made by China, indicated here by the figures for coal and steel production.

to life far different from those which inspired Karl Marx still prevail. To cite one example, whose far-reaching effect can be seen much more clearly in Fitzgerald's book: the Chinese language does not contain words for the concept of 'sin', so that according to Snow, there is no specific word for 'sinner', which is usually rendered by *tsui-jen*, 'criminal'. On the other hand, many subtle distinctions exist for the concept of 'shame'. Many puzzling matters are elucidated by comparing the concept of 'shame' with the Western concept of 'sin'.

If history is anything to go by China will not be confined to a slavish copy of Leninism, but will make radical alterations to it to suit her different geographical and human environment. This is what makes her such an interesting example of the contribution that can be made by the emergent countries to the models of a technological society epitomised respectively by the USA and the USSR. In particular, the basic role allotted by Mao to the peasants during the revolution affords a fundamental distinction, for Russian Marxism assigned the leading role to the industrial proletariat. Although this difference can be explained by the special characteristics of China and the overwhelming numerical superiority of workers on the land, this does not detract from its importance. In the first place, the basic fabric of the model clearly differs from the Russian; in the second place, this is just the feature of the Chinese model likely to appeal most to the numerous other countries where peasants form the majority of the population.

Another notable contribution, in contrast to typical Marxism, is the admission that contradictions can exist side by side in a socialist society, although they may differ from those which distinguish socialism from its opponents. This was the theme of the speech delivered by Mao Tse-tung on 27 February 1957, famous for its watchword, 'let a hundred flowers bloom and a hundred schools of ideology strive with each other'. Although this attitude stiffened later and although it is not easy to fathom its real meaning, such tolerance seems to be another offshoot of China's deep roots in the past. It is the same outlook which permitted the

Figures 26a and b. *The Sino-Soviet split in terms of foreign trade*. China's trade with the USSR suffered its first fall in 1957, following the policy of de-Stalinisation initiated by Moscow in February 1956. It picked up thereafter, but after the unsuccessful visit of Khruschev to Peking in October 1959 a definite decline set in

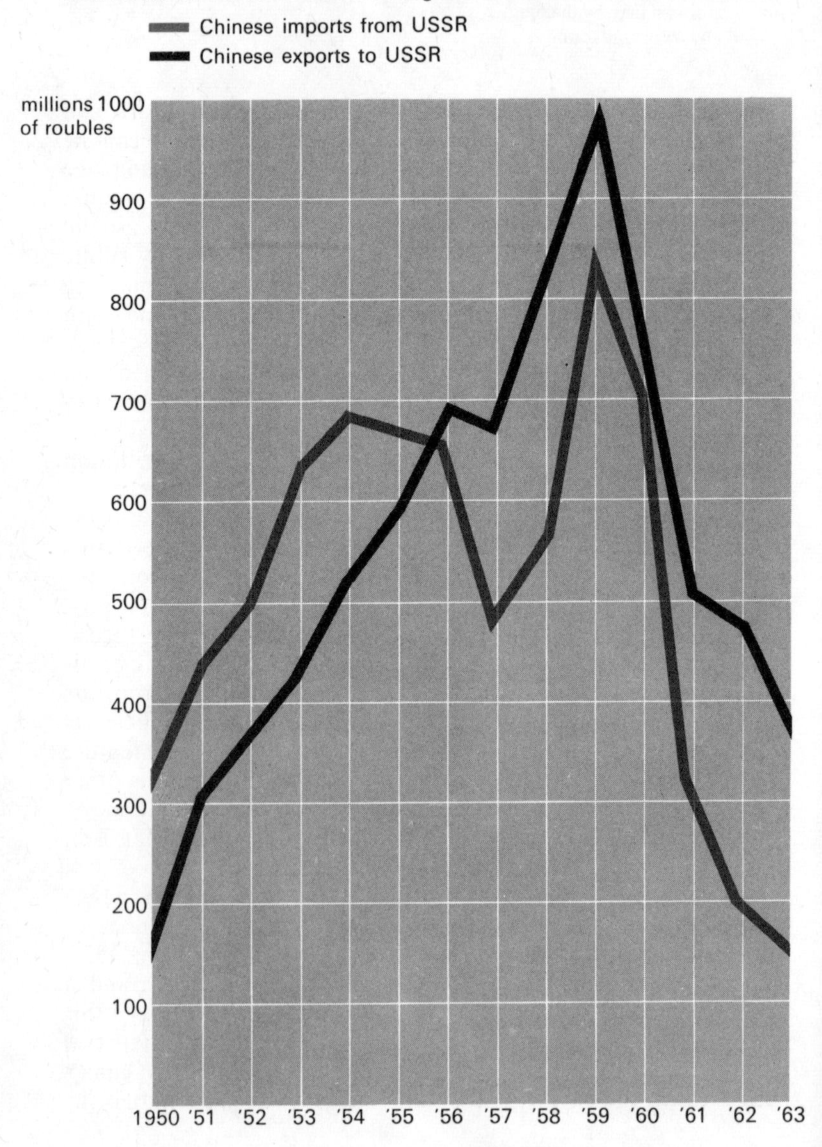

and gathered momentum until the total break in 1960. At the same time China's trade with the West, after an initial decline, reached levels in 1957–8 which have been maintained ever since.

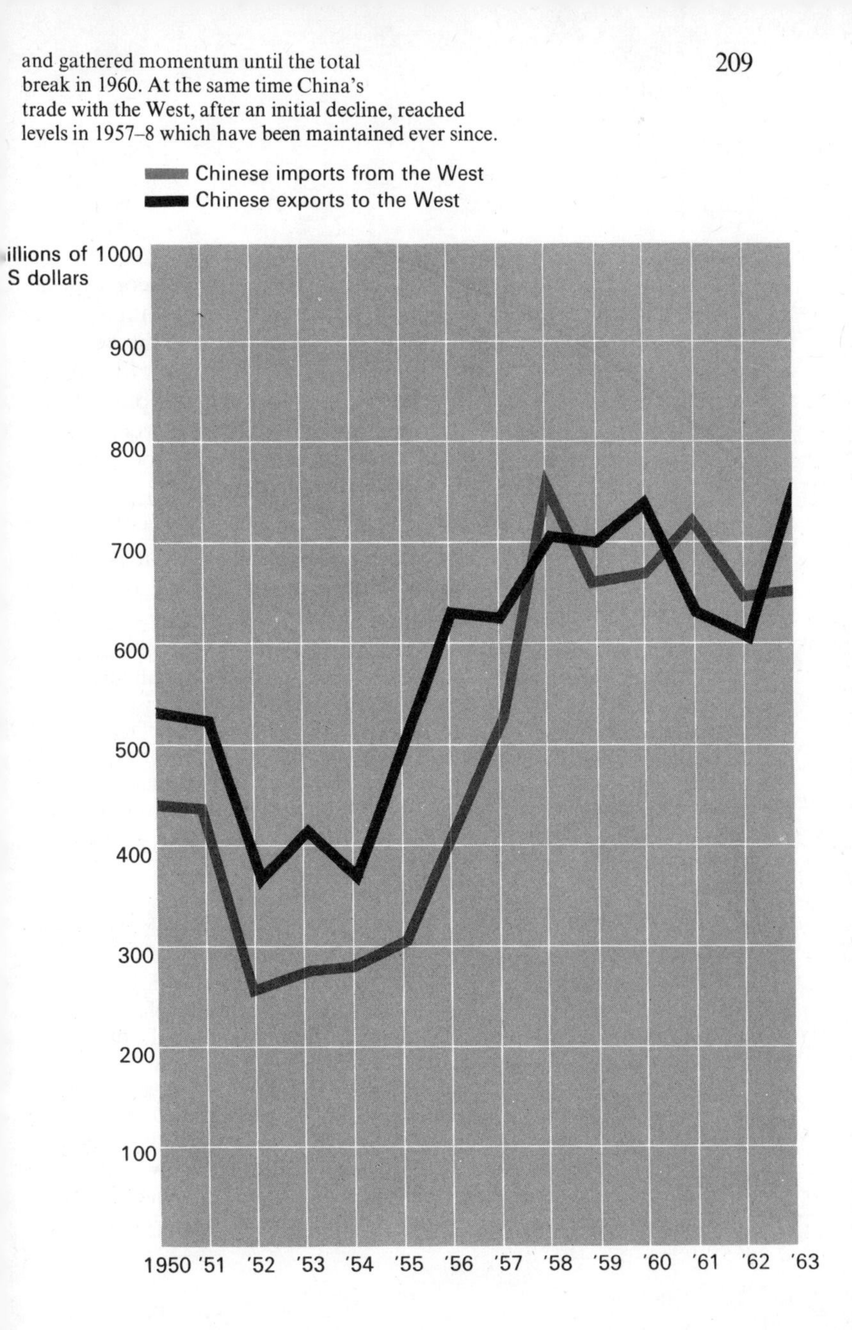

peaceful coexistence of the so-called *three roads* of religion: Buddhism, Confucianism and Taoism. Yet, it also corresponds to the Taoist belief in a duality in the nature of things, to be reconciled by an ineffable unifying principle which is the key to an understanding of the world; it is an irrational system of argument which, nevertheless, can be related on a metaphysical plane to the Hegelian origin of Marxism. This metaphysical interpretation was confirmed when Mao, in the same speech, quoted the words of Lao-Tse, who two thousand years before had taught:

In adversity dwells good fortune, in good fortune is adversity veiled.

In any event tolerance and the assimilation of what is contradictory have been defended by Mao time and again, as when he spoke thus about intellectuals:

Now that the social system of our country has changed and the economic foundation of the bourgeois ideology has been eradicated to all intents and purposes it is not only necessary for our intellectuals to revise their conception of the world, but also possible that many of them may do so. Nevertheless, something as final as one's conception of the world cannot be arrived at in a few moments. Rest assured, there will be many who will refuse to admit the ideology of Leninist–Marxist Communism. We must use no coercion with them. If they submit to the demands of the State and go about their lawful business, we must make it possible for them to do useful work.

As for the mistaken ideas among the people themselves, Mao declared that they must not be forbidden, because:

To apply methods of an over-simplified nature to deal with problems of ideology arising within the soul of the people, problems affecting man's spiritual existence, not only achieves nothing but is downright dangerous. The expression of mistaken ideas can be banned, but they continue to exist. On the other hand, if correct and well-founded ideas have been reared in a hot-house, if they have not been exposed to the elements, if they have not been immunised, they will not carry the day when an assault is made on them by the mistaken ideas. Therefore, to further the growth of proper ideas, we are in fact only permitted to use discussion, criticism and rational argument in order to vanquish false beliefs and find a solution to our problems.

It is easy to scoff at these remarks and dismiss them as pure propaganda, but even though the tolerance here preached by Mao was subsequently curtailed, there are many factors which confirm that this attitude is the true expression of the Chinese view of life. From many different cultural points of view – for instance by Jung in psychology – assessment has been made of the Chinese conception of the world as a great and embracing whole, where all events are interrelated, as against the Western analytic view, based on reason and the concept of cause and effect. The black and white distinction between yes and no, good and bad, is the product of the logical spirit of European rationalism, which develops in its extreme form into dogmatic Marxism. Its mechanical version in cybernetics has been interpreted by Wiener as a refutation of Manicheism and a confirmation of Saint Augustine, but China is beyond such scholastic disputes. However little anyone may have read about Oriental culture, he will not fail to hear echoes from the past in these words of an article published in *Jenmin Jihpao* on 23 February 1962:

> Truth and error usually cannot be distinguished from each other at a glance. . . . If we honestly analyse all opinions, we shall usually discover that there are similarities among different opinions and that there are some not quite correct points in every correct opinion . . . and some good points in every erroneous opinion.

It appears that Chinese Marxism, despite its claim to be the true successor to the Leninist–Marxist policy, is in fact introducing some important differences in ideology which have their origin without any doubt in the traditional past, as we saw when referring to the Taoist 'dialectics', and manifest the practical parallels between Confucianism and Marxism. I foresee this survival from the past into the present, equal in importance to the grafting of technology on to the ancient cultures, as the possible contribution of the emergent countries to the future. We will now turn to another country comparable with China, even if its traditions are now inseparably linked with capitalism.

In Japan Western technology and productive efficiency have

been grafted on to the old stock. Although this process has not long been in operation the cumulative effect is really staggering. The Japanese succeeds in being highly efficient during working hours when, attired in a lounge suit or wearing the modern workman's plastic cap, he takes his place at the office-desk or the factory-bench. But when he enters his house, he puts the West behind him and donning his kimono or his yukata he sinks once more into the milieu of traditional family life. A few minutes only divide him from his other life – only a paper-thin wall and the delicate cherry-tree branches in the miniature garden – but his soul has already ceased to balance uneasily on the tightrope of foreign technology and relaxes luxuriously in the secure haven of a way of life that has endured for a thousand years.

Japanese tradition is the reverse of modern Western individualism, because it implies an absolute submission to the community and its conventions. A similar subordination to the service of the community has been carried into the sphere of industrial labour relations. At first glance, a Japanese firm looks just like its Western counterpart, since the conditions imposed by technology demand a certain standard organisation everywhere, as we noted when we compared the capitalist corporation with the socialist state enterprise. Yet it is, in fact, an organisation completely different from the Western corporation; whereas the latter stresses the connection between money and goods (including labour), Japanese industrial relations are far removed from the mere payment of cash in return for human effort. In spite of their recent evolution, and allowing for the possibly brief duration of the present stage, they are akin to those that previously existed between the feudal lord and his serf: the employer, in return for the promise of an undivided allegiance, shelters and protects the employee throughout his life.

The methods employed in the recruitment of labour during the early days of industrialisation, when certain feudal families started to build up the huge *zaibatsu* or complex networks of companies, have perhaps contributed to this situation. There is scarcely any mobility of labour in Japan, and a worker hardly ever leaves one

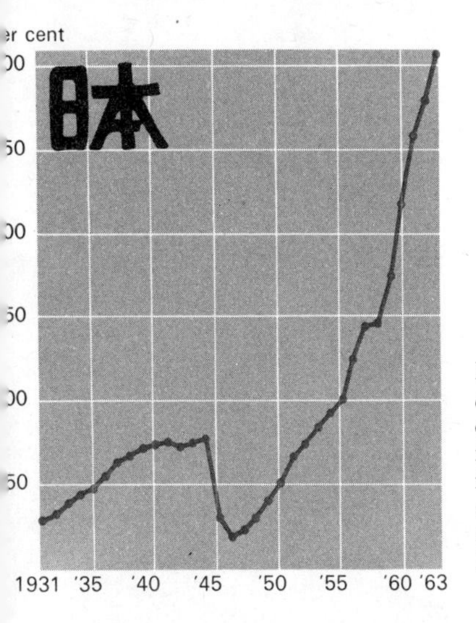

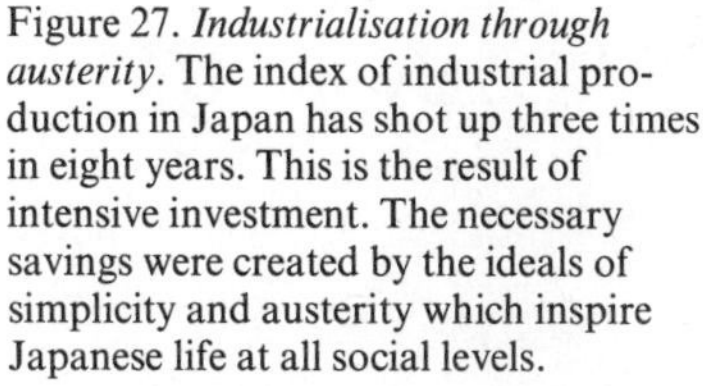
Figure 27. *Industrialisation through austerity*. The index of industrial production in Japan has shot up three times in eight years. This is the result of intensive investment. The necessary savings were created by the ideals of simplicity and austerity which inspire Japanese life at all social levels.

firm for another, as frequently occurs in the West. Wages are based on efficiency incentive schemes and labour is organised on a company basis in spite of the progress made in efforts to organise it by trades, on the pattern of the European Trades Unions. At the risk of oversimplification, it could be said that in Japan two mentalities coexist in every human being. It is as if one person were increasing production by modern methods so that another person – the same person in a different guise – could go on living according to the traditional pattern. The concept of life 'in the service of' the community and its accepted standards appears both in the personal submission of the employees to their particular firm, and in an equally scrupulous dedication to their work on the part of the governing body, which shows a degree of discipline very different from the profiteering motives inherent in capitalism. This attitude explains the high figure of personal savings in modern Japan and the country's consequent impressive rate of economic progress (figure 27). Japan seems to combine with unusual success technical advance and continued tradition, the mechanical horse and the mount of flesh and blood. This combination is an efficient producer, whose core is the spirit of the past acting within an expanding economy. It offers an example not of parasitism but of a highly profitable symbiosis.

It is impossible to form any judgment about the countries which

Portuguese traders seen through Japanese eyes, c. 1600. Note their clumsiness and inordinately large features – the Japanese view of barbarian Europe.

are neighbours of China, such as the People's Republics of Korea, Vietnam or Indonesia. Nor can the huge, vacillating world of India be given the space it deserves. The two principal examples cited must suffice to establish that the split between capitalism and socialism in the West may be considerably modified when these two forces are introduced into cultures rich in ancient tradition. One can understand the tenor of the remarks addressed by the leader of the modern 'Middle Empire' to young Chinese students in the USSR on 17 November 1957:

> The direction of the wind in the world has changed. In the struggle between the socialist camp and the capitalist camp, either the West wind prevails over the East wind; or the East wind prevails over the West wind. The whole world now has a population of 2700 million, of which the various socialist countries account for nearly 1000 million; the independent, former colonial countries make up more than 700 million; and the capitalist countries now struggling for independence or for complete independence and capitalist countries with neutral tendencies have 600 million. The population of the imperialist camp is only about 400 million; moreover, they are divided internally. 'Earthquakes' may occur there. At present, it is not the West wind which is prevailing over the East wind, but the East wind that is prevailing over the West wind.

African socialism

It seems impossible at first glance that modernity and traditionalism can be yoked together in Africa as they have been in Japan or China. The opinion commonly accepted in Europe is that black Africa's past was mere barbarism, an infertile soil in which the seeds of civilisation have scarcely taken root as yet. This view is completely without foundation, though some of the nationalistic vaunts of modern Africans are equally untrue. In their stand for independence Africans have, understandably, exaggerated the most brilliant passages of their history. However, after allowing for such exaggeration, recent research finds traces of a much less 'primitive' past than is usually supposed. New evidence of this past is continually being unearthed worthy to be ranked with such attested phenomena as the great Sudanese Empire or the bronze art of Benin.

It must also be remembered that, unlike China and Japan, Africa was the victim of the tremendous ravages of colonisation. We will not discuss here the undeniable economic exploitation practised by the colonising powers, nor the resulting benefits which they reaped. It would make a good motion for a debate, whose verdict, I fear, would not be in Europe's favour. However, our sole concern here is to prove that colonisation has had an inhibiting effect on the contribution of traditionalism to African society. When the occupying powers began to need labour for their capitalist enterprises and a ready response was not forthcoming from the natives, who were settled in their traditional societies, they made use of an expedient as simple as it was brutally effective, described in Basil Davidson's *Which way Africa?* as 'probably the most destructive element in the economic system of the invader'. They levied a tax on the country's population. What European conscience, however highly principled, could possibly be shocked by a tax? But in African society, where money was almost unknown, a demand for cash payment was equivalent to a demand for forced labour. For the native either had to go to the mines or the plantations to earn the sum demanded by the Treasury, or be hauled before the courts, where the legal penalty for non-payment was a certain period of forced labour.

Attempts at flight or evasion served only to heighten European prejudice that the Negro is lazy and incapable of a corporate sense of responsibility. It should also be noted that besides this indirect method, which was used in the former British and French colonies, forced labour was directly imposed in other places. Davidson recalls that when in 1905 King Leopold of the Belgians refused in his own interests to suspend the enforced collection of rubber, he justified himself on the grounds that this forced labour could only be waived 'when the Negro has generally shaken off his idleness and become ready to work for the lure of wages alone'.

It is not surprising that when the Congo ceased in 1908 to be a vast private estate of the King and became national property, Leopold II made a great bonfire of all the documents, declaring:

> They can have my Congo, but they've no right to know what I've done there.

This case, and others like it, show the power that colonialism has to uproot man from his native environment and destroy his connections with his society, and it throws light too on a fundamental aspect of that society. It shows clearly that traditional African society, unlike capitalism, was not an organisation based on money and the production of goods for sale. It demonstrates how mistaken those people are who believe that the profit motive is an innate drive in man and the foundation of his psychology. The individual entrepreneur of liberalism had no place in African society: this is the first step – there are other factors, as we shall see – towards understanding the trends which are becoming prominent in the new independent nations of Africa.

Because the prevailing mood in Africa in recent years has been an antipathy (which is quite understandable) towards Europe, the inevitable reaction has been to look back with nostalgia to African origins. Such an attitude not only explains the present in terms of the past but is rapidly leaving this present behind. If the era of colonial rule brought about upheavals comparable with, although much more grievous than, the havoc wrought by factories on the rural life of Europe by the Industrial Revolution, the Second World War and the post-war period created an awareness of history not only among the minority of Africans educated in Europe, but also among the masses; and to a greater degree than was suspected from outside. This awareness is so far beyond question that it now yields only to force, as Chief Albert Luthuli was sadly forced to state in his speech on acceptance of the Nobel Peace Prize:

> How great is the paradox, and how much greater the honour, that an award in support of peace and the brotherhood of man should come to one who is a citizen of a country where the brotherhood of man is an illegal doctrine.

Africans may exaggerate their past achievements, just as Europeans have tended to depreciate pre-colonial African culture. But the sixteenth-century bronze art of Benin was neither influenced by Europeans nor 'primitive'.

In contrast to capitalist values, a community and social sense which is scarcely comprehended by a Europe conditioned for several centuries by the doctrine of individualism is now being reborn from the deep recesses of African tradition. The polarity of these two concepts can be appreciated both by examining the general disagreements and by considering particular instances. Perhaps nobody, in our estimation, has given such wholehearted and selfless service to Africa as the now legendary Dr Albert Schweitzer. Yet, in the view of an African statesman like Alex Quaison-Sackey, Schweitzer never understood the people among whom he worked, though he devoted his entire life to them. Quaison-Sackey writes:

> Despite his erudition, he has apparently not appreciated how sensitive the Africans are to any slights to their dignity. That African culture differs from Dr Schweitzer's or anyone else's does not make the Africans inferior; yet that seems to have been the assumption, unconscious or otherwise, on which most Europeans have long operated.

We must observe in African cultures, therefore, not only the powerful vitality recognised by admirers of Negro music and dancing or of carved masks and sculpture, but a deep and universal sense of humanity, which might almost be termed a 'species experience'. The African seems to see himself as but a fragment of a vast community, which embraces all living men as well as all the dead and all who are yet to be born. In 1962, when a group of Uganda intellectuals founded a journal in London for the dissemination of their ideas, they deliberately called it *Ntu*, which is the root word in the Bantu language for Man or Humanity in exactly this sense. The same idea inspired the political philosophy of Kwame Nkrumah, when he declared that Socialism is only the rediscovery in modern dress of the communalism which is fundamental to traditional African society and which shows itself in a basic equality and in the idea that everyone is responsible for everyone else. In this sense 'socialism is the defence of the principles of communalism in a modern environment'. Another great ideologist of African socialism, Julius Nyerere, President of

Tanzania, is also convinced of this. His *Ujamaa* is a word which even if its literal meaning refers to connections within the family or with the neighbours is used to describe a socialism of the whole human race because in Africa there is in fact no other way of understanding human coexistence. Davidson recalls how he once asked an African in Tanganyika for an exact definition of *Ujamaa*. His companion said nothing but gestured towards a hut that several men were busy rebuilding. Pointing to an old man who was hobbling about on crutches, one of the workers explained: 'We are that man's neighbours and we are fixing his house for him'.

Yet African Socialism is not just the resurrection of communalism, which would be something as outmoded now as the Utopian Socialism which Marx fought so strenuously in his age. As Nkrumah himself explained, in a non-technical society with an economic organisation on the lines of a Liberal *laissez faire*, communalism could function quite unhampered by simply following traditional customs. But in a technical society, where methods of production are more complicated, this conception of free brotherhood can only be saved, paradoxically, by discipline exercised from the centre. Without this, economic disputes would arise among the different classes and political inequality would result. In African Socialism, therefore, communalism takes to itself only those methods of production and forms of organisation which are indispensable for achieving economic development under modern conditions, while retaining its traditional principles. Thus an attempt is being made in Africa to mature the new wine of modern life in the wine-skins of the old culture. The surprising yet perfectly natural result is the gradual evolution of 'communist man' sought, along other roads, by the Party Programme of the Soviets, already outlined in an earlier chapter.

In other words, it is clear that the most influential African leaders are tending towards a strong State control of the economy. Even when they do not adopt socialism, the majority of the new countries are turning to a planned type of capitalism, as Nigeria, with its more vigorous middle-class, is trying to do. Yet it is frequently felt that the only alternative to socialism is a sort of neo-colonialism, where the control of the national economy would still be in the hands of foreign private capital, either in the form of foreign aid or in the form of property in Africa, built up in the past by the efforts of Africans themselves. The idea of a *Welfare State* does not arise since, as Nkrumah observed, 'the welfare state is the climax of a highly developed industrialism. To assure its benefits in a less developed country is to promise merely the division of poverty'. In *Africa must unite*, Nkrumah justified State control in these words:

> Because colonialism prevented the emergence of a strong local capitalist class, because production for private profit is based on exploitation, and because the less developed nations need a high rate of economic growth, the government is obliged to play the role of main entrepreneur in laying the basis of national economic and social advancement.

Socialist ownership is essential for the institution of a national plan in the genuine interests of the people. To prefer capitalism would be to consign future economic expansion to long-term control by self-interested parties. Hence African Socialism has arisen to combine modern materialism with principles of equality and with an ethical concept of mankind in keeping with traditional communalism.

In brief, then, the principal contribution of Africa to modern political life, apart from her other cultural offerings, is a humanist socialism. I will make two further observations, both complementary to the central idea which I have put forward. The first is that any idea that nationalism will tend to break up economic unity in Africa should be dispelled. In an age in which, as we mentioned earlier, the great European powers of the nineteenth century have found themselves too small for the twentieth, it would be an anachronism to want to build up frontiers like the Great Wall of China around countries as reduced in size as some of those which have recently gained independence in Africa. The Africans are conscious of their basic unity, expressed in the French-

speaking areas, in the idea of *la négritude*, or of *African personality* among those in the former British Colonies. The conception of Pan-African unity is constantly being voiced even though the winning of independence may require that a sense of nationality be a prime consideration. The Conference of Addis Ababa, in May 1963, was a basic declaration among the African nations. It is true that it is a long way from declarations to facts, for it is impossible to ignore racial distrust or personal grudges among the leaders. Yet confidence is boosted by the fact that the old

The stained-glass window of the main lobby of Africa Hall, Addis Ababa, is the symbolical embodiment of the ideal of Pan-Africanism.

conception of the nation as the overall unit is gradually being superseded by technology. Thus unity does not rest on good intentions alone but also on those same unifying trends which we have seen manifested in Europe, despite some reactionary heads of State. The full economic consequences of these unifying influences will be equally felt in their neighbour continent, Africa.

The second observation is made, because all the above generalisations have dealt principally with what is called Black Africa. Alien to it in political ideology is the Republic of South Africa, whose racial policy seems an historical deadlock, which must inevitably be resolved one way or another. In the North lies Islamic Africa, where Arab Socialism, the 'democratic cooperative socialism' of Nasser, is in control. In 1955, shortly after he had accepted the Egyptian presidency, Nasser described its objectives as follows:

> This is a middle-class revolution against capitalism and against communism. . . . Politics for me means only one thing – solving the social problem. Somehow we have got to create a political party which people join not for what they get out of it but for what they put in. That's a completely new idea here, and that's why I have to exclude all the old politicians and prevent the capitalists and landlords from muscling in. The new party must be composed of people . . . with a sense of public service.

These views have been influenced by post-war vicissitudes: the culture of Islam and the Pharaonic tradition of strong central control have likewise left their mark on Nasserism. It is not easy to define briefly the basic characteristics of the North African region, which stretches from the Western Kingdom of Morocco to the United Arab Republic, when countries like Algeria are still at a transitional stage. But North Africa remains the hinge on which the whole continent turns in its historical and geographical relationships with Europe and Asia.

Finally one need hardly bring to the reader's attention what he can easily perceive by reading the daily press, viz. the overwhelming and pathetic instability of all African situations obtaining since the latest wave of decolonisation. The longstanding difficulties in the former Belgian Congo are merely one example of the numerous *coups d'état*, reversals and seizures of power which take place in new nations with fragile institutional structures. In the preceding comments we have referred to some of the causes of such instability – the destruction by colonists of traditional structures, the opposing temptations offered by the capitalist or the socialist model, outside influences and so on – but the problem is extraordinarily complex and presents itself in many different local forms. In short there is no doubt that in the immediate future there will be still more changes in the politico-economic orientation of the continent. Nevertheless, we are convinced that they will occur, broadly speaking, in the directions determined by the basic forces which we have studied here as the formative pressures of the future.

The new independence of South America

We have found Asia and Africa hovering on the brink of a decision between a brand of socialism or capitalism, adapted to their traditional way of life. It will be recalled that in general Latin American states gained their independence about the beginning of the nineteenth century and it seemed then that their choice had been made and all that remained was to make the best possible progress in the direction indicated. However, the disorders in the present political scene suggest that the politico–social problems are far from solved. In fact all America South of the Rio Grande is now facing a period of great decision. As the eminent Brazilian Josué de Castro has written, the South American continent is in its crucial decade, for the moment of choice is at hand.

The reason for this state of flux is not far to seek. The economic structure has been neo-colonial in fact, if not in name, since the granting of independence. Its purpose was production for subsistence with a special bias towards mineral or agricultural exports, according to the profit fluctuations on the world market. In the new countries the Spanish and Portuguese administrations of the eighteenth century continued unchanged in form, although they were already out of date at the time of the Industrial Revolution in Europe. Celso Furtado declares that up to 1930 Brazil was still in the grip of complex colonialist attitudes, and that even in the next ten years expensive efforts were made to produce and pay for surplus coffee because according to colonialist ideas coffee was the foundation of the Brazilian economy. Similar instances of this neo-colonialism in independent states could be cited for other countries. One of its legacies is the birth of too many new and uneconomic nations, such as followed the recent declarations of independence in Africa.

Another legacy of neo-colonialism is the sprawling landed estate, the pillar of Latin-American economic structures; even this is not indigenous but is a relic of the feudalism introduced from Spain and Portugal. For here too colonisation sowed the seed of destruction, and a situation continues which the distinguished Peruvian, Luis Alberto Sánchez, sometime Rector of the ancient San Marcos University in Lima, describes in these words:

> Just as under the Viceroy, the members of the Republican Governments lead lives of leisure like petty Colonial gentlemen. They live on Government loans (*cf* the Jewish merchants of the sixteenth century); they beautify certain cities (*cf* the castle of former days) caring nothing for the country, and they are invested with an overriding power, which turns the dictator into a lackey of the foreign entrepreneur. The luxury of such potentates is founded on a bubble.

And in the same breath he quotes Amanda Labarca, who writing of Chile, says:

> The fraudulent understanding between a wealthy minority and the impoverished masses, largely illiterate and oppressed, furnishes a favourable climate in which the feudal estates and Imperialism can go on draining the South American nations, even though the State seems to occupy the position of *nouveau riche*.

In short, society is still being strangled by inadequate institutions, the legacy of colonialism, the colonialism with one important difference: that the Spaniard has never practised racialism. His sense of the dignity of the whole human race, beyond distinctions of colour or class, compared with the attitude already noted in the African. The title given by the South African writer, Bloke Modisane, to one of his short stories, *The Dignity of the Beggar*, is readily intelligible to the Spaniard who is by nature fitted to perceive the self-respect present alike in murderer, hunchback and king. Velázquez invested his clowns with the same human dignity as his ladies-in-waiting, and in an age when cultured Europeans were still debating whether women had souls, Spain recognised the soul of the native of South America, if only to win it at sword-point in the name of the Cross. Unamuno took the title *On Human Dignity*, already used by his Renaissance predecessors, for an essay stressing what he calls 'the firm soil of our being, what we all have in common, *humanity*, true humanity, the quality of being of mankind', as against that 'desperate bourgeoisie seeking a god who would chain the working classes to machines'. This outlook on life, which does not exist in the former British or French Colonies, has produced today a mixture of races which is an essential problem in Latin America; yet it is also an organic growth, a unique cross-fertilisation of cultures.

South America is today in danger of having to win independence all over again because of her outmoded social and economic structure. Her nations, like Spain and Portugal or the other capitalist countries on the intermediate level, have never developed beyond the mercantile stage to industrial capitalism. The first serious attempts at industrialisation made a sporadic appearance in South America during the boom following the First World War and were mainly centred on food exports and a few manufactured goods, such as textiles. It was after the Second World War that a certain degree of industrialisation became fully established. This was more marked in countries like Mexico, though everywhere it was restricted in function by an unwieldy and archaic economic structure. The late appearance of this new trend contrasts with the early urbanisation of Latin America. Whereas a rash of conurbations was spread in Europe by the Industrial Revolution, in South America the growth of city life anticipated industry.

This urbanisation flourished with a truly remarkable vigour throughout the entire continent. When Vekemans and Segundo calculated the percentages of urban population in the various South American countries they found that the average for the most advanced was over forty. In Argentina, where the Greater Buenos Aires Area comprised a fifth of the whole population, it was 68 per cent; it reached 81 per cent in Uruguay, where a third of the people resided in Montevideo. This is why Latin America has not gone through the stage of the industrial proletariat. After the wholesale evacuation of the country districts in South America the farm and estates workers, in contrast to the European trend, gravitated towards jobs in the public services, which had expanded enormously owing to the urban concentration, and thus became civil servants.

It is generally accepted that the old-fashioned administration and the different pattern of urban evolution have, among other factors, made development along the lines of European capitalism impossible in South America. Occasionally the economist states – as Victor L. Urquidi did when he joined the National College of Mexico – that he has reached his present attitude 'after painfully retracing my steps along paths that were marked out by academic impressions received in early youth by being educated abroad, just over twenty years ago; a valuable education indeed, but inevitably tinged by the prejudices inherent in certain theoretical preconceptions.' Celso Furtado, one of the keenest minds in this field in South America, thinks likewise, for he concludes his essay about the training of the economist in the underdeveloped countries with the observation that:

> In Brazil, the economist with a solid background of methodology and a good understanding of general scientific principles is almost bound to veer towards heterodoxy. He will very soon learn that the well-trodden paths are of no use to him. He will then realise that the imagination is a useful tool of great power which it would be well to study. He will soon lose his awe of the textbooks and, as he begins to think independently he will regain his confidence and banish his hesitation.

In Latin America the urban revolution preceded the industrial revolution. Buenos Aires contains one fifth of the population of a country which is five and a half times the size of France and has an overall density of less than ten people per square kilometre.

The economic theory of capitalist growth, worked out by and for fully industrialised countries in Europe and North America, does not take into account the circumstances of countries like those of Latin America. Hence the failure of financial formulae prepared by the experts of international bodies, and the breakdown of such well-intentioned schemes as the Alliance for Progress, whose benefits are scarcely felt by the people in need, because they are channelled into the upper strata of the social structure and profit only the ruling factions. Liberal capitalism is not in fact bringing development quickly enough for a population which, as we have seen, has one of the most rapid rates of increases in the world. This increase absorbs almost the total annual rise in national production, which was estimated by Jorge Ahumada at 4·6 per cent between 1945 and 1958 over the whole continent. For this reason Urquidi states:

> Despite the blind, unthinking reverence in which many still hold the economic policy of Liberalism, the free play of social and economic forces – which has never existed in its pure form – would only aggravate the structural inequalities, hold up the integration of the Latin American economy into the trends of world economy by making it a servile dependent of the latter, and unleash social tensions which could not be resolved by peaceful means. Adam Smith's invisible hand, even if it was useful once, is wholly ineffective under the present conditions in Latin America and the under-developed world. In its stead the guiding hand and firm pulse of the State are needed.

This means that the inefficiency of liberalism has been realised on the other side of the Atlantic too. To counter the financial doctrines of the international experts, most of the Latin American economists support an economic theory which they call 'structuralism'. This new system can be seen taking shape in the succeeding issues of *El Trimestre Económico*, the most authoritative source for Latin American economic thought. Brothers, writing in number 116 of this review, explains:

> The arguments of the structuralists clearly point to the conclusion that the only visible method of promoting the economic development of Latin

America is the adoption of measures which will bring about radical changes in the productive structure of its economies.

It is not difficult to reach this conclusion if one admits the existence of the outmoded structures referred to above, and all the other factors, fiscal, administrative, political and social, which stem from them and whose regressive tendency has been described at length by numerous writers in similar terms. The two volumes published by UNESCO on the *Social Aspects of Economic Development in Latin America* are sufficient to show the grave view taken by several authors of the overwhelming problems created by the social structure.

Latin America has therefore reached a critical stage of development, where the introduction of far-reaching reforms has become essential. These reforms admit of no delay. The failure of liberal capitalism is evinced in the standard of living of the majority of the population, the serious inequalities of income, and the disasters that still afflict whole areas in countries as full of untapped resources as Brazil. A Brazilian structuralist already referred to, Celso Furtado, is in no doubt whatever:

In our countries *laissez faire* simply means the prolongation of misery.

State intervention, with centralised planning of the economy, cannot be avoided. The question that remains, however, is whether the State will exercise this control within a capitalist system, as in the most advanced industrial countries, or as a socialist organisation.

A definite solution is uncertain and in any case is likely to differ on a short-term basis from country to country. Yet it must be kept in mind that the adoption of State capitalism will slow down development to the gradual process experienced by industrialised countries during the past century. A gradual process was, I think, possible then, since expansion merely had to keep pace with maintenance of a standard of living already the highest in the world, but it would now be quite unacceptable. The same patience cannot be required of the masses concentrated in the huge and politically unstable suburban areas of South America, who can

Brazilian farmer hoping for rain. After a century and a half of independence, few Latin American economists put much trust in liberal capitalism as a means of solving such serious problems as the permanent threat of famine in North-east Brazil. Central planning, which is preferred by many, can be achieved either by State capitalism or by socialism. The former is Latin America's choice.

plainly see the rapid progress of other countries, and who are being increasingly influenced by modern methods of propaganda. I consider that these countries no longer have the option of electing for industrial capitalism; moreover State capitalism is already outmoded. The efforts made by many leaders to arrest the course of history do no more than build up the pressure of the masses behind barriers whose collapse is foreseeable.

Whether I am right or not, the trend towards reform with increased planning and State control within the various social systems of Latin America is indisputable. I believe too that these emergent countries may evolve a more humanised and less materialistic pattern of life than the capitalist world. In a lecture on the pre-revolutionary era in Brazil, delivered in Sao Paulo in 1962, Celso Furtado declared:

> Let us be in no doubt for a single moment that what is at the bottom of all these aspirations and ideals of youth today is a genuine humanism. What young people are concerned about is the anti-human aspect of our development; it is the fact that the contrast between extravagance and penury is growing daily more acute. Here we have rural populations who are living on the land, but they are unable to plant to eat and are suffering from hunger almost from one year's end to the other. Here we have cities, State capitals, where ten per cent of the population are on hospital records as tubercular. Yet we know that this can be put right, for it has already been banished from much of the world. Therefore the main consideration in the minds of the youth of today is Man; their compassion is aroused by his state of wretchedness and their consciences are awakened by the fact that we are partly responsible for this abject condition.

The continent may, then, discover new lines of economic development. Perhaps they are being laid down even now as structuralism gains impetus. A few pages back I referred to the mixture of races as a unique characteristic of South America. Luis Alberto Sánchez bears this out in the concluding words of his essay on Latin America:

> A hybrid continent, with a hybrid social organisation, a hybrid topography, a hybrid culture. The task before us is to canalise these facts towards

one positive meaning, of integration and rebirth. . . . Without exaggeration or rhetorical figure of speech, we have in our hands the responsibility for rebuilding the earth's culture by giving shape to a New World. We are no longer in debt to the past but to the present and the future. . . . A personal culture is being born for us which is lighting a beacon equally for the rest of the world's longing for something different.

Beyond the horizon

The 'longing for something different' evidently means a longing for something different from the present situation of the South American countries, where a defective capitalism survives based on disruptive individualism. Many sincere democrats in Latin America thus recognise the need for a central control of the economy which the State alone can accomplish. They agree with the entire emergent world in a unanimous resistance to the wholesale surrender of the helpless populace to the mechanical procedures of the market, and to the capitalist combines who for their own profit operate the 'automatisms' of supply and demand, by secretly manipulating the distributing channels of goods produced by collective effort. Differences will begin to show themselves in countries previously condemned to economic liberalism. While some adhere to State capitalism, others will advance towards socialism, arriving at one of the upper echelons of the centrally organised social scheme described by Mao Tse-tung.

Whatever the differences in development it is essential to realise that the forces operating in the Third World are both moving upwards towards higher technical levels, and horizontally, from right to left, away from systems based on a market controlled by individual decision and towards systems with central planning in which the individual is more clearly subordinated to the service of the community.

Whether the movement is marked or limited in extent, it is unmistakably towards the left. We can thus define another general factor in the whole trend of world economics: the emergent countries are moving further and further away from the old social structure bequeathed by their colonial past and maintained by the individualism of nineteenth-century capitalism. The eventual outcome of this movement is uncertain. Personally, I do not think that it is likely to be State capitalism, for this system requires social and political conditions which are not easy to bring about in the limited time available. Whatever the outcome, the trend of the forces in the vast economic periphery, which is collecting around the nuclei of capitalism and socialism, is the displacement of the social structure towards the left.

After all, to see how far left we have moved in the last hundred years, we need only read the tèn points proposed in the *Communist Manifesto* as a then revolutionary programme. Since 1848 several of them have become widely accepted: progressive income tax, national central banks, state transport and communications, and free education for all children.

We have now finished plotting the lines of force within the whole field: they tend towards a planned system in the capitalist world; towards a certain amount of decentralisation in the advanced socialist countries; in the emergent world towards a certain economic control, organised within any of the systems lying between State capitalism and advanced socialism, with probable leanings towards some form of the latter, since in my view the chance of capitalism has been lost in those countries; meanwhile, the tendency everywhere is towards scientific progress and an increasing application of technology.

These are the conclusions of reasoned argument; but human affairs are not governed by reason alone, as we have already stated. We must allow for the unforeseeable, for the unexpected complication. This is all the more necessary when we are dealing with basic trends in a vast and alien world on the threshold of upheaval, such as we have examined in this chapter. Traditional cultures have by their very traditions preserved many human qualities that have become outmoded or expressly denied by the obsession of technology with the profit motive of capitalism: a sense of rhythm, an aptitude for meditation, a spontaneous human friendliness, an unchecked emotional urge which even makes use of the escape valve of savagery and violence . . . in short, the art of living: this is what is preserved and put into practice better in these cultures than in the intellectually organised cultures self-styled as 'advanced'. It is significant that the citizens of the latter forsake their artificial metropolises from time to time for open country and a more human way of life.

The emergent peoples, whose knowledge springs from the well of family life, have much to teach the devotees of technology and efficiency about the complex levels of personality. Their outlook is already making an impact as distances on the earth's surface grow shorter and contact with others grows closer. Toynbee was entirely right when, in evoking the vision of our world in the eyes of the historians of the future, he considered that for them:

> The great event of the twentieth century will prove to be the clash of Western Civilisation with the other societies extant in the world at that time. . . . When a counter-radiation of influences has followed an earlier radiation, what will emerge will be one great single experience, shared by all humanity: that of having witnessed the shattering of the regional social inheritance of a civilisation by the shock of its encounter with the regional inheritances of other civilisations and of then discovering that a new life – a new, common life – was blooming from out of the ruins.

In this book I have given my reasons for believing that the 'new, common life', as described by Toynbee, is already moulding itself into an economic system the social structure of which will eliminate the independent capitalist of the recent past. What we may hope to see emerge is a new socialism more harmoniously blending the rationality and techniques of Western civilisation with that natural art of living which has been better preserved by other cultures.

As was emphasised at the beginning of this book these are critical times; they are so because of the net of contradictions in which we seem to be trapped; new techniques face old institutions, emergent needs face decaying systems, the wind from the East faces the wind from the West. Let us believe that the meeting of all peoples in the unique assembly hall of the UN is not just an empty symbol. Let us hope that, by means of the forces described in this book, those contradictions will adopt less disturbing proportions in the unified world that is awaiting us beyond the horizon.

Notes and bibliography

1 Introduction: an unsettled world

The quotation from Ortega y Gasset appears in *En torno a Galileo* (*Obras Completas*, Vol. V, Editorial Revista de Occidente, Madrid, 1955, 3rd edn., page 93). Valéry's comment from the opening of *Regards sur le monde actuel*, Gallimard, Paris, 1956.

The UN quotation is the opening paragraph of the report *The United Nations Development Decade. Proposals for Action*. United Nations, New York, 1962. The passage from Schumpeter is from *History of Economic Analysis*, Oxford University Press, 1954, 2nd edn., page 561. On page 472 (note) Schumpeter comes back to the same idea and complains that his American students have been crammed with historical facts, but lack the *sense* of history to acquire a wider knowledge. He concludes, 'It is much easier to make theorists of them than economists'.

2 The population explosion

The information in this chapter is based on the work of the United Nations, which includes the superb research of their technical experts, together with the work of the international conferences, in this case the one held in Rome in September 1954, *Proceedings of the World Population Conference. Summary Report*. United Nations, New York, 1955. In addition, I have made special use of the report entitled *The Future Expansion of the World Population*, ST/SOA/Series A/28, UN, 1959, from which came the data for the population curve from 1900 and those figures for the Table of growth rates (pages 25 and 35 in the report), as well as the sentences in the text and the map in figure 2. The table of future needs in food production is on page 35 of the FAO pamphlet *6 Billions to Feed*, FAO, Rome, 1962. The instance of 'the road that food built' is in *Basic Study No. 5, Nutrition and Working Efficiency*, FAO, Rome, 1962, page 24. Another more detailed study is *Basic Study No. 10, Possibilities of Increasing World Food Production*, FAO, Rome, 1963.

In addition, I have consulted several now classic works on the history of population and its problems, such as A. M. Carr-Saunders' *World Population: Past Growth and Present Trends*, Oxford University Press, London and New York, 1936, and M. R. Reinhard, *Histoire de la population mondiale de 1700 à 1948*, Domat-Montchrestien, Paris, 1949.

Another very useful source is the relevant chapters in W. S. and E. S. Woytinsky, *World Population and Production: Trends and Outlook*, The

Twentieth Century Fund, New York, 1953. The data on the Roman Empire and Antiquity come from the classic work of J. Beloch which I have taken, together with the figures relating to China, from Abbot P. Usher's *The History of Population and Settlement in Eurasia*, which is included in J. J. Spengler and O. D. Duncan (edd.), *Demographic Analysis: Selected Readings*, The Free Press, Glencoe, Illinois, 1957, page 9. Another useful anthology edited by the same authors is *Population Theory and Policy*, The Free Press, Glencoe, Illinois, 1956. Other studies which I have consulted are: A. Sauvy, *Théorie générale de la population*, Presses Universitaires de France, Paris, 1952 and 1954; *World Population and Resources*, Political and Economic Planning, London, 1955, and Essential Books, New York, 1955; C. M. Cipolla, *The Economic History of World Population*, Peter Smith, Gloucester, Mass., and Penguin Books, Harmondsworth, 1962; Kuan I-Chen, *World Population Growth and Living Standards*, Bookman Associates, New York, 1960; P. George, *Questions de géographie de la population du monde* and *Introduction à l'étude géographique de la population du monde*, Presses Universitaires de France, Paris, 1959 and 1951. The estimates of Kuczynski and Putman, quoted in the text, are taken from M. K. Bennet, *The World's Food*, Harper, New York, 1954. See also Kuczynski's now classic article 'Population: History and Statistics', printed in the *Encyclopaedia of the Social Sciences*, New York, 1934.

The Soviet view of the relative deterioration of the underdeveloped countries is drawn from L. Stepanov 'The Problem of Economic Independence' (included in T. P. Thornton (ed.) *The Third World in Soviet Perspective*, Princeton University Press, 1964, page 108). T. Kristensen and his collaborators published their figures in *The Economic World Balance*, North-Holland Publishing Company, Amsterdam, 1960.

For the general historical view of modern Europe see Charles Morazé, *Les bourgeois conquérants*, Armand Colin, Paris, 1957. The historical data regarding Spain are taken from J. Vicéns Vives (in collaboration with J. Nadal Oller), *Historia económica de España*, Editorial Vicéns Vives, Barcelona, 1964, 3rd edn., pages 379 and 562, and from the same author's *Historia social y económica de España y América*, Editorial Teide, Barcelona, 1959, vol. iv, part 2, page 22. See also E. Navarro Salvador, *La mortalidad infantil y la demografía general en España*, Madrid, 1922, which contains the complete series of birth and death rates in Spain from 1859.

I have also found several useful references to the history of the theory of population in E. Cannan, *Review of Economic Theory*, Messner, New York, 1940.

The theories of Hong Liang-Ki were brought to light by Jean Chesneaux in an artcle published in the French journal *Population*, Jan.-March 1960, page 89.

On the question of birth control, besides works already mentioned, I have drawn on the conclusions reached by the Conference Committee on Population Problems as they appear in F. Osborn, *Population: an International Dilemma*, The Population Council, New York, 1958, and the joint work of several Catholic authors in the Centre d'Études Laënnec, under the title *La régulation des naissances*, P. Lethielleux, Paris, 1961, where page 46 deals with the cultural difficulties in India. Recent information on American attitudes is taken from Tad Szulc, 'US is helping Latin Americans to Study Birth-Control Methods', The New York Times International Edition, 11 February 1965. Finally I would cite one of the latest, most vigorous and forthright pleas put forward in support of birth control in the underdeveloped countries – by J. K. Galbraith, in the closing pages of his *Economic Development in Perspective*, Harvard U.P. and Oxford U.P., 1962.

3 The technical acceleration

The bibliography of technology is very extensive. My information has come in the main from specialised works of reference, such as C. Singer, E. J. Holmyard, A. R. Hall, T. I. Williams (edd.) *A History of Technology*, Clarendon Press, Oxford, vols. 1–5, 1954–8. On a smaller scale, but also a mine of information, is Pierre Rousseau, *Histoire des Techniques*, Fayard, Paris, 1956. I have also made use of A. P. Usher, *History of Mechanical Inventions*, Harvard U.P. and Oxford U.P., 1954, and Lewis Mumford *Technics and Civilisation*, Harcourt Brace, New York, and Routledge, London, 1954. For a vivid account the reader should turn to V. Eco and G.B.Zorzoli, *Histoire illustrée des inventions*, Pont Royal, Paris, 1961, or J.Bronowski (ed.), *Technology: Man Remakes his World*, Macdonald, London, 1963. As an anthology of historical texts relating to technology there is also the very useful *A History of Western Technology*, by F. Klemm, Allen and Unwin, London, and Scribner, New York, 1959, from which I have taken the quotations from Paracelsus and Richard Baxter.

Particularly lucid as an interpretation of the technical phenomenon is J. Ellul, *The Technological Society*, Knopf, New York, 1964. A work which is very informative about the pros and cons of technology, although its bias is not one that I personally endorse, is the F. Dessauer, *Discusión sobre la técnica*, Rialp., Madrid, 1964, in which a modern (Darmstad, 1952) restatement will be found of the controversy over the inherent 'goodness' or 'evil' of technology – a controversy which is based on some curious Biblical beliefs.

The rationalism of technology was the subject of a special study by Max Weber. Apart from his voluminous *Theory of Social and Economic Organisation*, Free Press, Chicago, and Oxford U.P., 1947, his *General Economic History*, Free Press, Chicago, and Oxford U.P., 1950 (from which the quotation in the text was taken), also merits attention. Of considerable interest also is A. von Martin, *Sociology of the Renaissance*, Kegan Paul, London, 1944.

The quotations from Ortega are taken from *En torno a Galileo* and *Meditación de la técnica* (*Obras completas*, vol. V, Editorial Revista de Occidente, Madrid, 1947). The reference to Marc Bloch is to be found in his essay *Technique et évolution sociale. Réflexions d'un historien*, incorporated in the anthology *L'Homme, la technique et la nature*, Rieder, Paris, 1938. The references to Norbert Wiener are based on his *The Human Use of Human Beings*, Doubleday Anchor Books, New York, and Eyre and Spottiswoode, London, 1950.

The figures on power production are based on data published by the United Nations in *Besoins du monde en énergie en 1975 et en l'an 2000*, Geneva, 1956, which resulted from the International Conference on the use of atomic energy, together with data from other sources, such as S. N. Prokopovicz, *L'Industrialisation des pays agricoles et la structure de l'économie mondiale après la guerre*, Zeluck, Paris, 1946, and W. S. and E. S. Woytinsky, *World Population and Production: Trends and Outlook*, The Twentieth Century Fund, New York, 1953. For some of my figures I have used the work of P. Rousseau already mentioned above, and the same author's *Histoire de la vitesse*, Presses Universitaires de France, Paris, 1942. The dates attributed to W. W. Rostow will be found in his *The Stages of Economic Growth*, Cambridge U.P., London and New York, 1960. The remarks by Vance Packard are from *The Hidden Persuaders*, McKay, New York, and Longmans, London, 1957.

4 Social change

The initial reference to Tibor Mende is to his book *Regards sur l'histoire de demain*, Éditions du Seuil, Paris, 1954. The passage from Röpke is on page 15 of his *La communauté internationale*, Éditions du Cheval Ailé, Geneva, 1947. The passage from F. X. von Neumann-Spallart is taken from S. N. Prokopovicz, *L'Industrialisation des pays agricoles et la structure de l'économie mondiale après la guerre*, Zeluck, Paris, 1946, page 4. The reference to Keynes is to *The Economic Consequences of the Peace*, Macmillan, London, 1919. The passage from José de Cadalso is to be found in number 41 of his *Cartas marruecas*, Calleja, Madrid, 1917, pages 163–4. My own treatment of the changes in the centre of gravity in world economics is based on my works *Principales efectos de la unidad económica europea* and *El futuro europeo de España*, both of which are published by the Sociedad de Estudios Españoles y Europeos, Espasa-Calpe, Madrid, 1957 and 1961, respectively.

An abundant bibliography exists on the subject of historical materialism. References can be found in David Caute, *The Left in Europe*, World University Library, Weidenfeld and Nicolson, London and McGraw-Hill, New York, 1966.

There are also plenty of text-books on anthropology for which see especially E. E. Evans-Pritchard, *Social Anthropology*, Free Press, Chicago, and Cohen and West, London, 1957.

The UNESCO volume *Transformations sociales et développement économique*, Paris, 1962, contains, in addition to other reports, the deliberations of a Round Table convened by 'The International Bureau for investigating the social implications of technical progress', and my quotation from Raymond Firth will be found on pages 85–6. The reference to Unamuno is to his article 'Doctores en Industria', dated 16 October 1898 and included in M. García Blanco (ed.) under the title *España y los españoles*, Aguado, Madrid, 1955, page 57. Hoselitz's remarks are from his 'Tradition and Economic Growth', incorporated in R. Braibanti and J. J. Spengler (edd.) *Tradition, Values and Socio-Economic Development*, Cambridge U.P. and Duke U.P., 1961, pages 99–100. A systematic treatment of these themes will be found in E. E. Hagen, *On the Theory of Social Change*, Dorsey Press, Homewood, Illinois, 1962, and Tavistock Publications, London, 1964. I am indebted to pages 264 ff. for the inserted interpretation of English history.

Finally, the figures given by P. A. Sorokin are taken from his *Society, Culture and Personality*, Cooper, New York, 1962. Colin Clark's examples are to be found in his *Conditions of Economic Progress*, St Martin's Press, New York, and Macmillan, London, 1957, 3rd edn., pages 490 ff.

5 The resulting systems

The bibliography of economic systems has a long tradition behind it; yet no agreement has been reached on terminology. I have based this chapter on my personal research into the subject, using also material from a rich scientific tradition, which goes back to the ancient Greeks. The contents of my *Lecciones de estructura económica*, Madrid, 1965, which are here summarised, are being considerably amplified in a work in preparation, *Análisis estructural*. In E. Wagemann's book, *Economic Rhythm: a Theory of Business Cycles*, McGraw-Hill, New York, 1930, two criteria similar to those used here will be found in combination, but in a form which tends to compare the Soviet Union with the India of thirty years ago. The problems have also been studied in numerous American works on comparative economics such as G. N. Halm, *Economic Systems*, Holt, New York, 1960.

Typology based on the study of different historical periods has a lengthy tradition. Some distinguished German economists have treated this subject and their opinions can be examined in Bert Hoselitz's study, 'Theories of stages of Economic Growth', which he includes in his *Theories of Economic Growth*, Free Press, Chicago, 1960.

The work of Brian J. L. Berry, quoted in the text, will be found in N. Ginsburg, *Atlas of Economic Development*, University of Chicago Press, Chicago, and London, 1961. The work of R. H. Fitzgibbon appeared in *Inter-American Economic Affairs*, vol. 9, 1956, pages 65 ff., and that of Vekemans and Segundo in the UNESCO publication, *Aspectos sociales del desarrollo económico en América Latina*, vol. I, pages 72 ff.

The 'water-mill example' which starts the chapter was given by Marc Bloch in his essay, already cited, 'Technique et évolution sociale: Réflexions d'un historien', in *L'Homme, la technique et la nature*, Reider, Paris, 1938, pages 36 ff. There is a copious literature on the *yang* and *yin* philosophy, and I will mention only the brief but significant book of H. Wilhelm, *Change: Eight Lectures on the I-Ching*, Harper Torchbooks, New York, 1964.

Finally, Max Weber's definition of the economic order can be read on pages 302–3 of vol. II of his *Economia y sociedad* (Spanish version published by the Fondo de Cultura Económica, Mexico, 1944).

6 Towards a planning system

The basic ideas for this chapter are taken from an earlier work of mine, published in the *Revista de Occidente*, Madrid, November and December 1963. I am grateful to the Editor for his permission to use this material. I incorporated in it the quotation from Wallich, taken from the Spanish translation, *El coste de la libertad*, Editorial Ariel, Barcelona, 1962, page 223, as well as the one by Echegaray, to be found in an article in the journal *El financiero*, in the number dated 29 January 1909, which the same journal reprinted on 5 April 1926.

The influence on transportation of developments in harness was studied by Lefebvre des Noëttes, whose work is cited by Lynn White, Jr. in 'Technology and Invention in the Middle Ages', published in *Speculum*, April 1940, and reprinted in *The Pirenne Thesis*, Heath, Boston, 1958. The importance of the stern rudder has been recognised by many authors, and the references in this chapter are taken from Max Weber's *General Economic History*, Free Press, Chicago, and Oxford U.P., London.

The railway as a symbol of progress is already a commonplace. So too is the idea that the nations of Europe are no longer individually large enough to exist as separate units of economic organisation. This is a theme which I have myself dealt with at length in my book *El futuro europeo de España*, sponsored by the Sociedad de Estudios Económicos Españoles y Europeos, Espasa-Calpe, Madrid, 1961.

The quotation from A. A. Berle, Jr. comes from his *The 20th Century Capitalist Revolution*, Harcourt Brace, New York, 1954, and Macmillan, London, 1955, page 25, and F. L. Allen's from *Big Change: America Transforms Itself*, Harper, New York, and Hamish Hamilton, London, 1952.

The figures relating to the bureaucracy of the entrepreneur were given by Reinhard Bendix in *Work and Authority in Industry*, Wiley, New York, and Chapman and Hall, London, 1956, which deals with the matter in considerable detail. C. Wright Mills can be consulted in *Power Elite* Oxford U.P., London and New York, 1956. The book by James Burnham referred to is *The Managerial Revolution: What is Happening in the World*, John Day, New York, 1941, and the one by William H. Whyte is *The Organisation Man*, Simon & Schuster, New York, and Cape, London, 1956. The quotations from Vance Packard are from his *The Status Seekers*, McKay, New York, and Longmans, London, 1959. J. K. Galbraith's view is developed in his *American Capitalism: the Concept of Counter-vailing Power*, Houghton Mifflin, New York, and Hamish Hamilton, London, 1952. Michael Harrington's study of poverty in the USA is *The Other America*, Macmillan, New York and London, 1962.

There is an abundant bibliography on the future of capitalism. I will confine myself to mentioning the different points of view collected in Shigeto Tsuru (ed.), *Has Capitalism Changed?*, International Publications, New York and London, 1961. A recent, concise statement of the question as it appears to Soviet authors can be found in E. Varga, *Twentieth Century Capitalism*, Lawrence & Wishart, London, 1963.

7 Towards the new socialism

From the massive bibliography on this subject, I will select only those works which have a direct bearing on this chapter. The reader should consult in particular John Reed's classic account of the beginning of the revolution, *Ten Days that Shook the World*, Vintage, New York, and Lawrence and Wishart, London, 1962, and Bertrand Russell's *Practice and Theory of Bolshevism*, Allen and Unwin, London, and Macmillan, New York, 2nd edn., 1949, which was written soon after the Revolution.

The argument on the theoretical viability of socialism is now part of the history of economic thought. It is admirably discussed by Benjamin E. Lipincott in the introduction to his edition of the works of Lange and Taylor, quoted in the text, under the title of *On the Economic Theory of Socialism*, University of Minnesota Press, McGraw-Hill Paperback Edition, New York and London, 1964.

Alec Nove, *The Soviet Economy*, Allen and Unwin, London, and Praeger, New York, 1961, affords a very good introduction to the overall picture of Soviet organisation. The earlier period is dealt with in Harry Schwartz, *Russia's Soviet Economy*, Prentice-Hall, New York, 1950, and Cape, London, 1951. A more recent study is Pierre Sorlin, *La société soviétique*, Armand Colin, Paris, 1964. The specific problems of the year 1956 are analysed in the works presented in October 1957 at the 'Study week on the Soviet Economy' held at the Institut de Sociologie Solvay, and published by this body under the title *L'Économie soviétique en 1957*.

There are numerous comparisons and analyses of the relative power of the two systems. The following are of particular value: Jane Degras (ed.), *Soviet Planning: Essays in Honour of Naum Jasny*, Blackwell, Oxford, 1964, which contains the essays of Peter Wiles and M.C.Kaser; Harry G. Shaffer (ed.), *The Soviet Economy: A Collection of Soviet and Western Views*, Appleton, New York, Methuen, London, 1963, and Robert W. Campbell, *Soviet Economic Power*, Houghton Mifflin, New York, 1960.

Of the many accounts available use was made of Giuseppe Boffa, *Le grand tournant: De Staline à Khrouchtchev*, Maspero, Paris, 1960, and Harrison E. Salisbury, *A New Russia?*, Harper, New York, Secker & Warburg, London, 1962.

Among Soviet publications in translation use was made principally of

I. Evenko, *Planning in the USSR*, Universal Distributors, London, and New York, 1961, P. Alampiev, *Economic Areas in USSR*, Progress Publishers, Moscow, 1965, and statistics and data from the following official publications: *USSR in Figures, 1959*, *USSR Today and Tomorrow* and *Mémento du plan septennal*, all issued by Foreign Language Publications, Moscow. I have also made use of data contained in Khruschev's report to the 21st Congress of the Communist Party of the Soviet Union about the Seventh Plan. For a detailed study of the communist party one should consult Leonard Schapiro (ed.), *The USSR and the Future: an Analysis of the New Program of the CPSU*, Praeger, New York, and Pall Mall Press, London, 1963.

In my references to Soviet authorities I have been guided by the speech of Khruschev made on 8 March 1963 to the Soviet leaders and the representatives of literature and the arts, published in French by Collection Études Soviétiques, Paris, as well as that of Brezhnev on the 47th anniversary of the October Revolution, published in English by Novosti Press Agency Publishing House, Moscow, together with Kosygin's report to the Supreme Soviet at the session held on 9 December 1964, published in English by the same agency as *1965 State Plan for Economic Development of the USSR*.

The passage quoted from the *Les Principes du Marxisme–Leninisme*, Éditions en langues étrangères, Moscow, will be found on page 658. The data from Aganbegian on the Soviet consumer can be found in Shaffer, *The Soviet Economy*, cited earlier.

Liberman's proposals have received near-sensational coverage in the Western Press. Some of the works already mentioned discuss this affair, which is especially well outlined in B. Kerblay, *Cahiers du monde russe et soviétique*, issues for July–September 1963, École Pratique des Hautes Études, Mouton, Paris. The subject has also been treated by M. I. Goldman in the April 1963 issue of *Foreign Affairs*, Council on Foreign Relations, New York, under the heading 'Economic Controversy in the Soviet Union'. The latest articles by Liberman, Trapeznikov and Leontiev have been translated in their entirety in the supplement to number 128 of *Économie et politique: problèmes d'économie socialiste*, Paris. An interesting comparative report on the entrepreneur is David Granick's *Red Executive*, Doubleday, New York, and Macmillan, London, 1960.

Finally, on the growing importance of cybernetics in the Soviet system, the reader should consult G. Paloczi-Horvath, *The Facts Rebel: The Future of Russia and the West*, Secker and Warburg, London, 1964. See also Jacques Gillemaud, *Cybernétique et matérialisme dialetique*, Petite Encyclopédie Marxiste, Editions sociales, Paris, 1965. Several specialist journals have published articles on the state of sociology in the USSR, such as those by Talcott Parsons and Allen Kassof in the February 1965 issue of *American Sociological Review*. UNESCO's monograph issue of the *International Social Science Journal* on the teaching of the social sciences in USSR, clearly shows that up to a few years ago sociology was still only a minor appendage of philosophy and was regarded as simply the application of a bygone materialism, as in the article by V. S. Molodtsov in this Journal.

As that book had already been sent to press, it was not possible to take into account the full text of the proceedings of the Twenty-Third Congress of the CPSU (29 March to 8 April 1966). In general, it confirms the trends described in this book; it is published in English by the Novosti Press Agency Publishing House, under the title *23rd Congress of the CPSU, 1966*.

8 The emergent countries

A simple introduction to the economy of the Eastern countries is given in Stanislaw Wellisz, *The Economies of the Soviet Bloc*, McGraw-Hill, New York and London, 1964. The early part of its organisation is dealt with more fully in Jan Marczewski, *Planification et Croissance Économique des Démocracies Populaires*, Presses Universitaires de France, Paris, 1956. The reference to the article by Brus is in B. Kerblay *Cahiers du Monde Russe et Soviétique* for July–September 1963, École Pratique des Hautes Études, Mouton, Paris. The words in the text by Clinton Rossiter are contained in his article, 'The Paradox of India's Democracy', in V. M. Dean and H. D. Harootunian (edd.), *West and Non-West: New Perspectives*, Holt, New York, 1963, page 226. The Soviet points of view are taken from T. P. Thornton's interesting anthology, *The Third World in Soviet Perspective*, Princeton University Press, 1964. I have also paid special attention to the work of L. A. Gordon and L. A. Fridman in *Peculiarities in the Composition and Structure of the Working Class in the Economically Underdeveloped Countries of Asia and Africa* (page 154) and of R. Avakov and G. Mirskiy in *Class Structure in the Underdeveloped Countries* (page 276). J. K. Galbraith has written about Eastern Europe in his *Journey to Poland and Yugoslavia*, Harvard University Press, 1958, and Oxford U.P., 1959, and also about the respective advantages of capitalism and socialism for the emergent world in chapter three of his *Economic Development*, Harvard University Press and Oxford U.P., 1964.

The quotations from Mao Tse-tung are taken from the volumes published in Spanish by the 'Ediciones en Lenguas Extranjeras' of Peking. I have made special use of the *Proposición acerca de la línea general del movimiento comunista internacional* (the reply of the Central Committee of the Chinese Communist Party to its Soviet equivalent, on 14 June 1963), the *Class analysis in Chinese society* (the revised translation of 1960), *Sobre el tratamiento correcto de las contradicciones en el seno del pueblo* (revised translation of 1961, pages 45, 39 and 50) and the *Words of comrade Mao Tse-tung on 'Imperialism and all reactionaries are paper tigers*' (revised translation of 1960, page 29).

On the subject of China, I recommend Edgar Snow, *The Other Side of the River: Red China Today*, Random House, New York, 1962, and Gollancz, 1963, which is of more value than many other books with greater academic pretentions. Robert C. North, *Chinese Communism*, World University Library, Weidenfeld and Nicolson, London, and McGraw-Hill, New York, gives an excellent summary and analysis of Chinese history from the late 18th century to the present day. See also C. P. Fitzgerald, *The Chinese View of their Place in the World*, Chatham House Essays, Royal Institute of International Affairs, Oxford U.P., 1964, from page 57 of which I have taken a few sentences. I have quoted also from page 40 of A. Doak Barnett's *Communist China in Perspective*, Praeger, New York, 1962, at the same time taking into account the collection of reports selected by Dan. N. Jacobs and Hans H. Baerwald and entitled *Chinese Communism*, Harper Torchbooks, New York and London, 1963.

On the differences of opinion with the USSR I have consulted Edward Crankshaw, *The New Cold War*, Penguin, Harmondsworth, 1963. For Chinese history in general the classic work now is K. S. Latourette, *The Chinese: Their History and Culture*, Macmillan, New York, 4th edn., 1963. A recent economic study of fundamentals is *The Economy of the Chinese Mainland 1933–1959*, by Ta-Chung Liu and Kung-Chia Yeh, Princeton University Press, 1965. More elementary are A. Eckstein, *The National Income of Communist China*, Free Press, New York, 1961, and the revealing and useful *The Economic Development of Communist China 1949–60*, by T. J. Hughes and D. E. T. Luard, Oxford U.P., 2nd edn., 1962. A really vivid account is to be found in Jan Myrdal, *Report from a Chinese Village*, Pantheon, New York, and Heinemann, London, 1965. An introduction to the present situation is provided by S. Chandrasekhar, *Communist China Today*, Asia Publishing House, 1961. On the education of the young and present similarities with Confucianism see John K. Fairbank, *The United States and China*, Harvard University Press, 1958, and Oxford U.P., London, 1959. My references to the labour situation in Japan include the studies of two specialists in the subject, Makoto Sakurabayashi and R. J. Ballon entitled 'Labour-Management Relations in Modern Japan' and included in *Studies in Japanese Culture*, Sophia University, Tokyo, 1963.

An excellent general introduction to African problems can be obtained from Basil Davidson, *Which Way Africa?*, Penguin, Harmondsworth, 1964, from which I have taken the references to Leopold II's exploitation of the Congo (pages 37 and 40). A country-by-country examination has been produced by Helen Kitchen in *A Handbook of African Affairs*, Heinemann, London, and Praeger, New York, 1964. The Western point of view can be learned from A. Rivkin, *Africa and the West*, Thames and Hudson, London, and New York, 1962. A concise summary of the ideas of Kwame Nkrumah can be found in the pamphlet *Some Essential Features of Nkrumaism*, Spark Publications, Accra, 1964, and Lawrence and Wishart, London, from which I have taken a few references. The statement by Albert Luthuli appears at the beginning of Alex Quaison-Sackey, *Africa Unbound*, Deutsch, London, and Praeger, New York, 1963.

A first-class anthology of studies in sociology in Latin–America is the UNESCO publication, *Aspectos sociales del desarrollo económico en América Latina*, Paris, 1962 and 1963. This includes the work of Wekemans and Segundo quoted in the text (on pages 72 et seq. of vol. I) to reflect the percentage of urban population.

Another interesting collection of studies is afforded by *El Trimestre Económico*, a review published by the *Fondo de Cultura Económica*. I have used from it part of the article of Celso Furtado (page 377 of number 115, for July–September 1962) and some of Dwight S. Brothers' *Nexos entre la estabilidad monetaria y el desarrollo económico entre América Latina: un escrito doctrinal y de política* (page 593 of number 116, for October–December 1962). The same Review published the speech of Victor L. Urquidi, on his becoming a member of the National College of Mexico (page 1 of number 109, for January–March 1961), from which I have also borrowed a few sentences.

Urquidi has also written an introduction to the situation in the South American continent, under the title of *Viabilidad económica de América Latina*, Fondo de Cultura Económica, Mexico, 1962, page 90, which provided me with material for a quotation. I am similarly indebted to Celso Furtado, *Le Brésil à l'heure du choix*, Plon, Paris, 1964, page 133, and to Luis Alberto Sánchez, *Examen espectral de América Latina*, Losada, Buenos Aires, 2nd edn., 1962, pages 177 and 239. Unamuno's essay was published in *La dignidad humana*, Colección Austral, Espasa-Calpe, Buenos Aires, 1944.

Acknowledgments

Thanks are due to Mr Bruce Robertson who designed the diagrams and to the following sources for providing information or material for adaption (numbers refer to figures in the text):

1 8000 BC: C. Cipolla, *The Economic History of World Population*, London, 1962, p. 95.
Year 0: J. Beloch, as quoted by A. P. Usher in 'The History of Population and Settlement in Eurasia', included in *Demographic Analysis. Selected Readings*, edited by J. J. Spengler and O. D. Duncan, Glencoe, Illinois, 1956, p. 9.
1000–1900: M. K. Bennett, *The World's Food*, New York, 1954, p. 9.
1925–2000: *The Future Growth of World Population*, United Nations, New York, 1959.

2 *The Future Growth of World Population*, United Nations, New York, 1959.

3 *Six Billion to Feed*, Food and Agriculture Organisation, New York, 1962, p. 38.

4 Thorkil Kristensen and associates, *The Economic World Balance*, Copenhagen and Amsterdam, 1960, p. 266.

5 GREAT BRITAIN
1740–1920: M. R. Reinhard, *Histoire de la population mondiale de 1700 à 1948*, Paris, 1949, pp. 110–248.
1930: *The League of Nations Statistical Yearbook, 1934–5*, p. 52.
1940–60: *The UN Statistical Yearbook, 1948*, pp. 35, 41; and *The UN Statistical Yearbook, 1963*, pp. 45, 49; *The UN Demographic Yearbook 1956*, pp. 619, 643.
SPAIN
1880–1990: E. Navarro Salvador, *La mortalidad infantil y la demografia general en España*, Madrid, 1922, p. 42.
1910–40: *Anuario Estadístico, 1950*, p. 64.
1950 and 1960: Successive *Anuarios Estadísticos.*
CHILE
1920 and 1930: *The League of Nations Statistical Yearbook, 1934–5*, p. 52.
Following years: the same Yearbooks as for Great Britain.

6 1820–1948: W. S. and E. S. Woytinsky, *World Population and Production*,

New York, 1953, p. 930.
1963: *The UN Statistical Yearbook*, p. 327.
1980: Estimate by Thorkil Kristensen and associates, *The Economic World Balance*, Copenhagen and Amsterdam, 1960, p. 266.

7 *The UN Statistical Yearbook, 1963*, pp. 330–333.

9 R. Vekemans and J. L. Segundo, 'The Socio-Economic Typology of Latin America'. (A paper included in *Social Aspects of the Economic Development of Latin America*, Vol. I., United Nations Educational, Social and Cultural Organisation, Paris, 1962).

10 Brian J. L. Berry, 'Basic Patterns of Economic Development'. (Included as an Appendix in Norton Ginsburg's *Atlas of Economic Development*, Chicago, 1961).

13 American monthly *Fortune*, August, 1965, p. 170.

15 *The British Economy. Key Statistics 1900–1964*, London, 1965, p. 13.

16 The French weekly *Entreprise* as quoted by J. A. Lesourd and C. Gérard, *Histoire économique, XIX et XX siècles*, Paris, 1963, Vol. II, p. 445.

18 USSR official index: *L'URSS en chiffres*, Moscow, 1961, p. 57.
American estimates of USSR growth: National Bureau and Shimkin estimates combined, as quoted by R. W. Campbell, *Soviet Economic Power*, New York, 1960, pp. 48–9, for years 1928–55. Extended to 1961 according to R. V. Greenslade and P. Wallace as quoted by Frank O'Brien in *Crisis in World Communism*, New York and London, 1965, p. 73.
American official index: *Economic Report of the President, I*, 1962, p. 245.

19 A. Aganbegian, 'Living Standards of the Working People in the USSR and USA', included in *The Soviet Economy*, edited by Harry G. Shaffer, London, 1964, pp. 277–8.

20 P. Alampiev, *Economic Areas in the USSR*, Moscow, p. 52.

21 *The USSR Today and Tomorrow*, Moscow, 1959.

22 I. Evenko, *Present-day Planning in the USSR*, Moscow, 1961.

25 1926–33: *The League of Nations Statistical Yearbook, 1934–5*, pp. 129, 141.
1941–59: T. J. Hughes and D. E. T. Luard, *The Economic Development of Communist China, 1949–60*, London, 1962, p. 217.
1960: E. Snow, *La Chine en marche*, Paris, 1963, p. 134.

26 Yuan-Li Wu, *The Economy of Communist China*, London, 1965, pp. 178–9.

27 *The Statistical Survey of the Economy of Japan, 1959*, pp. 10–11. This is the official Japanese source.
More recent figures from *Bulletin statistique de l'OCDE*, Paris, and from the OECD report *Japan*, Paris, 1964.

Acknowledgment is due to the following for illustrations (the number refers to the page on which the illustration appears). Frontispiece, 231 (photo V. Bianohi) Food and Agriculture Organisation; 10 Michael Raeburn; 11, 22 (right), 145 Radio Times Hulton Picture Library; 12, 97 United States Information Service; 15 Albert Robida, *La vie électrique*; 22 (left) National Portrait Gallery; 32, 59, 62, 101, 105, 214 British Museum; 35 (top and bottom) Wellcome Historical Medical Museum (reproduction by courtesy of the Wellcome Trustees); 43 International Planned Parenthood Federation; 46, 54, 127 Science Museum; 72 British Film Institute; 91, 165, 201 (Rizzoli Press Service, Milan) Camera Press; 120, 164 (left and right), 166, 167 Novosti Press Agency; 125 (top) J. R. Freeman and Co.; 125 (bottom) Royal Commission for Historical Monuments; 130 Mansell Collection; 131 Marx Memorial Library; 136, 137 E. I. Du Pont de Nemours and Co.; 148, 149 Associated Press; 218 Werner Forman; 222 United Nations; 229 United Nations Educational, Social and Cultural Organisation.

Index

World University Library

Some books published or in preparation

Economics and Social Studies

The World Cities
Peter Hall, *London*

The Economics of Underdeveloped Countries
Jagdish Bhagwati, *Delhi*

Development Planning
Jan Tinbergen, *Rotterdam*

Decisive Forces in World Economics
J. L. Sampedro, *Madrid*

Key Issues in Criminology
Roger Hood, *Durham*

Human Communication
J. L. Aranguren, *Madrid*

Education in the Modern World
John Vaizey, *London*

History

The Emergence of Greek Democracy
W. G. Forrest, *Oxford*

Muhammad and the Conquests of Islam
Francesco Gabrieli, *Rome*

Humanism in the Renaissance
S. Dresden, *Leyden*

The Ottoman Empire
Halil Inalcik, *Ankara*

The Rise of Toleration
Henry Kamen, *Warwick*

The Left in Europe
David Caute, *Oxford*

The Rise of the Working Class
Jürgen Kuczynski, *Berlin*

Chinese Communism
Robert C. North, *Stanford*

Philosophy and Religion

Christianity
W. O. Chadwick, *Cambridge*

Monasticism
David Knowles, *London*

Judaism
J. Soetendorp, *Amsterdam*

The Modern Papacy
K. O. von Aretin, *Gottingen*

Sects
Bryan Wilson, *Oxford*

Language and Literature

A Model of Language
E. M. Uhlenbeck, *Leyden*

French Literature
Raymond Picard, *Paris*

Russian Writers and Society
Ronald Hingley, *Oxford*

Satire
Matthew Hodgart, *Sussex*

The Arts

Primitive Art
Eike Haberland, *Mainz*

The Language of Modern Art
Ulf Linde, *Stockholm*

Aesthetic Theories since 1850
J. F. Revel, *Paris*

Art Nouveau
S. T. Madsen, *Oslo*

Academic Painting
Gerald Ackerman, *Stanford*

Palaeolithic Cave Art
P. J. Ucko and A. Rosenfeld, *London*

Psychology and Human Biology

Eye and Brain
R. L. Gregory, *Cambridge*

The Ear and the Brain
Edward Carterette, *U.C.L.A.*

The Variety of Man
J. P. Garlick, *London*

The Biology of Work
O. G. Edholm, *London*

Psychoses
H. J. Bochnik, *Hamburg*

Child Development
Philippe Muller, *Neuchâtel*

Man and Disease
Gernot Rath, *Göttingen*

Chinese Medicine
P. Huard and M. Wong, *Paris*

The Psychology of Fear and Stress
J. A. Gray, *Oxford*

Zoology and Botany

Animal Communication
J. M. Cullen, *Oxford*

Mimicry
Wolfgang Wickler, *Seewiesen*

Migration
Gustaf Rudebeck, *Stockholm*

The World of an Insect
Rémy Chauvin, *Strasbourg*

Biological Rhythms
Janet Harker, *Cambridge*

Lower Animals
Martin Wells, *Cambridge*

Dinosaurs
Bjöon Kurtén, *Helsinki*

Physical Science and Mathematics

Mathematics Observed
H. Freudenthal, *Utrecht*

The Quest for Absolute Zero
K. Mendelssohn, *Oxford*

Particles and Accelerators
Robert Gouiran, *C.E.R.N., Geneva*

Optics
A. C. S. van Heel and
C. H. F. Velzel, *Eindhoven*

Waves and Corpuscles
J. L. Andrade e Silva and
G. Lochak, *Paris*
Introduction by Louis de Broglie

Energy
J. Fischhoff, *Paris*

Earth Sciences and Astronomy

The Electrical Earth
J. Sayers, *Birmingham*

Climate and Weather
H. Flohn, *Bonn*

The Structure of the Universe
E. L. Schatzman, *Paris*

Applied Science

Words and Waves
A. H. W. Beck, *Cambridge*

The Science of Decision-Making
A. Kaufmann, *Paris*

Bioengineering
H. S. Wolff, *London*

Bionics
Lucien Gerardin, *Paris*

Metals and Civilisation
R. W. Cahn, *Sussex*